Practical Machine Learning

Tackle the real-world complexities of modern machine learning with innovative and cutting-edge techniques

Sunila Gollapudi

PUBLISHING

BIRMINGHAM - MUMBAI

Practical Machine Learning

First published: January 2016

Production reference: 2270116

Published by Packt Publishing Ltd.
Livery Place
35 Livery Street
Birmingham B3 2PB, UK.

ISBN 978-1-78439-968-9

www.packtpub.com

Credits

Author
Sunila Gollapudi

Reviewers
Rahul Agrawal

Rahul Jain

Ryota Kamoshida

Ravi Teja Kankanala

Dr. Jinfeng Yi

Commissioning Editor
Akram Hussain

Acquisition Editor
Sonali Vernekar

Content Development Editor
Sumeet Sawant

Technical Editor
Murtaza Tinwala

Copy Editor
Yesha Gangani

Project Coordinator
Shweta H Birwatkar

Proofreader
Safis Editing

Indexer
Tejal Daruwale Soni

Graphics
Jason Monteiro

Production Coordinator
Manu Joseph

Cover Work
Manu Joseph

Foreword

Can machines think? This question has fascinated scientists and researchers around the world. In the 1950s, Alan Turing shifted the paradigm from "Can machines think?" to "Can machines do what humans (as thinking entities) can do?". Since then, the field of Machine learning/Artificial Intelligence continues to be an exciting topic and considerable progress has been made.

The advances in various computing technologies, the pervasive use of computing devices, and resultant Information/Data glut has shifted the focus of Machine learning from an exciting esoteric field to prime time. Today, organizations around the world have understood the value of Machine learning in the crucial role of knowledge discovery from data, and have started to invest in these capabilities.

Most developers around the world have heard of Machine learning; the "learning" seems daunting since this field needs a multidisciplinary thinking—Big Data, Statistics, Mathematics, and Computer Science. Sunila has stepped in to fill this void. She takes a fresh approach to mastering Machine learning, addressing the computing side of the equation-handling scale, complexity of data sets, and rapid response times.

Practical Machine Learning is aimed at being a guidebook for both established and aspiring data scientists/analysts. She presents, herewith, an enriching journey for the readers to understand the fundamentals of Machine learning, and manages to handhold them at every step leading to practical implementation path.

She progressively uncovers three key learning blocks. The foundation block focuses on conceptual clarity with a detailed review of the theoretical nuances of the disciple. This is followed by the next stage of connecting these concepts to the real-world problems and establishing an ability to rationalize an optimal application. Finally, exploring the implementation aspects of latest and best tools in the market to demonstrate the value to the business users.

V. Laxmikanth
Managing Director, Broadridge Financial Solutions (India) Pvt Ltd

About the Author

Sunila Gollapudi works as Vice President Technology with Broadridge Financial Solutions (India) Pvt. Ltd., a wholly owned subsidary of the US-based Broadridge Financial Solutions Inc. (BR). She has close to 14 years of rich hands-on experience in the IT services space. She currently runs the Architecture Center of Excellence from India and plays a key role in the big data and data science initiatives. Prior to joining Broadridge she held key positions at leading global organizations and specializes in Java, distributed architecture, big data technologies, advanced analytics, Machine learning, semantic technologies, and data integration tools. Sunila represents Broadridge in global technology leadership and innovation forums, the most recent being at IEEE for her work on semantic technologies and its role in business data lakes. Sunila's signature strength is her ability to stay connected with ever changing global technology landscape where new technologies mushroom rapidly , connect the dots and architect practical solutions for business delivery . A post graduate in computer science, her first publication was on Big Data Datawarehouse solution, Greenplum titled *Getting Started with Greenplum for Big Data Analytics, Packt Publishing*. She's a noted Indian classical dancer at both national and international levels, a painting artist, in addition to being a mother, and a wife.

Acknowledgments

At the outset, I would like to express my sincere gratitude to Broadridge Financial Solutions (India) Pvt Ltd., for providing the platform to pursue my passion in the field of technology.

My heartfelt thanks to Laxmikanth V, my mentor and Managing Director of the firm, for his continued support and the foreword for this book, Dr. Dakshinamurthy Kolluru, President, International School of Engineering (INSOFE), for helping me discover my love for Machine learning and Mr. Nagaraju Pappu, Founder & Chief Architect Canopus Consulting, for being my mentor in Enterprise Architecture.

This acknowledgement is incomplete without a special mention of Packt Publications for giving this opportunity to outline, conceptualize and provide complete support in releasing this book. This is my second publication with them, and again it is a pleasure to work with a highly professional crew and the expert reviewers.

To my husband, family and friends for their continued support as always. One person whom I owe the most is my lovely and understanding daughter Sai Nikita who was as excited as me throughout this journey of writing this book. I only wish there were more than 24 hours in a day and would have spent all that time with you Niki!

Lastly, this book is a humble submission to all the restless minds in the technology world for their relentless pursuit to build something new every single day that makes the lives of people better and more exciting.

About the Reviewers

Rahul Agrawal is a Principal Research Manager at Bing Sponsored Search in Microsoft India, where he heads a team of applied scientists solving problems in the domain of query understanding, ad matching, and large-scale data mining in real time. His research interests include large-scale text mining, recommender systems, deep neural networks, and social network analysis. Prior to Microsoft, he worked with Yahoo! Research, where he worked in building click prediction models for display advertising. He is a post graduate from Indian Institute of Science and has 13 years of experience in Machine learning and massive scale data mining.

Rahul Jain is a big data / search consultant from Hyderabad, India, where he helps organizations in scaling their big data / search applications. He has 8 years of experience in the development of Java- and J2EE-based distributed systems with 3 years of experience in working with big data technologies (Apache Hadoop / Spark), NoSQL(MongoDB, HBase, and Cassandra), and Search / IR systems (Lucene, Solr, or Elasticsearch). In his previous assignments, he was associated with IVY Comptech as an architect where he worked on implementation of big data solutions using Kafka, Spark, and Solr. Prior to that, he worked with Aricent Technologies and Wipro Technologies Ltd, Bangalore, on the development of multiple products.

He runs one of the top technology meet-ups in Hyderabad—*Big Data Hyderabad Meetup*—that focuses on big data and its ecosystem. He is a frequent speaker and had given several talks on multiple topics in big data/search domain at various meet-ups/conferences in India and abroad. In his free time, he enjoys meeting new people and learning new skills.

I would like to thank my wife, Anshu, for standing beside me throughout my career and reviewing this book. She has been my inspiration and motivation for continuing to improve my knowledge and move my career forward.

Ryota Kamoshida is the maintainer of Python library MALSS (`https://github.com/canard0328/malss`) and now works as a researcher in computer science at a Japanese company.

Ravi Teja Kankanala is a Machine learning expert and loves making sense of large amount of data and predicts trends through advanced algorithms. At Xlabs, he leads all research and data product development efforts, addressing HealthCare and Market Research Domain. Prior to that, he developed data science product for various use cases in telecom sector at Ericsson R&D. Ravi did his BTech in computer science from IIT Madras.

Dr. Jinfeng Yi is a research staff Member at IBM's Thomas J. Watson Research Center, concentrating on data analytics for complex real-world applications. His research interests lie in Machine learning and its application to various domains, including recommender system, crowdsourcing, social computing, and spatio-temporal analysis. Jinfeng is particularly interested in developing theoretically principled and practically efficient algorithms for learning from massive datasets. He has published over 15 papers in top Machine learning and data mining venues, such as ICML, NIPS, KDD, AAAI, and ICDM. He also holds multiple US and international patents related to large-scale data management, electronic discovery, spatial-temporal analysis, and privacy preserved data sharing.

www.PacktPub.com

Support files, eBooks, discount offers, and more

For support files and downloads related to your book, please visit www.PacktPub.com.

Did you know that Packt offers eBook versions of every book published, with PDF and ePub files available? You can upgrade to the eBook version at www.PacktPub.com and as a print book customer, you are entitled to a discount on the eBook copy. Get in touch with us at service@packtpub.com for more details.

At www.PacktPub.com, you can also read a collection of free technical articles, sign up for a range of free newsletters and receive exclusive discounts and offers on Packt books and eBooks.

https://www2.packtpub.com/books/subscription/packtlib

Do you need instant solutions to your IT questions? PacktLib is Packt's online digital book library. Here, you can search, access, and read Packt's entire library of books.

Why subscribe?

- Fully searchable across every book published by Packt
- Copy and paste, print, and bookmark content
- On demand and accessible via a web browser

Free access for Packt account holders

If you have an account with Packt at www.PacktPub.com, you can use this to access PacktLib today and view 9 entirely free books. Simply use your login credentials for immediate access.

I dedicate this work of mine to my father G V L N Sastry, and my mother, late G Vijayalakshmi. I wouldn't have been what I am today without your perseverance, love, and confidence in me.

Table of Contents

Preface

Finding something meaningful in increasingly larger and more complex datasets is a growing demand of the modern world. Machine learning and predictive analytics have become the most important approaches to uncover data gold mines. Machine learning uses complex algorithms to make improved predictions of outcomes based on historical patterns and the behavior of datasets. Machine learning can deliver dynamic insights into trends, patterns, and relationships within data, which is immensely valuable to the growth and development of business.

With this book, you will not only learn the fundamentals of Machine learning, but you will also dive deep into the complexities of the real-world data before moving onto using Hadoop and its wider ecosystem of tools to process and manage your structured and unstructured data.

What this book covers

Chapter 1, Introduction to Machine learning, will cover the basics of Machine learning and the landscape of Machine learning semantics. It will also define Machine learning in simple terms and introduce Machine learning jargon or commonly used terms. This chapter will form the base for the rest of the chapters.

Chapter 2, Machine learning and Large-scale datasets, will explore qualifiers of large datasets, common characteristics, problems of repetition, the reasons for the hyper-growth in the volumes, and approaches to handle the big data.

Chapter 3, An Introduction to Hadoop's Architecture and Ecosystem, will cover all about Hadoop, starting from its core frameworks to its ecosystem components. At the end of this chapter, readers will be able to set up Hadoop and run some MapReduce functions; they will be able to use one or more ecosystem components. They will also be able to run and manage Hadoop environment and understand the command-line usage.

Chapter 4, Machine Learning Tools, Libraries, and Frameworks, will explain open source options to implement Machine learning and cover installation, implementation, and execution of libraries, tools, and frameworks, such as Apache Mahout, Python, R, Julia, and Apache Spark's MLlib. Very importantly, we will cover the integration of these frameworks with the big data platform—Apache Hadoop

Chapter 5, Decision Tree based learning, will explore a supervised learning technique with Decision trees to solve classification and regression problems. We will cover methods to select attributes and split and prune the tree. Among all the other Decision tree algorithms, we will explore the CART, C4.5, Random forests, and advanced decision tree techniques.

Chapter 6, Instance and Kernel methods based learning, will explore two learning algorithms: instance-based and kernel methods; and we will discover how they address the classification and prediction requirements. In instance-based learning methods, we will explore the Nearest Neighbor algorithm in detail. Similarly in kernel-based methods, we will explore Support Vector Machines using real-world examples.

Chapter 7, Association Rules based learning, will explore association rule based learning methods and algorithms: Apriori and FP-growth. With a common example, you will learn how to do frequent pattern mining using the Apriori and FP-growth algorithms with a step-by-step debugging of the algorithm.

Chapter 8, Clustering based learning, will cover clustering based learning methods in the context of unsupervised learning. We will take a deep dive into k-means clustering algorithm using an example and learn to implement it using Mahout, R, Python, Julia, and Spark.

Chapter 9, Bayesian learning, will explore Bayesian Machine learning. Additionally, we will cover all the core concepts of statistics starting from basic nomenclature to various distributions. We will cover Bayes theorem in depth with examples to understand how to apply it to the real-world problems.

Chapter 10, Regression based learning, will cover regression analysis-based Machine learning and in specific, how to implement linear and logistic regression models using Mahout, R, Python, Julia, and Spark. Additionally, we will cover other related concepts of statistics such as variance, covariance, ANOVA, among others. We will also cover regression models in depth with examples to understand how to apply it to the real-world problems.

Chapter 11, Deep learning, will cover the model for a biological neuron and will explain how an artificial neuron is related to its function. You will learn the core concepts of neural networks and understand how fully-connected layers work. We will also explore some key activation functions that are used in conjunction with matrix multiplication.

Chapter 12, Reinforcement learning, will explore a new learning technique called reinforcement learning. We will see how this is different from the traditional supervised and unsupervised learning techniques. We will also explore the elements of MDP and learn about it using an example.

Chapter 13, Ensemble learning, will cover the ensemble learning methods of Machine learning. In specific, we will look at some supervised ensemble learning techniques with some real-world examples. Finally, this chapter will have source-code examples for gradient boosting algorithm using R, Python (scikit-learn), Julia, and Spark machine learning tools and recommendation engines using Mahout libraries.

Chapter 14, New generation data architectures for Machine learning, will be on the implementation aspects of Machine learning. We will understand what the traditional analytics platforms are and how they cannot fit in modern data requirements. You will also learn about the architecture drivers that promote new data architecture paradigms, such as Lambda architectures polyglot persistence (Multi-model database architecture); you will learn how Semantic architectures help in a seamless data integration.

Appendix, Data Exploration and Preparation, will cover the most important data exploration and preprocessing techniques like Aggregation, Dimensionality reduction, feature creation, attribute transformation that can be applied in the context of any learning algorithm explained throughput this book. You can find this chapter at `https://www.packtpub.com/sites/default/files/downloads/ Practical_Machine_Learning_Appendix.pdf`.

What you need for this book

You'll need the following softwares for this book:

- R (2.15.1)
- Apache Mahout (0.9)
- Python(sckit-learn)
- Julia(0.3.4)
- Apache Spark (with Scala 2.10.4)

Who this book is for

This book has been created for data scientists who want to see Machine learning in action and explore its real-world application. With guidance on everything from the fundamentals of Machine learning and predictive analytics to the latest innovations set to lead the big data revolution into the future, this is an unmissable resource for anyone dedicated to tackling current big data challenges. Knowledge of programming (Python and R) and mathematics is advisable, if you want to get started immediately.

Conventions

In this book, you will find a number of styles of text that distinguish between different kinds of information. Here are some examples of these styles, and an explanation of their meaning.

Code words in text, database table names, folder names, filenames, file extensions, pathnames, dummy URLs, user input, and Twitter handles are shown as follows: "The Map() function works on the distributed data and runs the required functionality in parallel."

A block of code is set as follows:

```
public static class VowelMapper extends Mapper<Object, Text, Text,
IntWritable>
{
private final static IntWritable one = new IntWritable(1);
private Text word = new Text();
public void map(Object key, Text value, Context context) throws
IOException, InterruptedException
{
StringTokenizer itr = new StringTokenizer(value.toString());
while (itr.hasMoreTokens())
{
word.set(itr.nextToken());
context.write(word, one);
}
}
```

Any command-line input or output is written as follows:

```
$ hadoop-daemon.sh start namenode
```

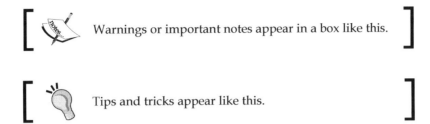

Warnings or important notes appear in a box like this.

Tips and tricks appear like this.

Reader feedback

Feedback from our readers is always welcome. Let us know what you think about this book—what you liked or may have disliked. Reader feedback is important for us to develop titles that you really get the most out of.

To send us general feedback, simply send an e-mail to feedback@packtpub.com, and mention the book title via the subject of your message.

If there is a topic that you have expertise in and you are interested in either writing or contributing to a book, see our author guide on www.packtpub.com/authors.

Customer support

Now that you are the proud owner of a Packt book, we have a number of things to help you to get the most from your purchase.

Downloading the example code

You can download the example code files for all Packt books you have purchased from your account at http://www.packtpub.com. If you purchased this book elsewhere, you can visit http://www.packtpub.com/support and register to have the files e-mailed directly to you.

The author will be updating the code on https://github.com/PacktCode/Practical-Machine-Learning for you to download as and when there are version updates.

Downloading the color images of this book

We also provide you with a PDF file that has color images of the screenshots/diagrams used in this book. The color images will help you better understand the changes in the output. You can download this file from `http://www.packtpub.com/sites/default/files/downloads/Practical_Machine_Learning_ColorImages.pdf`.

Errata

Although we have taken every care to ensure the accuracy of our content, mistakes do happen. If you find a mistake in one of our books — maybe a mistake in the text or the code — we would be grateful if you could report this to us. By doing so, you can save other readers from frustration and help us improve subsequent versions of this book. If you find any errata, please report them by visiting `http://www.packtpub.com/submit-errata`, selecting your book, clicking on the **Errata Submission Form** link, and entering the details of your errata. Once your errata are verified, your submission will be accepted and the errata will be uploaded to our website or added to any list of existing errata under the Errata section of that title.

To view the previously submitted errata, go to `https://www.packtpub.com/books/content/support` and enter the name of the book in the search field. The required information will appear under the **Errata** section.

Piracy

Piracy of copyright material on the Internet is an ongoing problem across all media. At Packt, we take the protection of our copyright and licenses very seriously. If you come across any illegal copies of our works, in any form, on the Internet, please provide us with the location address or website name immediately so that we can pursue a remedy.

Please contact us at `copyright@packtpub.com` with a link to the suspected pirated material.

We appreciate your help in protecting our authors, and our ability to bring you valuable content.

Questions

You can contact us at `questions@packtpub.com` if you are having a problem with any aspect of the book, and we will do our best to address it.

1
Introduction to Machine learning

The goal of this chapter is to take you through the Machine learning landscape and lay out the basic concepts upfront for the chapters that follow. More importantly, the focus is to help you explore various learning strategies and take a deep dive into the different subfields of Machine learning. The techniques and algorithms under each subfield, and the overall architecture that forms the core for any Machine learning project implementation, are covered in depth.

There are many publications on Machine learning, and a lot of work has been done in past in this field. Further to the concepts of Machine learning, the focus will be primarily on specific practical implementation aspects through real-world examples. It is important that you already have a relatively high degree of knowledge in basic programming techniques and algorithmic paradigms; although for every programming section, the required primers are in place.

The following topics listed are covered in depth in this chapter:

- Introduction to Machine learning
- A basic definition and the usage context
- The differences and similarities between Machine learning and data mining, **Artificial Intelligence (AI)**, statistics, and data science
- The relationship with big data
- The terminology and mechanics: model, accuracy, data, features, complexity, and evaluation measures

- Machine learning subfields: supervised learning, unsupervised learning, semi-supervised learning, reinforcement learning, and deep learning. Specific Machine learning techniques and algorithms are also covered under each of the machine learning subfields

- Machine learning problem categories: Classification, Regression, Forecasting, and Optimization

- Machine learning architecture, process lifecycle, and practical problems

- Machine learning technologies, tools, and frameworks

Machine learning

Machine learning has been around for many years now and all social media users, at some point in time, have been consumers of Machine learning technology. One of the common examples is face recognition software, which is the capability to identify whether a digital photograph includes a given person. Today, Facebook users can see automatic suggestions to tag their friends in the digital photographs that are uploaded. Some cameras and software such as iPhoto also have this capability. There are many examples and use cases that will be discussed in more detail later in this chapter.

The following concept map represents the key aspects and semantics of Machine learning that will be covered throughout this chapter:

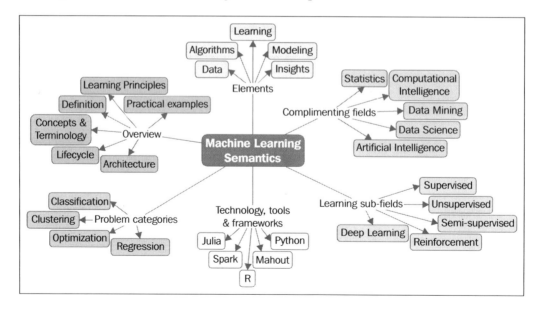

Definition

Let's start with defining what Machine learning is. There are many technical and functional definitions for Machine learning, and some of them are as follows:

> *"A computer program is said to learn from experience E with respect to some class of tasks T and performance measure P, if its performance at tasks in T, as measured by P, improves with experience E."*
>
> *– Tom M. Mitchell*

> *"Machine learning is the training of a model from data that generalizes a decision against a performance measure."*
>
> *– Jason Brownlee*

> *"A branch of artificial intelligence in which a computer generates rules underlying or based on raw data that has been fed into it."*
>
> *– Dictionary.com*

> *"Machine learning is a scientific discipline that is concerned with the design and development of algorithms that allow computers to evolve behaviors based on empirical data, such as from sensor data or databases."*
>
> *– Wikipedia*

The preceding definitions are fascinating and relevant. They either have an algorithmic, statistical, or mathematical perspective.

Beyond these definitions, a single term or definition for Machine learning is the key to facilitating the definition of a problem-solving platform. Basically, it is *a mechanism for pattern search* and building intelligence into a machine to be able to learn, implying that it will be able to do better in the future from its own experience.

Drilling down a little more into what a pattern typically is, pattern search or pattern recognition is essentially the study of how machines perceive the environment, learn to discriminate behavior of interest from the rest, and be able to take reasonable decisions about categorizing the behavior. This is more often performed by humans. The goal is to foster accuracy, speed, and avoid the possibility of inappropriate use of the system.

Machine learning algorithms that are constructed this way handle building intelligence. Essentially, machines make sense of data in much the same way that humans do.

The primary goal of a Machine learning implementation is to develop a general purpose algorithm that solves a practical and focused problem. Some of the aspects that are important and need to be considered in this process include data, time, and space requirements. Most importantly, with the ability to be applied to a broad class of learning problems, the goal of a learning algorithm is to produce a result that is a rule and is as accurate as possible.

Another important aspect is the big data context; that is, Machine learning methods are known to be effective even in cases where insights need to be uncovered from datasets that are large, diverse, and rapidly changing. More on the large scale data aspect of Machine learning will be covered in *Chapter 2, Machine Learning and Large-scale Datasets*.

Core Concepts and Terminology

At the heart of Machine learning is knowing and using the data appropriately. This includes collecting the *right* data, cleansing the data, and processing the data using learning algorithms iteratively to build models using certain key features of data, and based on the hypotheses from these models, making predictions.

In this section, we will cover the standard nomenclature or terminology used in machine learning, starting from how to describe data, learning, modeling, algorithms, and specific machine learning tasks.

What is learning?

Now, let us look at the definition of "learning" in the context of Machine learning. In simple terms, historical data or observations are used to predict or derive actionable tasks. Very clearly, one mandate for an intelligent system is its ability to learn. The following are some considerations to define a learning problem:

1. Provide a definition of what the learner should learn and the need for learning.
2. Define the data requirements and the sources of the data.
3. Define if the learner should operate on the dataset in entirety or a subset will do.

Before we plunge into understanding the internals of each learning type in the following sections, you need to understand the simple process that is followed to solve a learning problem, which involves building and validating models that solve a problem with maximum accuracy.

A model is nothing but an output from applying an algorithm to a dataset, and it is usually a representation of the data. We cover more on models in the later sections.

In general, for performing Machine learning, there are primarily two types of datasets required. The first dataset is usually manually prepared, where the input data and the expected output data are available and prepared. It is important that every piece of input data has an expected output data point available as this will be used in a supervised manner to build the rule. The second dataset is where we have the input data, and we are interested in predicting the expected output.

As a first step, the given data is segregated into three datasets: training, validation, and testing. There is no one hard rule on what percentage of data should be training, validation, and testing datasets. It can be 70-10-20, 60-30-10, 50-25-25, or any other values.

The training dataset refers to the data examples that are used to learn or build a classifier, for example. The validation dataset refers to the data examples that are verified against the built classifier and can help tune the accuracy of the output. The testing dataset refers to the data examples that help assess the performance of the classifier.

There are typically three phases for performing Machine learning:

- **Phase 1 — Training Phase**: This is the phase where training data is used to train the model by pairing the given input with the expected output. The output of this phase is the learning model itself.

- **Phase 2 — Validation and Test Phase**: This phase is to measure how good the learning model that has been trained is and estimate the model properties, such as error measures, recall, precision, and others. This phase uses a validation dataset, and the output is a sophisticated learning model.

- **Phase 3 — Application Phase**: In this phase, the model is subject to the real-world data for which the results need to be derived.

The following figure depicts how learning can be applied to predict the behavior:

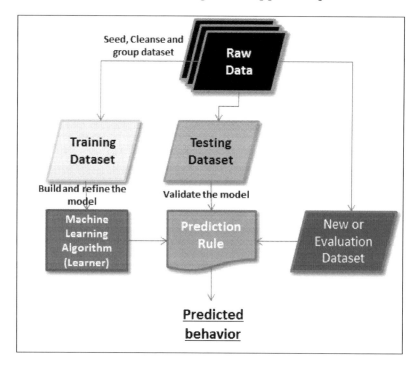

Data

Data forms the main source of learning in Machine learning. The data that is being referenced here can be in any format, can be received at any frequency, and can be of any size. When it comes to handling large datasets in the Machine learning context, there are some new techniques that have evolved and are being experimented with. There are also more big data aspects, including parallel processing, distributed storage, and execution. More on the large-scale aspects of data will be covered in the next chapter, including some unique differentiators.

When we think of data, dimensions come to mind. To start with, we have rows and columns when it comes to structured and unstructured data. This book will cover handling both structured and unstructured data in the machine learning context. In this section, we will cover the terminology related to data within the Machine learning context.

Term	Purpose or meaning in the context of Machine learning
Feature, attribute, field, or variable	This is a single column of data being referenced by the learning algorithms. Some features can be input to the learning algorithm, and some can be the outputs.
Instance	This is a single row of data in the dataset.
Feature vector or tuple	This is a list of features.
Dimension	This is a subset of attributes used to describe a property of data. For example, a date dimension consists of three attributes: day, month, and year.
Dataset	A collection of rows or instances is called a dataset. In the context of Machine learning, there are different types of datasets that are meant to be used for different purposes. An algorithm is run on different datasets at different stages to measure the accuracy of the model. There are three types of dataset: training, testing, and evaluation datasets. Any given comprehensive dataset is split into three categories of datasets and is usually in the following proportions: 60% training, 30% testing, and 10% evaluation.
a. Training Dataset	The training dataset is the dataset that is the base dataset against which the model is built or trained.
b. Testing Dataset	The testing dataset is the dataset that is used to validate the model built. This dataset is also referred to as a validating dataset.
c. Evaluation Dataset	The evaluation dataset is the dataset that is used for final verification of the model (and can be treated more as user acceptance testing).
Data Types	Attributes or features can have different data types. Some of the data types are listed here: • Categorical (for example: young, old). • Ordinal (for example: 0, 1). • Numeric (for example: 1.3, 2.1, 3.2, and so on).
Coverage	The percentage of a dataset for which a prediction is made or the model is covered. This determines the confidence of the prediction model.

Labeled and unlabeled data

Data in the Machine learning context can either be labeled or unlabeled. Before we go deeper into the Machine learning basics, you need to understand this categorization, and what data is used when, as this terminology will be used throughout this book.

Unlabeled data is usually the raw form of the data. It consists of samples of natural or human-created artifacts. This category of data is easily available in abundance. For example, video streams, audio, photos, and tweets among others. This form of data usually has no explanation of the meaning attached.

The unlabeled data becomes labeled data the moment a meaning is attached. Here, we are talking about attaching a "tag" or "label" that is required, and is mandatory, to interpret and define the relevance. For example, labels for a photo can be the details of what it contains, such as animal, tree, college, and so on, or, in the context of an audio file, a political meeting, a farewell party, and so on. More often, the labels are mapped or defined by humans and are significantly more expensive to obtain than the unlabeled raw data.

The learning models can be applied to both labeled and unlabeled data. We can derive more accurate models using a combination of labeled and unlabeled datasets. The following diagram represents labeled and unlabeled data. Both triangles and bigger circles represent labeled data and small circles represent unlabeled data.

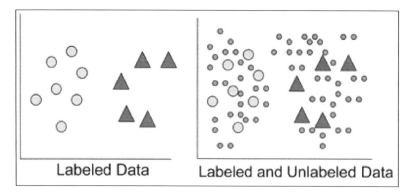

The application of labeled and unlabeled data is discussed in more detail in the following sections. You will see that supervised learning adopts labeled data and unsupervised learning adopts unlabeled data. Semi-supervised learning and deep learning techniques apply a combination of labeled and unlabeled data in a variety of ways to build accurate models.

Tasks

A task is a problem that the Machine learning algorithm is built to solve. It is important that we measure the performance on a task. The term "performance" in this context is nothing but the extent or confidence with which the problem is solved. Different algorithms when run on different datasets produce a different model. It is important that the models thus generated are not compared, and instead, the consistency of the results with different datasets and different models is measured.

Algorithms

After getting a clear understanding of the Machine learning problem at hand, the focus is on what data and algorithms are relevant or applicable. There are several algorithms available. These algorithms are either grouped by the learning subfields (such as supervised, unsupervised, reinforcement, semi-supervised, or deep) or the problem categories (such as Classification, Regression, Clustering or Optimization). These algorithms are applied iteratively on different datasets, and output models that evolve with new data are captured.

Models

Models are central to any Machine learning implementation. A model describes data that is observed in a system. Models are the output of algorithms applied to a dataset. In many cases, these models are applied to new datasets that help the models learn new behavior and also predict them. There is a vast range of machine learning algorithms that can be applied to a given problem. At a very high level, models are categorized as the following:

- Logical models
- Geometric models
- Probabilistic models

Logical models

Logical models are more algorithmic in nature and help us derive a set of rules by running the algorithms iteratively. A Decision tree is one such example:

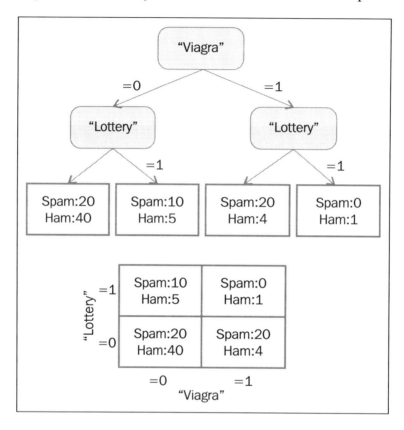

Geometric models

Geometric models use geometric concepts such as lines, planes, and distances. These models usually operate, or can operate, on high volumes of data. Usually, linear transformations help compare different Machine learning methods:

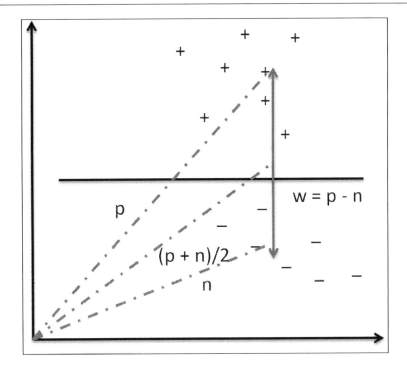

Probabilistic models

Probabilistic models are statistical models that employ statistical techniques. These models are based on a strategy that defines the relationship between two variables. This relationship can be derived for sure as this involves using a random background process. In most cases, a subset of the overall data can be considered for processing:

Viagra	Lottery	P(Y= Spam (Viagra, lottery))	P(Y= ham (Viagra, lottery))
0	0	0.31	0.69
0	1	0.65	0.35
1	0	0.80	0.20
1	1	0.40	0.60

Data and inconsistencies in Machine learning

This section details all the possible data inconsistencies that may be encountered while implementing Machine learning projects, such as:

- Under-fitting
- Over-fitting
- Data instability
- Unpredictable future

Fortunately, there are some established processes in place today to address these inconsistencies. The following sections cover these inconsistencies.

Under-fitting

A model is said to be under-fitting when it doesn't take into consideration enough information to accurately model the actual data. For example, if only two points on an exponential curve are mapped, this possibly becomes a linear representation, but there could be a case where a pattern does not exist. In cases like these, we will see increasing errors and subsequently an inaccurate model. Also, in cases where the classifier is too rigid or is not complex enough, under-fitting is caused not just due to a lack of data, but can also be a result of incorrect modeling. For example, if the two classes form concentric circles and we try to fit a linear model, assuming they were linearly separable, this could potentially result in under-fitting.

The accuracy of the model is determined by a measure called "power" in the statistical world. If the dataset size is too small, we can never target an optimal solution.

Over-fitting

This case is just the opposite of the under-fitting case explained before. While too small a sample is not appropriate to define an optimal solution, a large dataset also runs the risk of having the model over-fit the data. Over-fitting usually occurs when the statistical model describes noise instead of describing the relationships. Elaborating on the preceding example in this context, let's say we have 500,000 data points. If the model ends up catering to accommodate all 500,000 data points, this becomes over-fitting. This will in effect mean that the model is memorizing the data. This model works well as long as the dataset does not have points outside the curve. A model that is over-fit demonstrates poor performance as minor fluctuations in data tend to be exaggerated. The primary reason for over-fitting also could be that the criterion used to train the model is different from the criterion used to judge the efficacy of the model. In simple terms, if the model memorizes the training data rather than learning, this situation is seen to occur more often.

Now, in the process of mitigating the problem of under-fitting the data, by giving it more data, this can in itself be a risk and end up in over-fitting. Considering that more data can mean more complexity and noise, we could potentially end up with a solution model that fits the current data at hand and nothing else, which makes it unusable. In the following graph, with the increasing model complexity and errors, the conditions for over-fit and under-fit are pointed out:

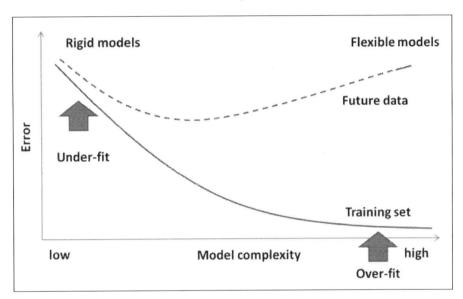

Data instability

Machine learning algorithms are usually robust to noise within the data. A problem will occur if the outliers are due to manual error or misinterpretation of the relevant data. This will result in a skewing of the data, which will ultimately end up in an incorrect model.

Therefore, there is a strong need to have a process to correct or handle human errors that can result in building an incorrect model.

Unpredictable data formats

Machine learning is meant to work with new data constantly coming into the system and learning from that data. Complexity will creep in when the new data entering the system comes in formats that are not supported by the machine learning system. It is now difficult to say if our models work well for the new data given the instability in the formats that we receive the data, unless there is a mechanism built to handle this.

Practical Machine learning examples

In this section, let's explore some real-world machine learning applications. We covered various examples within the introductory section of this chapter and we will now cover some domain-specific examples with a brief description of each problem.

For online and offline applications, some of the following examples can easily be guessed. In the chapters to follow, a subset of these examples will be picked to demonstrate the practical implementation aspects using suitable Machine learning algorithms.

Problem / problem Domain	Description
Spam detection	The problem statement here is to identify which e-mails are "spam". A Machine learning algorithm can categorize an e-mail to be marked as spam based on some rules that it builds using some key features of e-mail data. Once an e-mail is marked as spam, that e-mail is then moved to the spam folder and the rest are left in the inbox.
Credit card fraud detection	This is one of the recent problems that credit card firms need a solution for. Based on the usage patterns of the credit card by the consumer and the purchase behavior of the customer, the need is to identify any transaction that is not potentially made by the customer and mark them as fraudulent for necessary action to be taken.
Digit recognition	This is a very simple use case that requires the ability to group posts based on the zip code. This includes the need to interpret a handwritten numeric accurately and bucket the posts based on the zip code for faster processing.
Speech recognition	Automated call centers need this capability where a user's request on the phone is interpreted and mapped to one of the tasks for execution. The moment the user request can be mapped to a task, its execution can be automated. A model of this problem will allow a program to understand and make an attempt to fulfill that request. The iPhone with Siri has this capability.

Problem / problem Domain	Description
Face detection	This is one of the key features that today's social media websites provide. This feature provides an ability to tag a person across many digital photographs. This gives aptitude to a group or categorizes the photographs by a person. Some cameras and software such as iPhoto have this capability.
Product recommendation or customer segmentation	This capability is found in almost all of the top online shopping websites today. Given a purchase history for a customer and a large inventory of products, the idea is to identify those products that the customer will most likely be interested in buying, thus motivating more product purchases. There are many online shopping and social websites that support this feature (for example: Amazon, Facebook, Google+, and many others). There are other cases like the ability to predict whether a trial version customer opts for the paid version of the product.
Stock trading	This means predicting stock performance based on the current past stock movement. This task is critical to financial analysts and helps provide decision support when buying and selling stocks.
Sentiment analysis	Many times, we find that the customers make decisions based on opinions shared by others. For example, we buy a product because it has received positive feedback from the majority of its users. Not only in commercial businesses as detailed earlier, but sentiment analysis is also being used by political strategists to gauge public opinion on policy announcements or campaign messages.

Types of learning problems

This section focuses on elaborating different learning problem categories. Machine learning algorithms are also classified under these learning problems. The following figure depicts various types of learning problems:

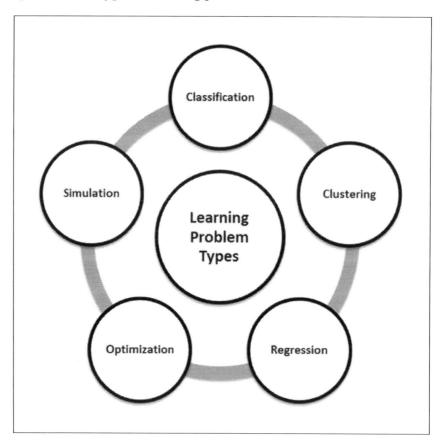

Classification

Classification is a way to identify a grouping technique for a given dataset in such a way that depending on a value of the target or output attribute, the entire dataset can be qualified to belong to a class. This technique helps in identifying the data behavior patterns. This is, in short, a discrimination mechanism.

For example, a sales manager needs help in identifying a prospective customer and wants to determine whether it is worth spending the effort and time the customer demands. The key input for the manager is the customer's data, and this case is commonly referred to as **Total Lifetime Value (TLV)**.

We take the data and start plotting blindly on a graph (as shown in the following graph) with the *x* axis representing the total items purchased and the *y* axis representing the total money spent (in multiples of hundreds of dollars). Now we define the criteria to determine, for example, whether a customer is good or bad. In the following graph, all the customers who spend more than 800 dollars in a single purchase are categorized as good customers (note that this is a hypothetical example or analysis).

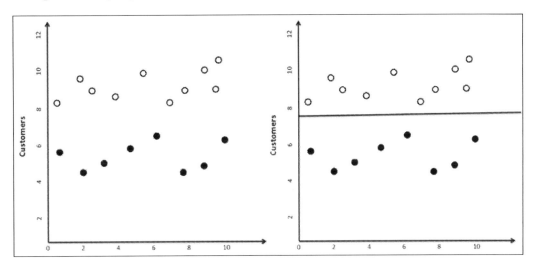

Now when new customer data comes in, the sales manager can plot the new customers on this graph and based on which side they fall, predict whether the customer is likely to be good or bad.

 Note that classification need not always be binary (yes or no, male or female, good or bad, and so on) and any number of classifications can be defined (poor, below average, average, above average, good) based on the problem definition.

Clustering

In many cases, the data analyst is just given some data and is expected to unearth interesting patterns that may help derive intelligence. The main difference between this task and that of a classification is that in the classification problem, the business user specifies what he/she is looking for (a good customer or a bad customer, a success or a failure, and so on).

Let's now expand on the same example considered in the classification section. Here the patterns to classify the customers are identified without any target in mind or any prior classification, and unlike running a classification, the results may always not be the same (for example, depending on how the initial centroids are picked). An example modeling method for clustering is k-means clustering. More details on k-means clustering is covered in the next section and in detail in the following chapters.

In short, clustering is a classification analysis that does not start with a specific target in mind (good/bad, will buy/will not buy).

Forecasting, prediction or regression

Similar to classification, forecasting or prediction is also about identifying the way things would happen in the future. This information is derived from past experience or knowledge. In some cases, there is not enough data, and there is a need to define the future through regression. Forecasting and prediction results are always presented along with the degree of uncertainty or probability. This classification of the problem type is also called **rule extraction**.

Let's take an example here, an agricultural scientist working on a new crop that she developed. As a trial, this seed was planted at various altitudes and the yield was computed. The requirement here is to predict the yield of the crop given the altitude details (and some more related data points). The relationship between yield gained and the altitude is determined by plotting a graph between the parameters. An equation is noted that fits most of the data points, and in cases where data does not fit the curve, we can get rid of the data. This technique is called regression.

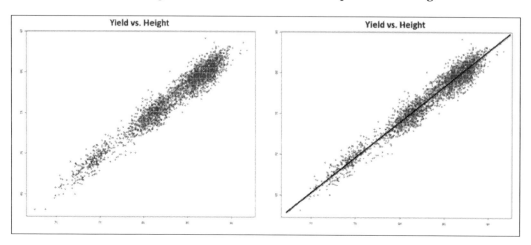

Simulation

In addition to all the techniques we defined until now, there might be situations where the data in context itself has many uncertainty. For example, an outsourcing manager is given a task and can estimate with experience that the task can be done by an identified team with certain skills in 2-4 hours.

Let's say the cost of input material may vary between $100-120 and the number of employees who come to work on any given day may be between 6 and 9. An analyst then estimates how much time the project might take. Solving such problems requires the simulation of a vast amount of alternatives.

Typically in forecasting, classification, and unsupervised learning, we are given data and we really do not know how the data is interconnected. There is no equation to describe one variable as a function of others.

Essentially, data scientists combine one or more of the preceding techniques to solve challenging problems, which are:

- Web search and information extraction
- Drug design
- Predicting capital market behavior
- Understanding customer behavior
- Designing robots

Optimization

Optimization, in simple terms, is a mechanism to make something better or define a context for a solution that makes it the best.

Considering a production scenario, let's assume there are two machines that produce the desired product but one machine requires more energy for high speed in production and lower raw materials while the other requires higher raw materials and less energy to produce the same output in the same time. It is important to understand the patterns in the output based on the variation in inputs; a combination that gives the highest profits would probably be the one the production manager would want to know. You, as an analyst, need to identify the best possible way to distribute the production between the machines that gives him the highest profit.

The following image shows the point of highest profit when a graph was plotted for various distribution options between the two machines. Identifying this point is the goal of this technique.

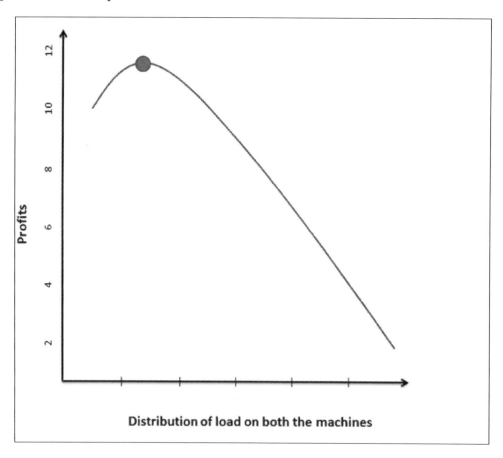

Distribution of load on both the machines

Unlike the case of simulations where there is uncertainty associated with the input data, in optimization we not only have access to data, but also have the information on the dependencies and relationships between data attributes.

One of the key concepts in Machine learning is a process called **induction**. The following learning subfields use the induction process to build models. Inductive learning is a reasoning process that uses the results of one experiment to run the next set of experiments and iteratively evolve a model from specific information.

The following figure depicts various subfields of Machine learning. These subfields are one of the ways the machine learning algorithms are classified.

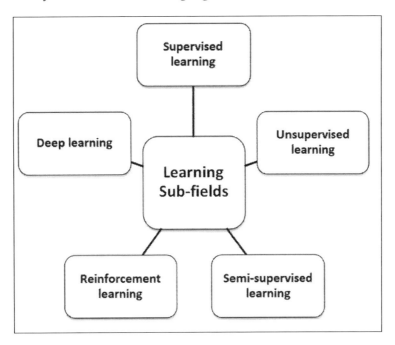

Supervised learning

Supervised learning is all about operating to a known expectation and in this case, what needs to be analyzed from the data being defined. The input datasets in this context are also referred to as "labeled" datasets. Algorithms classified under this category focus on establishing a relationship between the input and output attributes, and use this relationship speculatively to generate an output for new input data points. In the preceding section, the example defined for the classification problem is also an example of supervised learning. Labeled data helps build reliable models but is usually expensive and limited.

When the input and output attributes of the data are known, the key in supervised learning is the mapping between the inputs to outputs. There are quite a few examples of these mappings, but the complicated function that links up the input and output attributes is not known. A supervised learning algorithm takes care of this linking, and given a large dataset of input/output pairs, these functions help predict the output for any new input value.

Unsupervised learning

In some of the learning problems, we do not have any specific target in mind to solve. In the earlier section, we discussed clustering, which is a classification analyses where we do not start with a specific target in mind (good/bad, will buy/will not buy) and is hence referred to as unsupervised analyses or learning. The goal in this case is to decipher the structure in the data against the build mapping between input and output attributes of data and, in fact, the output attributes are not defined. These learning algorithms operate on an "unlabeled" dataset for this reason.

Semi-supervised learning

Semi-supervised learning is about using both labeled and unlabeled data to learn models better. It is important that there are appropriate assumptions for the unlabeled data and any inappropriate assumptions can invalidate the model. Semi-supervised learning gets its motivation from the human way of learning.

Reinforcement learning

Reinforcement learning is learning that focuses on maximizing the rewards from the result. For example, while teaching toddlers new habits, rewarding them every time they follow instructions works very well. In fact, they figure out what behavior helps them earn rewards. This is reinforcement learning, and it is also called credit assessment learning.

The most important thing is that in reinforcement learning the model is additionally responsible for making decisions for which a periodic reward is received. The results in this case, unlike supervised learning, are not immediate and may require a sequence of steps to be executed before the final result is seen. Ideally, the algorithm will generate a sequence of decisions that helps achieve the highest reward or utility.

The goal in this learning technique is to measure the trade-offs effectively by exploring and exploiting the data. For example, when a person has to travel from a point A to point B, there will be many ways that include travelling by air, water, road or by walking, and there is significant value in considering this data by measuring the trade-offs for each of these options. Another important aspect is the significance of a delay in the rewards. How would this affect learning? For example, in games like chess, any delay in reward identification may change the result.

Deep learning

Deep learning is an area of Machine learning that focuses on unifying Machine learning with artificial intelligence. In terms of the relationship with artificial neural networks, this field is more of an advancement to artificial neural networks that work on large amounts of common data to derive practical insights. It deals with building more complex neural networks to solve problems classified under semi-supervised learning and operates on datasets that have little labeled data. Some Deep learning techniques are listed as follows:

- Convolutional Networks
- **Restricted Boltzmann Machine (RBM)**
- **Deep Belief Networks (DBN)**
- Stacked Autoencoders

Performance measures

Performance measures are used to evaluate learning algorithms and form an important aspect of machine learning. In some cases, these measures are also used as heuristics to build learning models.

Now let's explore the concept of the **Probably Approximately Correct (PAC)** theory. While we describe the accuracy of hypothesis, we usually talk about two types of uncertainties as per the PAC theory:

- **Approximate**: This measures the extent to which an error is accepted for a hypothesis
- **Probability**: This measure is the percentage certainty of the hypothesis being correct

The following graph shows how the number of samples grow with error, probability, and hypothesis:

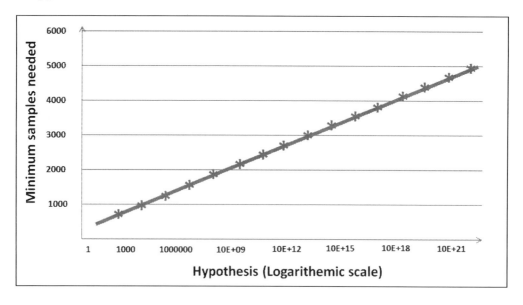

Is the solution good?

The error measures for a classification and prediction problem are different. In this section, we will cover some of these error measures followed by how they can be addressed.

In a classification problem, you can have two different types of errors, which can be elegantly represented using the "confusion matrix". Let's say in our target marketing problem, we work on 10,000 customer records to predict which customers are likely to respond to our marketing effort.

After analyzing the campaign, you can construct the following table, where the columns are your predictions and the rows are the real observations:

Action	Predicted (that there will be a buy)	Predicted (that there will be no buy)
Actually bought	TP: 500	FN: 400
Actually did not buy	FP: 100	TN: 9000

In the principal diagonal, we have buyers and non-buyers for whom the prediction matched with reality. These are correct predictions. They are called true positive and true negative respectively. In the upper right-hand side, we have those who we predicted are non-buyers, but in reality are buyers. This is an error known as a false negative error. In the lower left-hand side, we have those we predicted as buyers, but are non-buyers. This is another error known as false positive.

Are both errors equally expensive for the customers? Actually no! If we predict that someone is a buyer and they turn out to be a non-buyer, the company at most would have lost money spent on a mail or a call. However, if we predicted that someone would not buy and they were in fact buyers, the company would not have called them based on this prediction and lost a customer. So, in this case, a false negative is much more expensive than a false positive error.

The Machine learning community uses three different error measures for classification problems:

- **Measure 1: Accuracy** is the percent of predictions that were correct.

  Example: The "accuracy" was (9,000+500) out of 10,000 = 95%

- **Measure 2: Recall** is the percent of positives cases that you were able to catch. If false positives are low, recall will be high.

  Example: The "recall" was 500 out of 600 = 83.33%

- **Measure 3: Precision** is the percent of positive predictions that were correct. If false negatives are low, precision is high.

  Example: The "precision" was 500 out of 900 = 55.55%

In forecasting, you are predicting a continuous variable. So, the error measures are fairly different here. As usual, the error metrics are obtained by comparing the predictions of the models with the real values of the target variables and calculating the average error. Here are a few metrics.

Mean squared error (MSE)

To compute the MSE, we first take the square of the difference between the actual and predicted values of every record. We then take the average value of these squared errors. If the predicted value of the ith record is Pi and the actual value is Ai, then the MSE is:

$$MSE = \frac{\sum_{i=1}^{n}\left(P_i - A_i\right)^2}{n}$$

It is also common to use the square root of this quantity called **root mean square error (RMSE)**.

Mean absolute error (MAE)

To compute the MAE, we take the absolute difference between the predicted and actual values of every record. We then take the average of those absolute differences. The choice of performance metric depends on the application. The MSE is a good performance metric for many applications as it has more statistical grounding with variance. On the other hand, the MAE is more intuitive and less sensitive to outliers. Looking at the MAE and RMSE gives us additional information about the distribution of the errors. In regression, if the RMSE is close to the MAE, the model makes many relatively small errors. If the RMSE is close to the MAE2, the model makes a few but large errors.

$$MAE = \frac{\sum_{i=1}^{n}\left|P_i - A_i\right|}{n}$$

Normalized MSE and MAE (NMSE and NMAE)

Both the MSE and MAE do not indicate how big the error is as they are numeric values depending on the scale of the target variable. Comparing with a benchmarking index provides a better insight. The common practice is to take the mean of the primary attribute we are predicting and assume that our naïve prediction model is just the mean. Then we compute the MSE based on the naïve model and the original model. The ratio provides an insight into how good or bad our model is compared to the naïve model.

$$NMSE = \frac{MSE \ of \ developed \ model}{MSE \ of \ naive \ model}$$

A similar definition can also be used for the MAE.

Solving the errors: bias and variance

This trap of building highly customized higher order models is called over-fitting and is a critical concept. The resulting error is known as the **variance** of the model. Essentially, if we had taken a different training set, we would have obtained a very different model. Variance is a measure of the dependency of model on the training set. By the way, the model you see on the right most side (linear fit) is called under-fitting and the error caused due to under-fitting is called bias. In an under-fitting or high bias situation, the model does not explain the relationship between the data. Essentially, we're trying to fit an overly simplistic hypothesis, for example, linear where we should be looking for a higher order polynomial.

To avoid the trap of over-fitting and under-fitting, data scientists build the model on a training set and then find the error on a test set. They refine the model until the error in the test set comes down. As the model starts getting customized to the training data, the error on the test set starts going up. They stop refining the model after that point.

Let's analyze bias and variance a bit more in this chapter and learn a few practical ways of dealing with them. The error in any model can be represented as a combination of bias, variance, and random error. With $Err(x)=Bias2+Variance+Irred ucible \ Error$ in less complex models, the bias term is high, and in models with higher complexity, the variance term is high, as shown in the following figure:

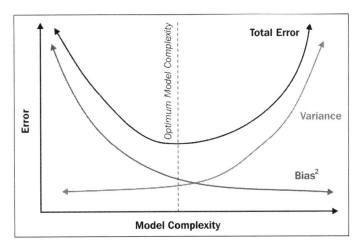

To reduce bias or variance, let's first ask this question. If a model has a high bias, how does its error vary as a function of the amount of data?

At a very low data size, any model can fit the data well (any model fits a single point, any linear model can fit two points, a quadratic can fit three points, and so on). So, the error of a high bias model on a training set starts minuscule and goes up with increasing data points. However, on the test set, the error remains high initially as the model is highly customized to the training set. As the model gets more and more refined, the error reduces and becomes equal to that of the training set.

The following graph depicts the situation clearly:

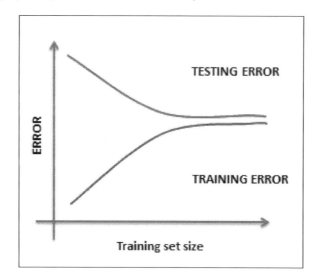

The remedy for this situation could be one of the following:

- Most likely, you are working with very few features, so you must find more features
- Increase the complexity of the model by increasing polynomials and depth
- Increasing the data size will not be of much help if the model has a high bias

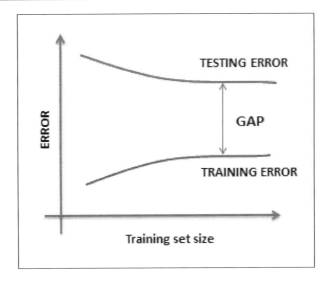

When you face such situations, you can try the following remedies (the reverse of the previous ones):

- Most likely, you are working with too many features, so, you must reduce the features
- Decrease the complexity of the model
- Increasing the data size will be some help

Some complementing fields of Machine learning

Machine learning has a close relationship to many related fields including artificial intelligence, data mining, statistics, data science, and others listed shortly. In fact, Machine learning is in that way a multi-disciplinary field, and in some ways is linked to all of these fields.

In this section, we will define some of these fields, draw parallels to how they correlate to Machine learning, and understand the similarities and dissimilarities, if any. Overall, we will start with the core Machine learning definition as a field of science that includes developing self-learning algorithms. Most of the fields we are going to discuss now either use machine learning techniques or a superset or subset of machine learning techniques.

Data mining

Data mining is a process of analyzing data and deriving insights from a (large) dataset by applying business rules to it. The focus here is on the data and the domain of the data. Machine learning techniques are adopted in the process of identifying which rules are relevant and which aren't.

Machine learning versus Data mining		
Similarities with Machine learning	**Dissimilarities with Machine learning**	**Relationship with Machine learning**
Both Machine learning and data mining look at data with the goal of extracting value from it. Most of the tools used for Machine learning and data mining are common. For example, R and Weka among others.	While Machine learning focuses on using known knowledge or experience, data mining focuses on discovering unknown knowledge, like the existence of a specific structure in data that will be of help in analyzing the data. Intelligence derived is meant to be consumed by machines in Machine learning compared to data mining where the target consumers are humans.	The fields of Machine learning and data mining are intertwined, and there is a significant overlap in the underlying principles and methodologies.

Artificial intelligence (AI)

Artificial intelligence focuses on building systems that can mimic human behavior. It has been around for a while now and the modern AI has been continuously evolving, now includes specialized data requirements. Among many other capabilities, AI should demonstrate the following:

- Knowledge storage and representation to hold all the data that is subject to interrogation and investigation
- **Natural Language Processing** (NLP) capabilities to be able to process text
- Reasoning capabilities to be able to answer questions and facilitate conclusions
- The ability to plan, schedule, and automate
- Machine learning to be able to build self-learning algorithms
- Robotics and more

Machine learning is a subfield of artificial intelligence.

Machine learning versus Artificial Intelligence		
Similarities with Machine learning	Dissimilarities with Machine learning	Relationship with Machine learning
Both machine learning and artificial intelligence employ learning algorithms and focus on automation when reasoning or decision-making.	Though Machine learning is considered to be in the AI's range of interests, Machine learning's primary focus is to improve on a machine's performance of a task, and the experience built need not always be human behavior. In the case of artificial intelligence, human inspired algorithms are employed.	Machine learning is often considered as a subfield of artificial intelligence.

Statistical learning

In statistical learning, the predictive functions are arrived at and primarily derived from samples of data. It is of great importance how the data is collected, cleansed, and managed in this process. Statistics is pretty close to mathematics, as it is about quantifying data and operating on numbers.

Machine learning versus Statistical learning		
Similarities with Machine learning	Dissimilarities with Machine learning	Relationship with Machine learning
Just like Machine learning, statistical learning is also about building the ability to infer from the data that in some cases represents experience.	Statistical learning focuses on coming up with valid conclusions while Machine learning is about predictions. Statistical learning works on and allows assumptions as against Machine learning. Machine learning and statistics are practiced by different groups. Machine learning is a relatively new field when compared to statistics.	The Machine learning technology implements statistical techniques.

Data science

Data science is all about turning data into products. It is analytics and machine learning put into action to draw inferences and insights out of data. Data science is perceived to be a first step from traditional data analysis and knowledge systems, such as **Data Warehouses** (**DW**) and **Business Intelligence** (**BI**), which considers all aspects of big data.

The data science lifecycle includes steps from data availability/loading to deriving and communicating data insights up to operationalizing the process, and Machine learning often forms a subset of this process.

Machine learning versus Data science		
Similarities with Machine learning	**Dissimilarities with Machine learning**	**Relationship with Machine learning**
Machine learning and data science have prediction as a common binding outcome given the problem's context.	One of the important differences between Machine learning and data science is the need for domain expertise. Data science focuses on solving domain-specific problems, while Machine learning focuses on building models that can generically fit a problem context.	Data science is a superset of Machine learning, data mining, and related subjects. It extensively covers the complete process starting from data loading until production.

Machine learning process lifecycle and solution architecture

In this section, we will discuss the machine learning implementation process and solution architecture:

1. The first step toward defining the solution architecture is defining the problem statement, which includes defining the goal, process, and assumptions.

2. Determine what problem type is this problem classified under? Whether it is a classification, regression, or optimization problem?

3. Choose a metric that will be used to measure the accuracy of the model.

4. In order to ensure the model works well with the unseen data:

    1. Build the model using training data.

    2. Tweak the model using test data.

    3. Declare an accuracy based on the final version.

The following figure explains the flow and architecture of the underlying system:

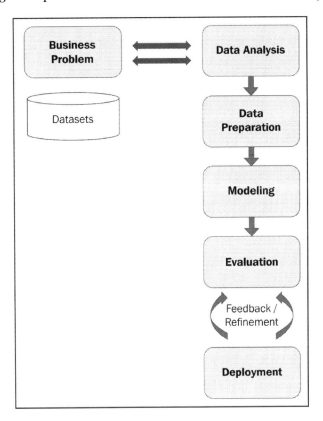

Machine learning algorithms

Now, let's look at the important machine learning algorithms and some brief details about each of them. In-depth implementation aspects for each of the algorithms will be covered in later chapters. These algorithms are either classified under the problem type or the learning type. There is a simple classification of the algorithms given but it is intuitive and not necessarily exhaustive.

There are many ways of classifying or grouping machine learning algorithms, and in this book we will use the learning model based grouping. In each chapter, starting from *Chapter 5, Decision Tree based learning*, we will cover one or more learning models and associated algorithms. The following concept model depicts a listing of learning models:

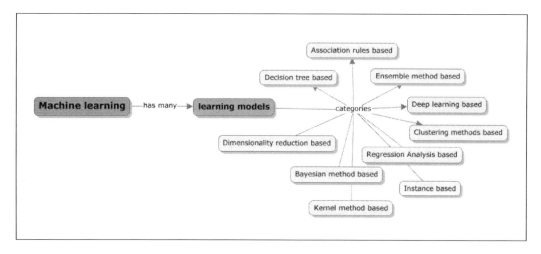

Decision tree based algorithms

Decision tree based algorithms define models that are iteratively or recursively constructed based on the data provided. The goal of Decision tree based algorithms is to predict the value of a target variable given a set of input variables. Decision trees help solve classification and regression problems using tree based methods. Decisions fork in tree structures until a prediction decision is made for a given record. Some of the algorithms are as follows:

- Random forest
- **Classification and Regression Tree (CART)**
- C4.5 and C5.0
- Chi-square
- **Gradient boosting machines (GBM)**
- **Chi-Squared Automatic Interaction Detection (CHAID)**
- Decision stump
- **Multivariate adaptive regression splines (MARS)**

Bayesian method based algorithms

Bayesian methods are those that explicitly apply the Bayesian inference theorem and again solve classification and regression problems. Bayesian methods facilitate subjective probability in modeling. The following are some of the Bayesian based algorithms:

- Naïve Bayes
- **Averaged one-dependence estimators (AODE)**
- **Bayesian belief network (BBN)**

Kernel method based algorithms

When we hear about kernel methods, the first thing that comes to mind is **Support Vector Machines (SVM)**. These methods are usually a group of methods in themselves. kernel methods are concerned with pattern analysis and as explained in the preceding sections, that crux of pattern analysis includes various mapping techniques. Here, the mapping datasets include vector spaces. Some examples of kernel method based learning algorithms are listed as follows:

- SVM
- **Linear discriminant analysis (LDA)**

Clustering methods

Clustering, like regression, describes a class of problems and a class of methods. Clustering methods are typically organized by the modeling approaches such as centroid-based and hierarchical. These methods organize data into groups by assessing the similarity in the structure of input data:

- K-means
- **Expectation maximization (EM)** and **Gaussian mixture models (GMM)**

Artificial neural networks (ANN)

Similar to kernel methods, artificial neural networks are again a class of pattern matching techniques, but these models are inspired by the structure of biological neural networks. These methods are again used to solve classifications and regression problems. They relate to Deep learning modeling and have many subfields of algorithms that help solve specific problems in context.

Some of the methods in this category include:

- **Learning vector quantization (LVQ)**
- **Self-organizing maps (SOM)**
- Hopfield network
- Perceptron
- Backpropagation

Dimensionality reduction

Like clustering methods, dimensionality reduction methods work iteratively and on the data structure in an unsupervised manner. Given the dataset and the dimensions, more dimensions would mean more work in the Machine learning implementation. The idea is to iteratively reduce the dimensions and bring more relevant dimensions forward. This technique is usually used to simplify high-dimensional data and then apply a supervised learning technique. Some example dimensionality reduction methods are listed as follows:

- **Multidimensional scaling (MDS)**
- **Principal component analysis (PCA)**
- **Projection pursuit (PP)**
- **Partial least squares (PLS)** regression
- Sammon mapping

Ensemble methods

As the name suggests, ensemble methods encompass multiple models that are built independently and the results of these models are combined and responsible for overall predictions. It is critical to identify what independent models are to be combined or included, how the results need to be combined, and in what way to achieve the required result. The subset of models that are combined is sometimes referred to as weaker models as the results of these models need not completely fulfill the expected outcome in isolation. This is a very powerful and widely adopted class of techniques. The following are some of the Ensemble method algorithms:

- Random forest
- Bagging
- AdaBoost
- Bootstrapped Aggregation (Boosting)

- Stacked generalization (blending)
- **Gradient boosting machines (GBM)**

Instance based learning algorithms

Instances are nothing but subsets of datasets, and instance based learning models work on an identified instance or groups of instances that are critical to the problem. The results across instances are compared, which can include an instance of new data as well. This comparison uses a particular similarity measure to find the best match and predict. Instance based methods are also called case-based or memory-based learning. Here the focus is on the representation of the instances and similarity measures for comparison between instances. Some of the instance based learning algorithms are listed as follows:

- **k-Nearest Neighbour (k-NN)**
- Self-Organizing
- **Learning vector quantization (LVQ)**
- **Self-organizing maps (SOM)**

Regression analysis based algorithms

Regression is a process of refining the model iteratively based on the error generated by the model. Regression also is used to define a machine learning problem type. Some example algorithms in regression are:

- Ordinary least squares linear regression
- Logistic regression
- **Multivariate adaptive regression splines (MARS)**
- Stepwise regression

Association rule based learning algorithms

Given the variables, association rule based learning algorithms extract and define rules that can be applied on a dataset and demonstrate experienced-based learning, and thus prediction. These rules when associated in a multi-dimensional data context can be useful in a commercial context as well. Some of the examples of Association rule based algorithms are given as follows:

- The Apriori algorithm
- The Eclat algorithm

Machine learning tools and frameworks

Machine learning adoption is rapidly increasing among technology and business organizations. Every organization is actively strategizing on how to capitalize on their data and use it to augment their client's experiences and build new businesses. When it comes to tools or frameworks for Machine learning, there are many open source and commercial options on the market. The new age tools are all built to support big data, distributed storage, and parallel processing. In the next chapter, we will cover some aspects of handling large scale data in the context of Machine learning.

At a very high level, there are three generations of Machine learning tools.

The first generation of Machine learning tools is focused on providing a richness of the Machine learning algorithms and supporting deep analytics. These tools haven't been built to focus on handling large scale data or for supporting distributed storage and parallel processing. Some of them still handle volumes as a result of their support for vertical scalability. Some of the tools that come under this category are SAS, SPSS, Weka, R, and more. Having said that, most of these tools are now being upgraded to support big data requirements too.

The second generation tools are focused on supporting big data requirements, most of them work on the Hadoop platform, and they provide capabilities to run machine learning algorithms in a MapReduce paradigm. Some of the tools that are categorized here are Mahout, RapidMiner, Pentaho, and MADlib. Some of these tools do not support all the machine learning algorithms.

The third generations tools are the smart kids on the road, breaking the traditional norms of operating in batch mode, supporting real-time analytics, providing support for advanced data types of big data, and at the same time supporting deeper analytics. Some of the tools that are categorized under this are Spark, HaLoop, and Pregel.

In *Chapter 4*, *Machine Learning Tools, Libraries, and Frameworks*, we will cover some of the key machine learning tools and demonstrate how they can be used based on the problem's context. Implementation details for tools such as R, Julia, Python, Mahout, and Spark will be covered in depth. Required technology primers and installation or setup-related guidance will be provided.

Summary

In this chapter, which forms the basis for the rest of the chapters of this book, we covered the basics of Machine learning and the landscape of Machine learning semantics. We started by defining Machine learning in simple terms and introduced Machine learning jargon or the commonly used terms.

There are many competing and complementing fields of Machine learning. We have thoroughly explained the similarities, dissimilarities, and the relationship of Machine learning with fields such as artificial intelligence, data mining, data science, and statistics. Overall, all these fields are very similar and have overlapping goals. In most cases, the practitioners of these fields were different. Even in terms of the tools being used, there were many common points.

We have also looked at some of the latest and best-of-breed tools that can be employed in Machine learning. Some of these tools will be demonstrated in the chapters using practical examples.

In the next chapter, we will cover a unique aspect of Machine learning that has pretty much changed the way Machine learning implementations have been looked at. We will explore how the big data, or large dataset, aspect of Machine learning has impacted the choice of tools and implementation approaches.

2
Machine learning and Large-scale datasets

We have seen a dramatic change in the way data has been handled in the recent past with the advent of big data. The field of Machine learning has seen the need to include scaling up strategies to handle the new age data requirements. This actually means that some of the traditional Machine learning implementations will not all be relevant in the context of big data now. Infrastructure and tuning requirements are now the challenges with the need to store and process large scale data complimented by the data format complexities.

With the evolution of hardware architectures, accessibility of cheaper hardware with distributed architectures and new programming paradigms for simplified parallel processing options, which can now be applied to many learning algorithms, we see a rising interest in scaling up the Machine learning systems.

The topics listed next are covered in-depth in this chapter:

- An introduction to big data and typical challenges of large-scale Machine learning
- The motivation behind scaling up and scaling out Machine learning, and an overview of parallel and distributed processing for huge datasets
- An overview of Concurrent Algorithm design, Big O notations, and task decomposition techniques for achieving parallelism
- The advent of cloud frameworks to provide cloud clustering, distributed data storage, fault tolerance, and high availability coupled with effective utilization of computational resources
- Frameworks and platform options for implementing large-scale Machine learning (Parallel Processing Frameworks such as MapReduce in **Massive Parallel Processing (MPP)**, MRI, platforms as GPU, FPGA, and Multicore)

Big data and the context of large-scale Machine learning

I have covered some of the core aspects of big data in my previous Packt book titled *Getting Started with Greenplum for Big Data Analytics*. In this section, we will quickly recap some of the core aspects of big data and its impact in the field of Machine learning:

- The definition of large-scale is a scale of terabytes, petabytes, exabytes, or higher. This is typically the volume that cannot be handled by traditional database engines. The following chart lists the orders of magnitude that represents data volumes:

Multiples of bytes		
SI decimal prefixes		Binary Usage
Name(Symbol)	Value	
Kilobyte (KB)	103	210
Megabyte (MB)	106	220
Gigabyte (GB)	109	230
Terabyte (TB)	1012	240
Petabyte (PB)	1015	250
Exabyte (EB)	1018	260
Zettabyte (ZB)	1021	270
Yottabyte (YB)	1024	280

- Data formats that are referred to in this context are distinct; they are generated and consumed, and need not be structured (for example, DBMS and relational data stores). Now, there are new sources of data; this data can be generated by social networking sites, equipment, and more. This can be streaming data that is heterogeneous in nature (for example, videos, emails, tweets, and so on). Again, none of the traditional data marts / data stores and data mining applications support these formats today.

- Additionally, all the large-scale processing always happened in batches, but we are now seeing the need to support *real-time* processing capabilities. The new **Lambda Architectures (LA)** address the need to support both batch and real-time data ingestion and processing.

- Overall, the response time windows are shrinking and this adds to the challenge.

Let's recap the four key characteristics of big data. All of these need special tools, frameworks, infrastructure, and capabilities:

- Higher volumes (to the degree of petabytes)
- The need for availability/accessibility of data (more real-time)
- Diversified data formats
- The increase in unlabeled data, and thus the **Noise**

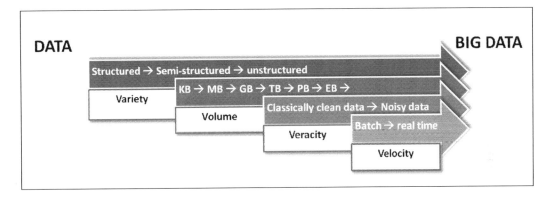

Functional versus Structural – A methodological mismatch

We could never have imagined even five years ago that Relational Databases or non-relational databases like object databases will become only a single kind of database technology, and not the database technology in itself. Internet-scale data processing has changed the way we process data.

The new generation architectures, such as Facebook, Wikipedia, Salesforce, and more, are founded on principles and paradigms, which are radically different from the well-established theoretical foundations on which the current data management technologies are developed.

Commoditizing information

The Apple App Store, SaaS, Ubiquitous Computing, Mobility, Cloud-Based Multi-Tenant architectures have unleashed, in business terms, an ability to commoditize information delivery. This model changes almost all the architecture decision making—as we now need to think in terms of what is the "units of information" that can be offered and billed as services, instead of thinking in terms of the **Total Cost of Ownership (TCO)** of the solution.

Theoretical limitations of RDBMS

As Michael Stonebreaker, the influential database theorist, has been writing in recent times, at the heart of the Internet-Scale Architectures is a new theoretical model of data processing and management. The theories of database management are now more than three decades old, and they were designed for mainframe-type computing environments and unreliable electronic components. Nature and the capabilities of systems and applications have since evolved significantly. With reliability becoming a quality attribute of the underlying environment, systems are composed of parallel processing cores, and the nature of data creation and usage has undergone tremendous change. In order to conceptualize solutions for these new environments, we need to approach the designing of solution architectures from a computing perspective and not only from an engineering perspective.

Six major forces that are driving the data revolution today are:

- Massive Parallel Processing
- Commoditized Information Delivery
- Ubiquitous Computing and Mobile Devices
- Non-RDBMS and Semantic Databases
- Community Computing
- Cloud Computing

Hadoop and **MapReduce** have unleashed massive parallel processing of data on a colossal scale, and have made the complex computing algorithms in a programmatic platform. This has changed analytics and Business Intelligence forever. Similarly, the web services and API-driven architectures have made information delivery commoditized on an enormous scale.

Today, it is possible to build very large systems in such a way that each subsystem or component is a complete platform in itself, hosted and managed by a different entity altogether.

Dijkstra once made an insightful remark that:

> *"Computer Science is no more about computers than astronomy is about telescopes"*

He would perhaps be a happy man today, as computing has liberated itself from the clutches of a personal computer, also known as workstations and servers. Most of our information consumption today is from the devices that we hardly call computers. Mobile devices, wearable devices, and information everywhere are changing the way data is created, assembled, consumed, and analyzed.

As the limitations of the traditional databases have been exposed, in recent years, many special purpose databases have emerged—in-memory, columnar, graph-DB, and semantic stores are all now commercially available.

The previously mentioned innovations have changed the traditional data architecture completely. Especially, the semantic computing, ontology-driven modelling of information has turned data design over its head. Philosophically, data architecture is going through an factual underpinning. In the traditional data models, we first design the "data model"—a fixed, design time understanding of the world and its future. A data model fixes the meaning of data forever into a fixed structure. A table is nothing but a category, a set of something. As a result, data has to mean if we understand the set/category to which it belongs. For example, if we design an automobile processing system into some categories, such as four-wheelers, two-wheelers, commercial vehicles, and so on, then this division itself has a relevant meaning embedded into it. The data that is stored in each of these categories does not reveal the purpose of the design that is embedded in the way the categories are designed. For example, another system might view the world of automobiles regarding of its drivetrain—electric, petroleum powered, nuclear powered, and so on.

This categorization itself reveals the purpose of the system in some manner, which is impossible to obtain the attributes of any single record. Semantic and Metadata-Driven architectures can turn such a data model over its head. In a metadata model, it is the object that exists first.

Some of the core characteristics of how data is stored and managed in an RDBMS-based storage system are as follows:

- Data is stored in a table that is typically characterized by rows and columns
- Tables are linked using relationships between data attributes
- It is known for efficiency and flexibility
- This supports normalization techniques that reduce data duplication

On the other hand:

- The metadata driven / NoSQL / Semantic data architectures are free from relationships that tie down the purpose of the usage of data
- The focus is more on accommodating constant changes in business requirements that results in least changes in the software system being built
- Support for large datasets with distributed storage techniques, with lowered storage costs is of great importance in the metadata driven / NoSQL /semantic data architecture

Scaling-up versus Scaling-out storage

With the advent of big data, there is now a need to scale data storage equipment to be able to store the petabyte-scale data. There are two ways of scaling storage equipment:

- Scaling-up (vertical scalability)
- Scaling-out (horizontal scalability)

Scaling up or vertical scalability is about adding more resources to the existing system that in turn increases the ability to hold more data. Here, resources can mean RAM, computation power, hard drive, and more.

Scaling out or horizontal scalability is about adding new components to the system. This requires the data to be stored and distributed, and there are tasks that can be parallelized. This usually adds complexity to the system, and most of the time requires a redesign of the system.

All the big data technologies work on and support the scaling out of the infrastructure.

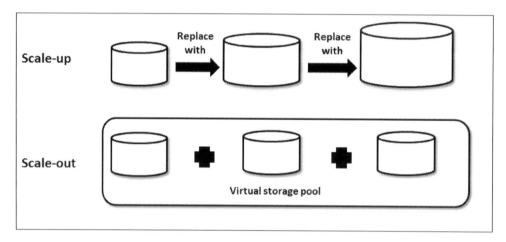

Scaling up (Vertical Scalability)	Scaling out (Horizontal Scalability)
Lesser and high capacity server	More and moderate, or low capacity server
There could be a threshold beyond which an infrastructure can cease to scale vertically	There is no limit, the infrastructure can be scaled on a need basis without any impact on the design
Can accommodate larger VMs	Runs with lower VMs and can be affected by failure in the host
Shared everything data architecture	Shared nothing data architecture

Scaling up (Vertical Scalability)	Scaling out (Horizontal Scalability)
Higher TCO	Relatively lower and variable costs
Lower network equipment	Needs relatively larger number of equipments (routers, switches, and more…)

Distributed and parallel computing strategies

Though distributed and parallel processing have been around for several years now, but with the advent of usability priorities needed for cost-effective solutions, these strategies have become critical for the Machine learning tasks.

The following diagram depicts Flynn's taxonomy for computing. The categorization is done based on the number of data streams versus the number of instruction streams.

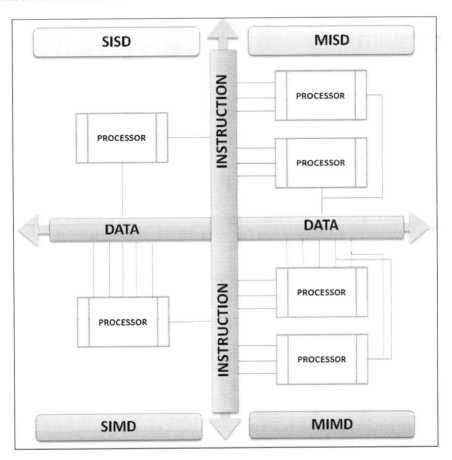

- **Single Instruction Single Data (SISD)**: This is a case of a single processor with no parallelism in data or instruction. A single instruction is executed on a single data in a sequential manner, for example, a uniprocessor.

- **Multiple Instruction Single Data (MISD)**: Here, multiple instructions operate on a single data stream; a typical example can be fault tolerance.

- **Single Instruction Multiple Data (SIMD)**: This is a case of natural parallelism; a single instruction triggers operation on multiple data streams.

- **Multiple Instructions Multiple Data (MIMD)**: This is a case where multiple independent instructions operate on multiple and independent data streams. Since the data streams are multiple, the memory can either be shared or distributed. Distributed processing can be categorized here. The previous figure depicts MIMD and a variation in a "distributed" context.

The following diagram explains parallel processor architectures and categorization:

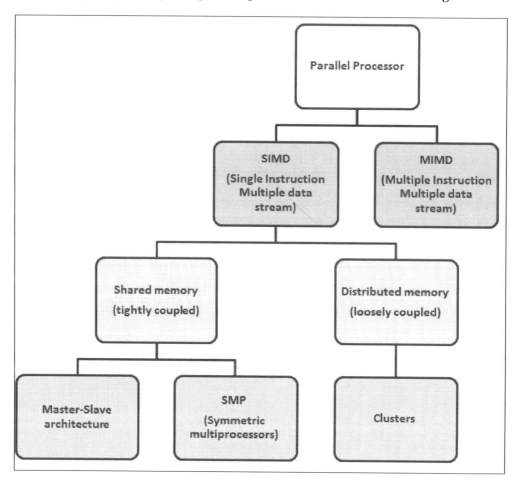

One of the critical requirements of parallel/distributed processing systems is High Availability and fault tolerance. There are several programming paradigms to implement parallelism. The following list details the important ones:

- **The Master/Workers Model**: Master model is the driver where the work is held and then disseminated to the workers. Pivotal Greenplum Database and HD (Pivotal's Hadoop's distribution) modules implement this pattern.

- **The Producer/Consumer Model**: Here, there is no owner who triggers the work. Producer generates work items and consumer subscribes and executes asynchronously. The **Enterprise Service Bus (ESB)** based data integration systems implement this pattern.

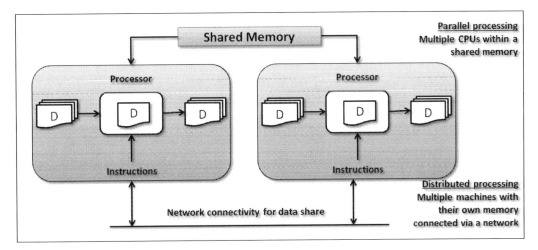

In theory, there are two types of parallelization; one is data parallelization, the other one is execution or task parallelization:

- **Data parallelization**: It deals with running the same computations with multiple inputs in parallel. In the Machine learning world, this is a case where we consider running the same algorithm across different data samples without really worrying about how the data samples are distributed.

- **Execution or Task parallelization**: Unlike data parallelization, this is about breaking the functionality into multiple pieces and running them in a parallel manner. These pieces of work may work on the same dataset, but this is possible only for the tasks that can be parallelized and have no dependencies between the sub tasks.

Task parallelization can be fine grained or coarse grained.

There are many distributed platform options to bring efficiency and scale to Machine learning algorithms and can process large datasets. Some of the options include:

- **Field-Programmable Gate Arrays (FPGAs)**
- **Graphics Processing Units (GPUs)**
- **High-Performance Computing (HPC)**
- Multicore and multi-processor parallel systems
- Cloud Infrastructures for virtual-large scale clusters

Besides the multiple platform options available, there are other highly adopted frameworks available that have out-of-box APIs for building Machine learning algorithms. The choice of this framework depends on the choice of hardware in particular.

It is important that we take an option that can take maximum advantage of the existing architecture, and suits the choice of learning algorithm and the data structure.

Machine learning: Scalability and Performance

There are two important ways in which Machine learning algorithms can be scaled:

- Sampling
- Distributed systems with parallel processing

It is possible to concurrently execute a given learning algorithm as separate chunks of work and consolidate the results. This sounds like a fairly simple way of parallelizing and being able to scale and perform well on a bigger dataset. This comes with an assumption that the datasets are discrete and there isn't any dependency between these distributed sets of data.

By the virtue of the proliferation of data sources, we now have access to large sets that are already distributed, and this brings in a need for the ability to have the learning algorithms running in a distributed mode.

There are now a variety of options for distributed and parallel framework for Machine learning. Let's look at some key differentiating factors between these platforms:

- The degree of granularity in parallelization is a critical aspect. Support for fine-grained versus coarse-grained parallelization is what it refers to. A lower degree of granularity defines a fine-grained task parallelization, while a higher level of granularity defines coarse-grained task parallelization.

- The degree to which algorithm customization is supported.
- Support for mixing a variety of programming paradigms.
- The ease with which datasets can be scaled-out.
- The degree to which batch and real-time processing is supported.

Given a problem context, the choice of the platform and programming framework should be guided by the previous criteria.

Following are some key metrics to measure the computational performance of parallel algorithms:

- **Performance** is the ratio of solution time for the sequential algorithms versus parallel process
- **Efficiency** or **Throughput** measures the ratio of performance across multiple processors
- **Scalability** is the percentage improvement in efficiency with the growing number of processors

The next section covers some key characteristics of the Machine learning problem that motivate scaling-up the Machine learning algorithms.

Too many data points or instances

We now see that in most of the Machine learning problems, there is an abundance of datasets and in many cases, all these data points are relevant in model building and refining. These data points can potentially run into terabyte scale with all their relevance.

This brings in a need to support distributed storage and a bandwidth to process these data points in the cluster. High-capacity storage systems with the ability to run parallel programming language paradigms like MapReduce and LINQ are used here.

Too many attributes or features

The datasets that form an input to a building model can come with too many features, attributes, or dimensions. In this case, the Machine learning algorithms group the dependent or more relevant attributes and run the algorithms in iteration. These kind of datasets can be seen in case of Text mining and **Natural language processing (NLP)**, where the number of features can run into multiples of millions. In this case, parallelizing the computation across features can get us to solve the problem effectively by the way of eliminating irrelevant features. Random forest and Decision trees are some of the examples. Also, some specific feature selection techniques such as the regularization methods will be covered in the chapters to come.

Shrinking response time windows – need for real-time responses

There are certain Machine learning requirements such as speech recognition that will demand a real-time response from the systems. In these applications, response time from a Machine learning implementation is critical, and the response itself will become irrelevant otherwise. Parallelization can bring in this efficiency.

Latency and performance of the model are more important a problem to deal with than the throughput. There are many use cases where this latency in inference can invalidate the model itself, as the response becomes obsolete.

For these kinds of problems, highly parallelized hardware architectures such as GPUs or FPGAs will be very effective.

Highly complex algorithm

This is a case where the algorithm of choice itself is complex, for example, a computational intensive function or any non-linear models. Let's take an example of a text or image content; it is inherently non-linear in nature. This complexity can easily be addressed using distributed computing.

There are many ways we can solve these problems and one way is to prioritize features and still target for higher accuracies. However this will remove the automation part in the learning. There always needs to be a step that engineers the features before running the algorithm.

The cases where there is more data complexity, there is a computational complexity. Unless the platform is scaled, there is no way to get the learning process run faster.

Multicore and GPU systems are apt for this kind of requirement. They bring in both; storage scale and computational efficiency.

Feed forward, iterative prediction cycles

There are some unique use cases in the Machine learning space that do not stop at one level of execution of the algorithm. The algorithm runs iteratively and sequentially where the output from an iteration feeds into another iteration. This is critical for the outcome of the model. There can also be a need to consolidate the inferences across all the iterations that are run sequentially. This can make the model execution process quite complex. We can deal with inference process as a one-shot process, which will bring up the computational costs, or there can be stages of parallelization of individual tasks.

Some real-world examples are:

- Speech recognition
- Machine translation

Model selection process

In some cases, we will need to run multiple models in parameters on the same training and test sets with the different priority of features, and compare the accuracy to choose an appropriate model for the given problem domain. These trials can run in parallel as there will not be any dependencies between these models. The complexity increases when we will have to tune the parameters of learning algorithms and evaluate across multiple executions to infer from the learning.

The very fact that there is no dependency between the executions makes it highly parallelizable and requires no intercommunication. One of the examples of this use case is statistical significance testing. The usefulness of the parallel platforms is obvious for these tasks, as they can be easily performed concurrently without the need to parallelize actual learning and inference algorithms.

Potential issues in large-scale Machine learning

Let's now look at some potential issues encountered in the large-scale Machine learning implementations:

- **Parallel execution**: Managing the accuracy of the parallel execution requires special care and a different design paradigm.
- **Load balancing** and **managing skews**: With data and execution now distributed and running parallel, it is very imperative to manage the data and compute skews. No single node will need to take relatively more data storage or computations.
- **Monitoring**: With a variety of hardware, effective monitoring and automatic recovery systems need to be placed.
- **Fault tolerance**: A foolproof failover and recovery system is a mandate.
- **Auto scaling**: The scaling out and scaling up process is automatic.
- **Job scheduling**: *Batch* jobs will need to be scheduled.
- **Workflow Management**: Choreography and Orchestration process to coordinate and monitor work execution among the nodes of the cluster.

Algorithms and Concurrency

Let's now look at some basics of algorithms in general, the time complexity; and the order of magnitude measurements, before we start talking about building concurrency in executing algorithms, then explore the approaches to parallelizing algorithms.

An algorithm can be defined as a sequence of steps that takes an input to produce the desired output. They are agnostic technology representations; let's look at a sorting algorithm example:

```
Input: A sequence of n number—a1, a2, ...,an
Output: A permutation (reordering)—a1', a2', ...,an' such that a1'<=a2'<=...
<=an'
```

The following algorithm is an insertion-sort algorithm:

```
INSERTION-SORT(A)
1. for j = 2 to length[A]
2. dokey<-A[j]
3. //insert A[j] to sorted sequence A[1..j-1]
4. i<-j-1
5. while i>0 and A[i]>key
6. do A[i+1] <- A[i] //move A[i] one position right
7. i<-i-1
8. A[i+1]<-key
```

For measuring the time and space complexity of algorithms, one of the elements is the input size. The time complexity is a measure of how "fast enough" the algorithm is for the defined needs; more importantly, how the algorithm would react when the volume of the data is increased.

Frequency count is one of the key measures for an algorithm. It is a prediction of how many times each instruction of the algorithm will run for an execution. For example:

Instruction	Code	Frequency count (FC)
1	`for (int i=0; i< n ; i++)`	n+1
2	`count << i`	N
3	`p = p + 1`	N
4		3n +1

The FC measure is relatively meaningless unless it considers the relative performance to volume. There is another measure called "order of magnitude" that is an estimate of performance versus data volume. The *Big-O* is a measure of the rate at which the algorithm performance degrades as the function of the amount of data that it requires to process.

For example, *O(n)* represents linear performance degradation and *O(n2)* represents quadratic performance degradation.

Developing concurrent algorithms

The first step in developing a parallel algorithm is to decompose the problem into tasks that can be executed concurrently. A given problem may be decomposed into tasks in many different ways. Tasks may be of same or different sizes:

Task dependency graph is a directed graph with nodes corresponding to tasks and edges indicating that the result of one task is required for processing the next task.

Example: This is the database query processing.

Consider the following execution of the query:

```
MODEL = ``CIVIC'' AND YEAR = 2001 AND (COLOR = ``GREEN'' OR COLOR =
``WHITE)
```

on the following database:

ID#	Model	Year	Color	Dealer	Price
4523	Civic	2002	Blue	MN	$18,000
3476	Corolla	1999	White	IL	$15,000
7623	Camry	2001	Green	NY	$21,000
9834	Prius	2001	Green	CA	$18,000
6734	Civic	2001	White	OR	$17,000
5342	Altima	2001	Green	FL	$19,000
3845	Maxima	2001	Blue	NY	$22,000
8354	Accord	2000	Green	VT	$18,000
4395	Civic	2001	Red	CA	$17,000
7352	Civic	2002	Red	WA	$18,000

There can be fine-grained and coarse-grained task decomposition. The degree of concurrency increases as the decomposition becomes finer.

There are many decomposition techniques and there is no single best way of doing it. Following are some techniques:

- Recursive decomposition
- Data decomposition
- Exploratory decomposition
- Speculative decomposition

Decomposition results in several tasks and some characteristics of these tasks critically affect the performance of the parallel algorithms. Some of these features are task interactions (inter-task communication), the size of data that each task handles, and the task size. Some important aspects that need to be kept in mind while designing parallel execution algorithms include decoupling tasks in such a way that there is minimal interaction and handling granularity trade-offs.

Technology and implementation options for scaling-up Machine learning

In this section, we will explore some parallel programming techniques and distributed platform options that Machine learning implementations can adopt. The Hadoop platform will be introduced in the next chapter, and we will look into some practical examples starting from *Chapter 3, An Introduction to Hadoop's Architecture and Ecosystem* with some real-world examples.

MapReduce programming paradigm

MapReduce is a parallel programming paradigm that abstracts the parallelizing computing and data complexities in a distributed computing environment. It works on the concept of taking the compute function to the data rather than taking the data to the compute function.

MapReduce is more of a programming framework that comes with many built-in functions that the developer need not worry about building, and can alleviate many implementation complexities like data partitioning, scheduling, managing exceptions, and intersystem communications.

The following figure depicts a typical composition of the MapReduce function:

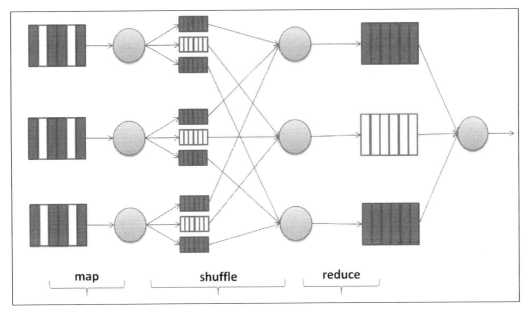

MapReduce was originally designed and adopted by Google as a programming model for processing large data sets on a cluster with parallel processing over distributed storage.

The MapReduce paradigm now has become an industry standard and many platforms are internally built on this paradigm and support MapReduce implementation. For example, Hadoop is an open source implementation that can be run either in-house or on cloud computing services such as, **Amazon EC2** with elastic MapReduce.

This has, at the core, the Map() and Reduce() functions that are capable of running in parallel across the nodes in the cluster. The Map() function works on the distributed data and runs the required functionality in parallel, and the Reduce() function runs a summary operation of the data.

High Performance Computing (HPC) with Message Passing Interface (MPI)

MPI is designed to provide access to advanced parallel hardware, and is meant to work with heterogeneous networks and clusters. It is an impressive specification and provides a portable way to implement the parallel programs.

Message passing is a process of data transfer and synchronization between the sender and the receiver. The following figure demonstrates the message passing between sender and receiver:

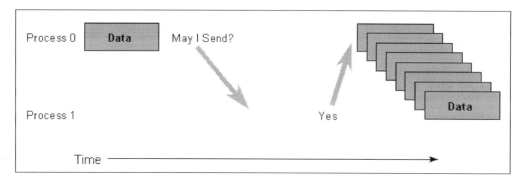

The processes can be grouped; the message sharing between the sender and the receiver needs to happen in the same context. Communicator thus is a combination of a group and the context. The data in a message is sent or received as triples.

MPI can be used to achieve portability and can improve performance through parallel processing. It can support unique data structures, and libraries can be built for reuse. MPI does not support liberal fault tolerance.

Language Integrated Queries (LINQ) framework

The LINQ framework is a general-purpose system for large-scale data and parallel computing. Similar to the MapReduce paradigm, it comes with a high level of abstraction that comes with base implementations, and helps developers reduce the development complexities of the parallel and distributed execution.

With the Machine learning functions moving out of general data handling and operating on diverse data types including documents, images, and graphs, the need for generic implementation paradigms is increasing. This framework pertains to the .NET languages only.

Manipulating datasets with LINQ

LINQ is shipped with a set of functions that operate on collections of .NET objects. These collections are modified by the LINQ functions that contain the .NET datatypes.

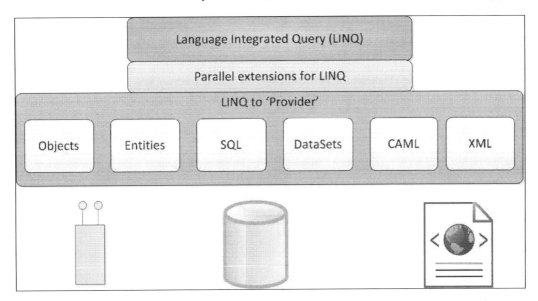

Graphics Processing Unit (GPU)

GPUs are electronic circuits designed to handle the memory requirements and rapidly create images in the frame buffers for visual display.

GPUs have been consistently supporting growing computational capabilities. They were initially meant to handle image processing and rendering, but the advanced GPUs are now positioned as self-contained, general purpose computing platforms.

While CPUs are designed to perform well on heterogeneous workloads, GPUs are built for tasks that are meant to ensure the availability of massive datasets and run in a parallel manner.

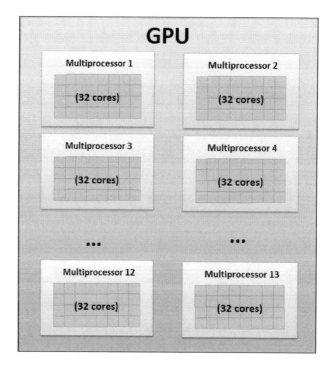

GPUs are mainly used in deep learning and training neural networks that can potentially need larger training datasets, lesser computational power, and storage space optimization. They are being employed in solving both classification and prediction problems in the cloud. Most of the social media companies have been in the list of early adopters for GPUs.

 With GPUs, pre-recorded speech or multimedia content can be transcribed much more quickly. Compared to a CPU implementation we are able to perform recognition up to 33x faster.

Field Programmable Gate Array (FPGA)

FPGAs are emerging in many areas of HPC. FPGAs can be used in the context of massive parallel processing. In this section, we will look at understanding some of the architecture and implementation aspects of FPGA.

FPGAs are known to provide high performance. They support different parallel computation applications. They have an on-chip memory to facilitate easy memory access to the processor. Above all, the memory is coupled to the algorithm logic and this means that we will not need any additional high-speed memory.

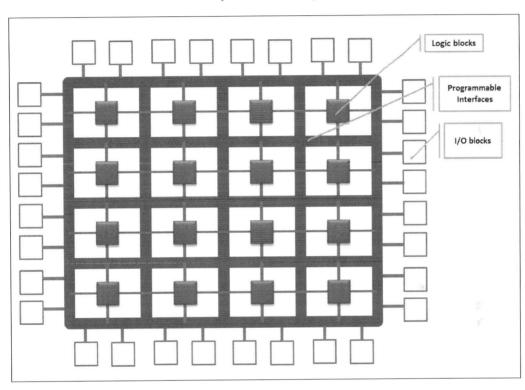

FPGA contains an enormous number of **Configurable Logical Blocks (CLB)**; each of these CLBs are connected using programmable interfaces that pass signals among them. The I/O blocks are the connections points for CLBs to the outside world.

FPGAs offer a variety of paradigms that help speed up computations in a hardware and software design. FPGAs are cost effective and the hardware resources are used in an optimal way. IBM Netezza leverages FPGA architecture.

Multicore or multiprocessor systems

Multiprocessor systems usually have multiple CPUs that need not necessarily be on the same chip. The new age multiprocessors are on the same physical board, and the communication happens via high-speed connection interfaces.

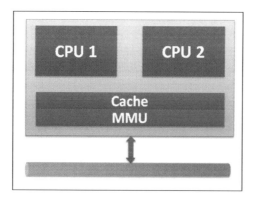

Multicore processors represent a family of processors that may contain many CPUs on one chip (such as two, four, and eight. In case of multicore systems, the efficiency of the multi-threading implementation is determined by how well-parallel the code is written).

Further to all the hardware and infrastructure advancements, we have just seen that the cloud frameworks for Machine learning are picking up considerable traction based on their ability to scale Machine learning processes at an optimal cost.

With the emergence of cloud computing, infrastructure service providers, such as Amazon Web Services, offer access to virtually unlimited computing power on demand that can be paid for, based on the usage.

Summary

In this chapter we have explored the qualifiers of large datasets, their common characteristics, the problems of repetition, and the reasons for the hyper-growth in volumes; in fact, the big data context.

The need for applying conventional Machine learning algorithms to large datasets has given rise to new challenges for Machine learning practitioners. Traditional Machine learning libraries do not quite support, processing huge datasets. Parallelization using modern parallel computing frameworks, such as MapReduce, have gained popularity and adoption; this has resulted in the birth of new libraries that are built over these frameworks.

The concentration was on methods that are suitable for massive data, and have potential for the parallel implementation. The landscape of Machine learning applications has changed dramatically in the last decade. Throwing more machines doesn't always prove to be a solution. There is a need to revisit traditional algorithms and models in the way they are being executed as now an another dimension in the study of Machine learning techniques is the scalability, parallel execution, load balancing, fault tolerance, and dynamic scheduling.

We have also taken a look at the emerging parallelization and distribution architectures and frameworks in the context of large datasets, and understood the need for scaling up and scaling out Machine learning. Furthermore, we have recapped the internals of some parallel and distributed platform techniques for Machine learning such as MapReduce, GPUs, FGPA, and more.

In the next chapter, we will look at how Hadoop is the best platform for large-scale Machine learning.

3
An Introduction to Hadoop's Architecture and Ecosystem

From this chapter onwards, we start with the implementation aspects of Machine learning. Let's start learning the platform of choice—a platform that can scale to Advanced Enterprise Data needs (big data needs of Machine learning in specific)—Hadoop.

In this chapter, we cover Hadoop platform and its capabilities in addressing large-scale loading, storage, and processing challenges for Machine learning. In addition to an overview of Hadoop Architecture, its core frameworks, and the other supporting ecosystem components, also included here is a detailed installation process with an example deployment approach. Though there are many commercial distributions of Hadoop, our focus in this chapter is to cover the open source, Apache distribution of Hadoop (latest version 2.x).

In this chapter, the following topics are covered in-depth:

- An introduction to Apache Hadoop, its evolution history, the core concepts, and the ecosystem frameworks that comprise Hadoop

- Hadoop distributions and specific offerings

- Installation and set up of the Hadoop environment

- Hadoop 2.0—HDFS and MapReduce (also **YARN (Yet Another Resource Negotiator)**) architectures with example implementation scenarios, using different components of the architecture

- Understanding the purpose of the core ecosystem components, setting up and learning to build and run the programs using examples

- Exploring Machine learning specific ecosystem extensions such as Mahout and R Connectors (*Chapter 4, Machine Learning Tools, Libraries, and Frameworks,* covers the implementation details)

Introduction to Apache Hadoop

Apache Hadoop is an open source, Java-based project from the Apache Software Foundation. The core purpose of this software has been to provide a platform that is scalable, extensible, and fault tolerant for the distributed storage and processing of big data. Please refer to *Chapter 2, Machine learning and Large-scale Datasets* for more information on what data qualifies as big data. The following image is the standard logo of Hadoop:

At the heart of it, it leverages clusters of nodes that can be commodity servers and facilitates parallel processing. The name Hadoop was given by its creator Doug Cutting, naming it after his child's yellow stuffed toy elephant. Till date, Yahoo! has been the largest contributor and an extensive user of Hadoop. More details of Hadoop, its architecture, and download links are accessible at `http://hadoop.apache.org/`.

Hadoop is an industry standard platform for big data, and it comes with extensive support for all the popular Machine learning tools in the market. This platform is now used by several big firms such as Microsoft, Google, Yahoo!, and IBM. It is also used to address specific Machine learning requirements like sentiment analysis, search engines, and so on.

The following sections cover some key characteristics of the Hadoop platform that make it ideal for facilitating efficiency in large-scale data storage and processing capabilities.

Evolution of Hadoop (the platform of choice)

The following figure (Source Cloudera Inc.) explains the evolution of the Hadoop platform. With Doug Cutting and Mike Cafarella starting it all in 2002 to build a greatly scalable search engine that is open source and hence extensible and running over a bunch of machines. Some important milestones in this evolution phase have been by Google that released the **Google File System** (**GFS**) in October 2003, followed by the MapReduce framework in December 2004 that evolved to form the core frameworks HDFS and MapReduce/YARN respectively.

The other significant milestone had been Yahoo's contribution and adoption around February 2008 when Yahoo implemented a production version that had indexing of searches implemented over 10,000 Hadoop cluster nodes. The following table depicts the evolution of Hadoop:

Year	Evolution / Progress
2002-2003	Work on Nutch was started by Doug Cutting and Mike Cafarella
2003 - 2004	Google published work on GFS and MapReduce
2004	Doug Cutting added suport for GFS and MapReduce to Nutc
2006	Hadoop spins out of Nutch when Yahoo hired Doug Cutting
2007	NY Times converts 4TB of image archives over 100 EC2s
	Facebook launched Hive, an SQL support for Hadoop
2008	Fastest sort over 910 nodes taking 3.5 mins
	Cloudera founded
2009	First Hadoop Summit with 750 attendeed
	Doug Cutting joined Cloudera

Hadoop and its core elements

The following concept map depicts the core elements and aspects of the Hadoop platform:

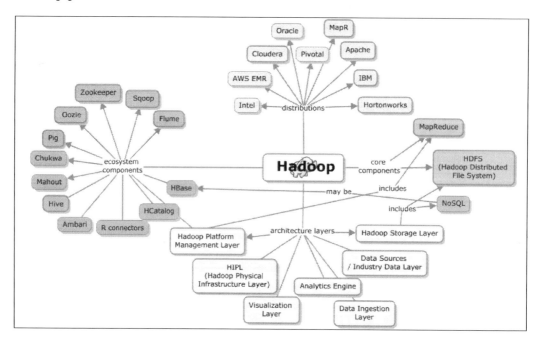

Machine learning solution architecture for big data (employing Hadoop)

In this section, let us look at the essential architecture components for implementing a Machine learning solution considering big data requirements.

The proposed solution architecture should support the consumption of a variety of data sources in an efficient and cost-effective way. The following figure summarizes the core architecture components that should potentially be a part of the Machine learning solution technology stack. The choice of frameworks can either be open source or packaged license options. In the context of this book, we consider the latest version of open source (Apache) distribution of Hadoop and its ecosystem components.

 Vendor specific frameworks and extensions are out of scope for this chapter.

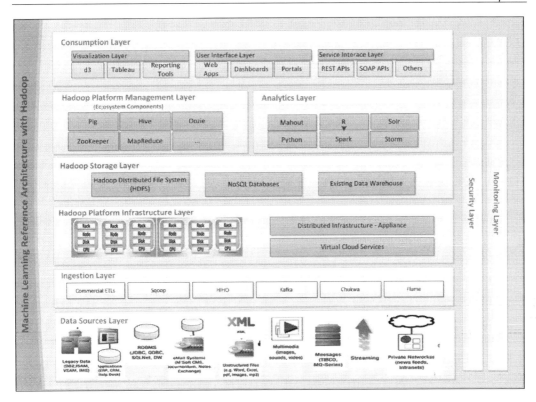

In the next sections, we'll discuss in detail each of these Reference Architecture layers and the required frameworks in each layer.

The Data Source layer

The Data Source layer forms a critical part of the Machine learning Reference Architecture. There are many internal and external data feeds that form an input to solving a Machine learning problem. These feeds can be structured, unstructured, or semi-structured in nature. Moreover, in real-time, batch, or near real time mode, they need to be seamlessly integrated and consolidated for analytics engines and visualization tools.

Before ingesting this data into the system for further processing, it is important to remove the irrelevance or the noise in the data. Some unique techniques can be applied to clean and filter the data.

These consolidated datasets are also called data lakes in big data and the data aggregation context. Hadoop is one of the storage options of choice for Data Lakes.

The following diagram shows the variety of data sources that form a primary source of input.

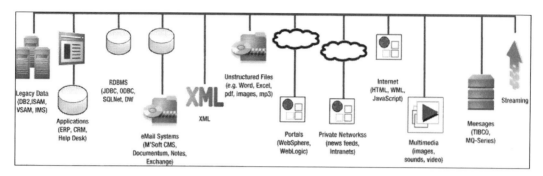

Data architectures have always been designed to support some of the protocols such as JMS, HTTP, XML, and so on. However, now, the recent advancements in the field of big data have brought about significant changes. So now, the new age data sources include data streams from social networking sites, GPS data, machine-generated data such as user access logs, and other proprietary data formats.

The Ingestion layer

The Data Ingestion layer is responsible for bringing data in from multiple data sources into the system, with a primary responsibility to ensure data quality. This layer has the capability to filter, transform, integrate, and validate data. It is important that the choice of technology to implement this layer should be able to support high volumes and other characteristics of data. The following meta model shows the composition and flow of functions of the Ingestion Layer. An ingestion layer could potentially be an **ETL** short for (**Extract, Transform, and Load**) capability in the architecture.

Listed below are a set of basic requirements for an ingestion layer:

- High-speed transformation of data from any source system in any manner
- Processing large volumes of records in minimal time
- Producing output in a semantically rich format so that any target system can query for **smart data**

The architecture framework for ingestion layer needs to provide the following capabilities; the upcoming model depicts various layers and compositions:

- An Adapter Framework—any product group or application should be able to use the Adapter Framework to quickly, reliably, and programmatically develop connectors to different data sources (Files, CSV format, and DB)

- A high speed, parallel transformation execution engine

- A job execution framework

- Semantified output generator framework

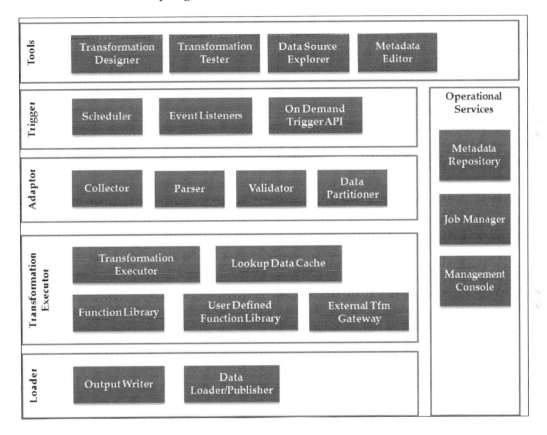

The Ingestion layer loads the relevant data into the storage layer, which in our current context is the Hadoop Storage Layer that is primarily a file-based storage layer.

The concept map below lists ingestion core patterns (these patterns address performance and scalability needs of a Machine learning architecture):

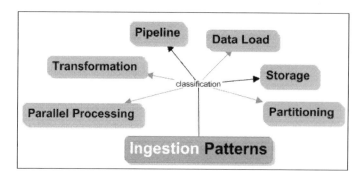

- **Parallel Processing and Partitioning Patterns**: The fundamental architecture for handling large volume ingestion requirements is to parallelize the execution. Running transformations on different input data in parallel and partitioning a single, large volume input into smaller batches for processing in parallel helps achieve parallelization.

- **Pipeline design patterns**: When designing the workflows for ingestion jobs, there are specific issues that need to be addressed, such as avoiding large sequential pipelines that enable parallel processing. Similarly, from the data reliability point of view, creating appropriate audit and execution logs is important to manage the entire ingestion execution.

- **Transformation patterns**: There are different categories of transformation. One of the main aspects of the transformation designs is to handle dependency. The patterns mentioned in the first category (parallelization) also handle dependency requirements. Other issues relate to the dependency on the past and historical data, which is especially significant when processing additional loads.

- **Storage Design**: When loading data into the target data store, there are issues such as recovering from failed transformations or reloading data for specific feeds (for example, when there should be a fixed transformation rule).

- **Data Load patterns**: One of the biggest performance bottlenecks in data ingestion is the speed of loading data into the target data mart. Especially when the target is an RDBMS, parallelization strategies lead to concurrency issues while loading the data, limiting the throughput of the ingestion that is possible. The patterns present certain techniques of how to realize the data load and address performance and concurrency issues while loading data.

The Hadoop Storage layer

Machine learning architecture has a distributed storage layer that supports parallel processing for running analytics or heavy computations over big data. The usage of distributed storage and processing large volumes in parallel is a fundamental change in the way an enterprise handles big data.

A typical distributed storage facilitates high performance by parallel processing the algorithms that run over petabyte scale data with fault-tolerance, reliability, and parallel processing capabilities.

In the current context of Hadoop architecture, **Hadoop Distributed File System (HDFS)** is the core storage mechanism. In this section, let us have a brief look at HDFS and NoSQL (Not-only-SQL) storage options. The following sections cover HDFS and its architecture in more detail.

HDFS is one of the core components and acts as a database for Hadoop. It is a distributed file system that stores large-scale data across a cluster of nodes. It comes with a framework to ensure data reliability and fault tolerance. Applications can store files in parts or whole depending on the size, and it facilitates the write once read many times.

Since HDFS is a file system, access to data for consumption or manipulation is not simple and requires some complex file operation programs. Another way of bringing in easier data management is by using non-relational stores called NoSQL stores.

The following model represents various NoSQL data store categories that are available with examples for each of the categories. Every data store category caters to a particular business requirement, and it is important to understand the purpose of each of these categories of NoSQL store to make the right choice for a given requirement. The CAP theorem (that stands for consistency, availability, and partition tolerance) attributes are satisfied to a varying degree for each of the NoSQL stores, resulting in support for optimized storage systems that are expected to work for combinations of these attributes. In reality, these NoSQL stores may have to coexist with relational stores as they would need a system of record to sync up on a need basis, or a better case is where we would need to use a combination of relational and non-relational data.

The following figure depicts types of NoSQL databases and some of the products in the market:

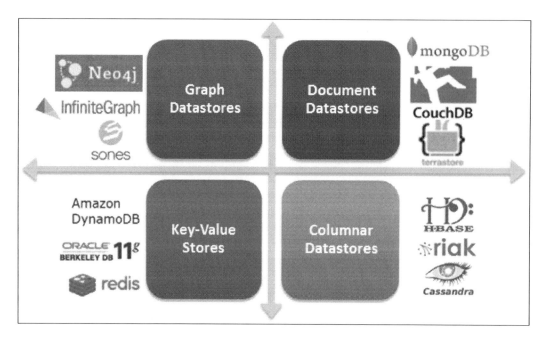

Hadoop was originally meant for \batch processing where the data into HDFS is loaded in batch or a scheduled manner. Usually, the storage layer has data loaded in batch. Some of the core and ecosystem components that facilitate data loading or ingestion into HDFS are Sqoop, **HIHO (Hadoop-in Hadoop-out)** MapReduce function, and ETL functions among others.

The Hadoop (Physical) Infrastructure layer – supporting appliance

The difference between the traditional architectures and big data (for Machine learning) architecture is the importance that the underlying infrastructure grabs. Performance, Scalability, Reliability, Fault Tolerance, High Availability, and Disaster Recovery are some of the important quality attributes that this architecture is required to support. The underlying infrastructure of the platform handles these requirements.

The Hadoop Infrastructure is a distributed architecture or model where data is not stored in one place, but is distributed across multiple or a cluster of nodes. The data distribution strategy can be intelligent (as in the case of Greenplum) or can be simply mathematical (as in the case of Hadoop). The distributed file system nodes are linked over a network. This is referred to as **Shared Nothing Architecture (SNA)**, and the big data solutions work on this reference architecture. Along with the data being distributed across multiple nodes, the processes run locally to the data nodes.

This is first cited in Michael Stonebraker's paper that can be accessed at `http://db.cs.berkeley.edu/papers/hpts85-nothing.pdf`.

Nodes that have data stored are called data nodes and those where processing happens are called compute nodes. The data and compute nodes can be collocated or decoupled. The following figure represents an SNA context that has data and compute nodes collocated:

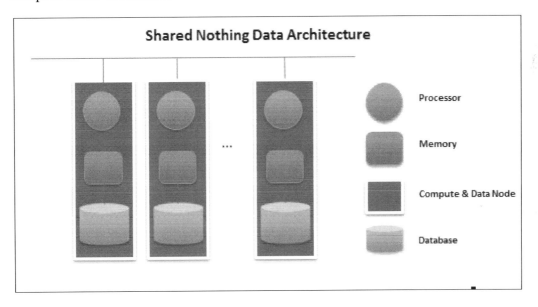

Shared nothing data architecture supports parallel processing. Redundancy is a default expectation as it deals with a variety of data from diverse sources.

Hadoop and HDFS, over a grid infrastructure connected, over a fast gigabit network, or a virtual cloud infrastructure, forms the infrastructure layer that supports large-scale Machine learning architecture.

The following figure illustrates big data infrastructure setup using commodity servers:

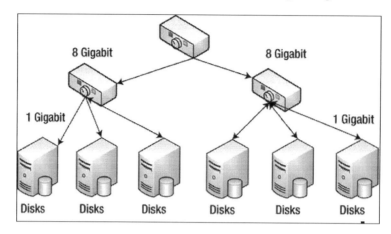

Hadoop platform / Processing layer

The platform or processing layer for Hadoop is the core data processing layer of the Machine learning architecture tools. This layer facilitates querying or accessing data stored in Hadoop's storage layer (NoSQL databases that use the HDFS storage file system typically), sitting at the top of the Hadoop infrastructure layer.

As learned in *Chapter 2, Machine learning, and Large-scale datasets*, technological advancements in the field of computing now facilitate handling large volumes of distributed computing and parallel processing.

The MapReduce framework of Hadoop helps to store and analyze large volumes of data efficiently and in an inexpensive way.

The key components of the Hadoop platform or processing layer are listed next; these components are a part of the ecosystem and are discussed in detail in the sections that follow in this chapter:

- **MapReduce**: MapReduce is a programming paradigm that is used to efficiently execute a function over a larger volume of data, typically in a batch mode. The *map* function is responsible for distributing the tasks across multiple systems, distributing the load equally and managing the processing in parallel. Post processing; the *reduce* function assimilates and combines the elements to provide a result. A step-by-step implementation on Hadoop's native MapReduce architecture, MapReduce v2, and YARN is covered in the *Hadoop ecosystem components* section.

- **Hive**: Hive is a data warehouse framework for Hadoop and is responsible for aggregating high volumes of data with SQL-like functions. Hive facilitates an efficient way of storing data that uses resources optimally. The configuration and implementation aspects of Hive are covered in the *Hadoop ecosystem components* section.

- **Pig**: Pig is a simple scripting language that facilitates querying and manipulating data held on HDFS. It internally runs the functions in a MapReduce paradigm and is often perceived to simplify building MapReduce functions. A detailed step-by-step guide to configuring, learning the syntax, and building essential functions is covered in the *Hadoop ecosystem components* section.

- **Sqoop**: Sqoop is a data import tool for Hadoop that has inbuilt functions to import data from specific tables, columns, or complete database onto the file system. Post processing, Sqoop supports extracting data from several Relational databases and NoSQL data stores.

- **HBase**: HBase is a Hadoop compliant NoSQL data store (a columnar NoSQL data store) that uses HDFS as the underlying file system. It supports distributed storage and automatic linear scalability.

- **ZooKeeper**: ZooKeeper is a monitoring and coordinating service that helps keep a check on the Hadoop instances and nodes. It is responsible for keeping the infrastructure synchronized and protects the distributed system from partial failures and ensures data consistency. The ZooKeeper framework can work standalone or outside Hadoop.

More of these ecosystem components are discussed in depth in the following sections.

The Analytics layer

More often, enterprises have some real **Business Intelligence** (**BI**) tools that are responsible for running some analytical queries and producing some MIS reports or dashboards. There is a need for modern Machine learning or analytics tools and frameworks to coexist with them. There is now a need for the analytics to run either in a traditional way on the data warehouses or big data stores as well that can handle structured, semi-structured, and unstructured data.

In this case, we can expect the data flow between the traditional data stores and the big data stores using tools such as Sqoop.

NoSQL stores are known for low latency; they facilitate real-time analytics. Many open source analytics frameworks have simplified building models, and run complex statistical and mathematical algorithms using simple out-of-box functions. All that is required now is to understand the relevance of each of the algorithms and the ability to choose a suitable algorithm or approach, given a specific problem.

Let us look into the below listed open source Analytics and Machine learning frameworks in the chapters to follow.

- R
- Apache Mahout
- Python (scikit-learn distribution)
- Julia
- Apache Spark

An introduction to one of the upcoming Spring projects called **Spring XD** is covered, as it looked like a comprehensive Machine learning solution that can run on Hadoop.

The Consumption layer

The insights generated from the analytics layer or the results of data processing are consumed in many ways by the end clients. Some of the ways this data can be made available for consumption are:

- Service APIs (for example, Web Service Interfaces (SOAP based or REST))
- Web applications
- Reporting engines and data marts
- Dashboard and Visualization tools

Of all the options, **Visualization** is core and not only an important way of distributing or communicating the results of Machine learning but also a good way of representing data in a way that helps in decision making. Very evidently data visualization is gaining traction in the field of big data and analytics. A visualization that best represents the data and the underlying patterns and the relationships is what is the key to decision making.

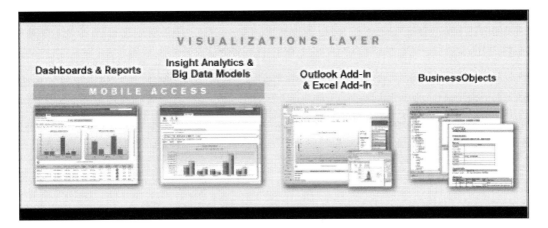

There are two types of visualizations; one is those that explain the data, and second is those that explore data and the underlying patterns. Visualization is now being looked at as a new language to communicate.

Explaining and exploring data with Visualizations

Visualizations for explaining and exploring data are unique and are used for different purposes.

The Visualizations for explaining are the typical ones we see in marketing and sales presentations. This is the case where data on the hand is clean to the maximum extent. The meaning of the data is clear, and communication is done by the final decision makers.

On the other hand, Visualizations for exploring help to correct data and link the related and useful attributes of data in the quest for understanding the data as such. Visualization for exploring sometimes can be inaccurate. The exploration usually happens iteratively, and there might be several rounds of refining the Visualizations before some sense is made out of the data on hand. There is a need to get rid of some irrelevant attributes in data or even the data itself (the one identified to be *noise*). This step of data exploration using Visualization sometimes replaces running complex algorithms and often requires statistical acumen.

Some popular visualization tools in the market (both open source and commercial) are Highcharts JS, D3, Tableau, and others. Although we use some of these frameworks to demonstrate how to depict and communicate insights, we are not explicitly covering any of the visualization options in depth.

Another important aspect is that these visualization tools usually need to leverage, traditional data warehousing tools and big data analysis tools. The following figure depicts how the proposed Machine learning architecture can support having existing data warehouses or BI tools coexist with big data analysis tools. As explained in *Chapter 1, Introduction to Machine learning,* the aggregated data and the data lakes become the core input to any big data analysis tools that run the Machine learning tools. The new age data storage mantra is semantic data structures. More on semantic data architectures are covered as a part of emerging data architectures in *Chapter 14, New generation data architectures for Machine learning.* The following figure depicts a high-level view of visualization in the context of data lakes and data warehouses:

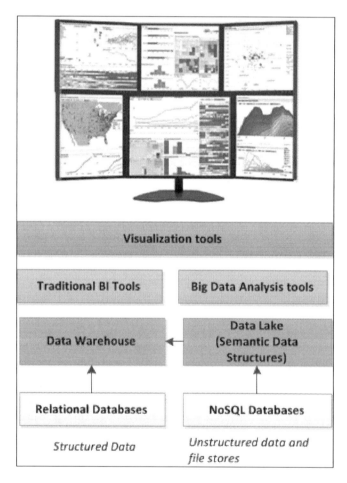

Security and Monitoring layer

When large volumes of data are being processed and consolidated across a variety of sources, security becomes of utmost importance and, in the case of sensitive data, the need for protecting data privacy is critical and sometimes the key compliance requirement too. The required authentication and authorization checks need to be implemented as a part of executing Machine learning algorithms. This is more of a prerequisite and cannot be an afterthought in the Machine learning architecture.

Data Ingestion and the processing function are the main areas that require strict security implementation, given the criticality of controlling data access.

By the virtue of distributed architecture, big data applications are inherently prone to security vulnerabilities; it is necessary that security implementation is taken care of, and it does not impact performance, scalability, or functionality with the ease of execution and maintenance of these applications.

The Machine learning architecture as such should support the following as a basic necessity for security:

- Authentication for each node in the cluster with the support for standard protocols like Kerberos
- Since it is a file system, there needs to be a minimum support for encryption
- Communication with the nodes should always use **SSL (Secure Socket Layer)**, TLS, or others that include NameNode
- Secure keys and tokens and usage of standard key management systems
- The implementation of distributed logging for tracking to trace any issues across layers easily

The next significant requirement is monitoring. The distributed data architecture comes with robust monitoring and support tools that can handle large clusters of nodes that are connected in a federated model.

There are always SLAs for the downtime of an application, and it is important that the recovery mechanism adheres to these SLAs while ensuring the availability of the application.

It is important that these nodes and clusters communicate with the monitoring system in a machine independent way, and the usage of XML-like formats is key. The data storage needs for the monitoring systems should not impact the overall performance of the application.

Usually, every big data stack comes with an in-built monitoring framework or tool. Also, there are open source tools such as Ganglia and Nagios that can be integrated and used for monitoring the big data applications.

Hadoop core components framework

Apache Hadoop has two core components:

- Hadoop Distributed File System also called HDFS
- MapReduce (in the version 2.x of Hadoop, this is called YARN)

The rest of the Hadoop components are represented in the Machine learning solution architecture. Using Hadoop we work around these two core components and form the eco-system components for Hadoop.

The focus of this chapter is Apache Hadoop 2.x distribution. There have been few architectural changes to HDFS and MapReduce in this version. We first cover the core architecture, and then the changes that have come in as a part of the 2.x architecture.

Hadoop Distributed File System (HDFS)

HDFS is inspired and built from **GFS (Google File System)**. It is a distributed file system that is elastically scalable, with support load balancing and fault tolerance to ensure high availability. It has data redundancy built in to demonstrate reliability and consistency in data.

HDFS implements the Master-slave architecture. Here, the master node is called NameNode, and the slave nodes are called DataNodes. NameNode is the entry point for all client applications, and the distribution of data across the DataNodes happens via the NameNode. The actual data is not passed through NameNode server to ensure that NameNode does not become a bottleneck for any data distribution. Only the metadata is communicated to the client, and the actual data movement happens directly between the clients and DataNodes.

Both NameNode and DataNode are referred to as daemons in the Hadoop architecture. NameNode requires a high-end machine and is expected to run only the NameNode daemon. The following points justify the need for a high-end machine for NameNode:

- The entire cluster's metadata is held in the memory for quicker access, and there is a need for more memory
- NameNode is both the single point of entry and failure for the Hadoop cluster

- The NameNode coordinates with several hundreds or thousands of DataNodes and manages batch jobs

HDFS is built on the traditional hierarchical file system where the creation of new directories, adding new files, deletion directories or subdirectories, removal of files, renaming, and moving or updating a file are common tasks. Details of the directories, files, data nodes, and blocks created and stored in each of the DataNodes are stored as metadata in the NameNode.

There is another node in this architecture that NameNode communicates with, called secondary Namenode. The secondary Namenode is not a backup for NameNode and hence, does not failover to the secondary Namenode. Instead, it is used to store a copy of the metadata and log files from NameNode. NameNode holds the metadata for the data blocks and related distribution details in a file called `fsimage`. This image file is not updated for every data operation in the file system and is tracked periodically by logging them in separate log files. This ensures faster I/O and thus the efficiency of the data import or export operations.

The secondary Namenode has a specific function with this regard. It periodically downloads the image and log files, and creates a new image by appending the current operations from the log file into the fsimage, then uploading the new image file back to NameNode. This eliminates any overhead on NameNode. Any restart on NameNode happens very quickly, and the efficiency of the system is ensured. The following figure depicts the communication workflow between the client application and HDFS:

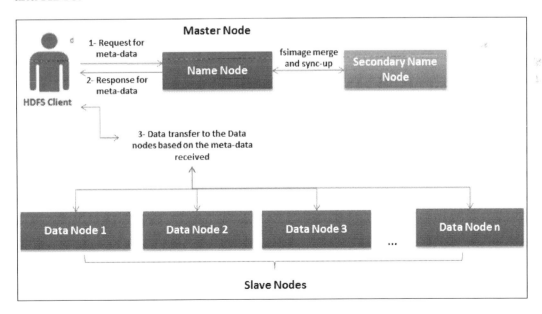

HDFS is built for reading and writing large volumes of data between DataNodes. These large files are split into blocks of smaller files, usually of a fixed size such as 64 MB or 128 MB, and these blocks are distributed across DataNodes. For each of these blocks, overall three copies are stored to ensure redundancy and support fault tolerance. The number of copies can be changed, which is a configuration of the system. More information on the HDFS architecture and specific functions is covered in the following section.

Secondary Namenode and Checkpoint process

While defining the purpose and function of the secondary Namenode, we have learned one important function that takes care of updating or preparing the metadata for NameNode that is stored in a file called fsimage. This process of generating a new fsimage by merging the existing fsimage and the log file is called **Checkpoint**. The following figure depicts the checkpoint process:

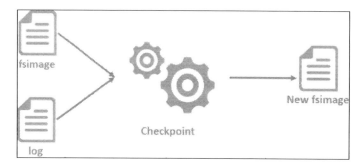

Some configurations changes are to be done to the cross-site.XML file related to checkpoint process.

Property	Purpose
dfs.namenode.checkpoint. dir	This is the directory path where the temporary fsimage files are held to run the merge process.
dfs.namenode.checkpoint. edits.dir	This is the directory path where the temporary edits are held to run the merge process. The default value for this parameter is same as dfs. namenode.checkpoint.dir
dfs.namenode.checkpoint. period	The time gap between two checkpoint runs (in seconds).

Property	Purpose
`dfs.namenode.checkpoint.txns`	Irrespective of the time gap configurations, this property defines after how many transactions a checkpoint process needs to be triggered.
`dfs.namenode.checkpoint.check.period`	This property defines the frequency (in seconds) in which the NameNode is polled to check the un-checkpointed transactions.
`dfs.namenode.checkpoint.max-retries`	In the case of failure, the secondary Namenode retry is checkpointing. This property defines the number of times a secondary Namenode attempts a retry for checkpointing before it gives up.
`dfs.namenode.num.checkpoints.retained`	This property represents the number of checkpoint files retained by both the NameNode and the secondary Namenode.

The checkpoint process can be triggered by both NameNode and the secondary Namenode. Secondary Namenode is also responsible for taking backup of the `fsimage` files periodically, which will further help in recovery.

Splitting large data files

HDFS stores smaller chunks of huge files across the data nodes distributed over the cluster. Before the files are stored, HDFS internally splits the entire file content into multiple data blocks each of a fixed size (default 64 MB). This size is configurable. There is no specific business logic followed to split the files and build the data blocks; it is purely driven by the file size. These data blocks are then stored on the DataNodes for the data read and write to happen in parallel. Each data block is again a file in itself in the local file system.

The following figure depicts how a large file is split into smaller chunks or blocks of fixed size:

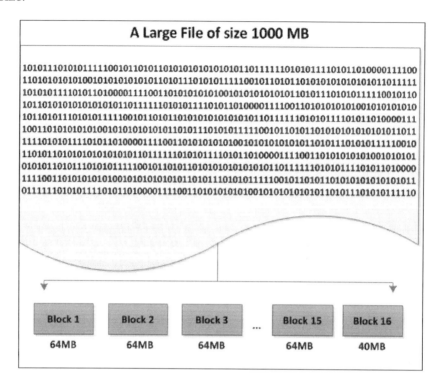

The size of each block can be controlled by the following configuration parameter in `hdfs-site.xml`. The cluster-wide block size is controlled by the `dfs.blocksize` configuration property in `hdfs-site.XML` The default value in Hadoop 1.0 is 64 MB and in Hadoop 2.x is 128 MB. The block size is determined by the effectiveness of the infrastructure and can get bigger with higher transfer speeds and the usage of the new age drives:

Property	Purpose
`dfs.blocksize`	The value is 134217728. The previous value in bytes represents 128 MB, alternatively any value suffixed by a measure can be defined. For example, 512m, 1g, 128k, and so on.

Any update to the value in the block size will not be applied to the existing blocks; only new blocks are eligible.

Block loading to the cluster and replication

Once the file is split, the data blocks are formed of a fixed block size and are configured for the environment.

By virtue of the distributed architecture, there is a strong need to store replicas of the data blocks to handle data reliability. By default, three copies of each data block are stored. The number of the copies configuration property is called replication factor. The following table lists all the configurations related to data loading and replication:

Property	Purpose
dfs.replication	The value is 3. This defines the number of replicas that need to be stored in each block.
dfs.replication.max	Maximal block replication.
dfs.namenode.replication. min	Minimal block replication.

The NameNode is responsible for ensuring the block placement and replication as per the configuration is done. With these data blocks placed onto DataNodes, each DataNode in the cluster sends block status periodically to the NameNode. The fact that NameNode receives a signal from the DataNode implies that the DataNode is active and functioning properly.

HDFS uses a **default block placement policy** that is targeted to achieve load balancing across the available nodes. Following is the scope of this policy:

- First, the copy or replica is written to the DataNode that is creating the file; this facilitates a higher write performance
- Second, the copy or replica is written to another DataNode from the same rack; this minimizes network traffic
- Third, the replica is written to a DataNode in a different rack; this way even if a switch fails, there still is a copy of the data block available

A default block placement policy is applied that uses all the nodes on the rack without compromising on the performance, data reliability, and availability. The following image depicts how three blocks of data are placed across four nodes with a replication strategy of two extra copies. Some of these nodes are located in the racks for optimal fault tolerance.

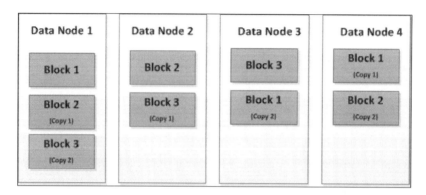

Overall, the flow of loading data into HDFS is shown in the following flow diagram:

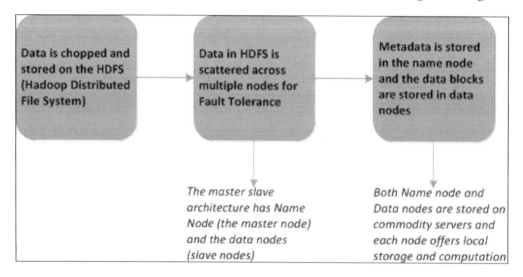

Writing to and reading from HDFS

While writing a file to HDFS, the client first contacts NameNode and passes the details of the file that needs to be written to HDFS. NameNode provides details on the replication configurations and other metadata details that specify where to place the data blocks. The following figure explains this flow:

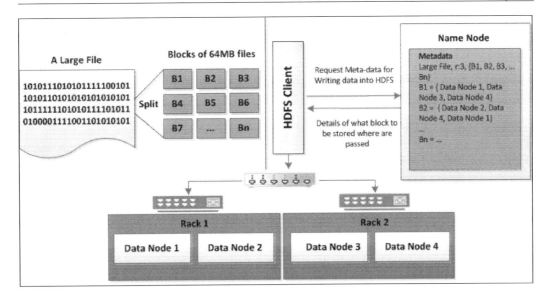

Handling failures

When the Hadoop cluster starts up, the NameNode gets into a safe-mode state and receives a heartbeat signal from all the data nodes. The fact that the NameNode receives a block report from DataNodes indicates that the DataNodes are up and functioning.

Let's now say that **Data Node 4** goes down; this would mean that **Name Node** does not receive any heartbeat signals from **Data Node 4**. **Name Node** registers the unavailability of **Name Node** and hence, whatever **Data Node 4** does is load balanced to the other nodes that have the replicas. This data is then updated in the metadata register by **Name Node**. The following figure illustrates the same:

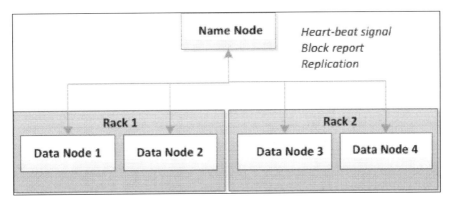

HDFS command line

HDFS has a command line interface called **FS Shell**. This facilitates the usage of shell commands to manage HDFS. The following screenshot shows the `Hadoop fs` command, and its usage/syntax:

```
                        Hadoop Command Line                    _  □  x

C:\apps\dist\hadoop-2.4.0.2.1.3.0-1948>hadoop fs
Usage: hadoop fs [generic options]
        [-appendToFile <localsrc> ... <dst>]
        [-cat [-ignoreCrc] <src> ...]
        [-checksum <src> ...]
        [-chgrp [-R] GROUP PATH...]
        [-chmod [-R] <MODE[,MODE]... | OCTALMODE> PATH...]
        [-chown [-R] [OWNER][:[GROUP]] PATH...]
        [-copyFromLocal [-f] [-p] <localsrc> ... <dst>]
        [-copyToLocal [-p] [-ignoreCrc] [-crc] <src> ... <localdst>]
        [-count [-q] <path> ...]
        [-cp [-f] [-p] <src> ... <dst>]
        [-createSnapshot <snapshotDir> [<snapshotName>]]
        [-deleteSnapshot <snapshotDir> <snapshotName>]
        [-df [-h] [<path> ...]]
        [-du [-s] [-h] <path> ...]
        [-expunge]
        [-get [-p] [-ignoreCrc] [-crc] <src> ... <localdst>]
        [-getfacl [-R] <path>]
        [-getmerge [-nl] <src> <localdst>]
        [-help [cmd ...]]
        [-ls [-d] [-h] [-R] [<path> ...]]
        [-mkdir [-p] <path> ...]
        [-moveFromLocal <localsrc> ... <dst>]
        [-moveToLocal <src> <localdst>]
        [-mv <src> ... <dst>]
        [-put [-f] [-p] <localsrc> ... <dst>]
        [-renameSnapshot <snapshotDir> <oldName> <newName>]
        [-rm [-f] [-r|-R] [-skipTrash] <src> ...]
        [-rmdir [--ignore-fail-on-non-empty] <dir> ...]
        [-setfacl [-R] [{-b|-k} {-m|-x <acl_spec>} <path>]|[--set <acl_spec> <pa
th>]]
        [-setrep [-R] [-w] <rep> <path> ...]
        [-stat [format] <path> ...]
        [-tail [-f] <file>]
        [-test -[defsz] <path>]
        [-text [-ignoreCrc] <src> ...]
        [-touchz <path> ...]
        [-usage [cmd ...]]

Generic options supported are
-conf <configuration file>     specify an application configuration file
-D <property=value>            use value for given property
-fs <local|namenode:port>      specify a namenode
-jt <local|jobtracker:port>    specify a job tracker
-files <comma separated list of files>    specify comma separated files to be co
pied to the map reduce cluster
-libjars <comma separated list of jars>    specify comma separated jar files to
include in the classpath.
-archives <comma separated list of archives>    specify comma separated archives
 to be unarchived on the compute machines.

The general command line syntax is
bin/hadoop command [genericOptions] [commandOptions]


C:\apps\dist\hadoop-2.4.0.2.1.3.0-1948>_
```

RESTFul HDFS

To have external applications, especially web applications or similar applications, have easy access to the data in HDFS over HTTP. HDFS supports an additional protocol called WebHDFS that is based on the RESTful standards that facilitate giving access to HDFS data over HTTP, without any need for Java binding or the availability of a complete Hadoop environment. Clients can use common tools such as curl/wget to access the HDFS. While providing web services-based access to data stored in HDFS, WebHDFS the built-in security and parallel processing capabilities of the platform, are well retained.

To enable WebHDFS, make the following configuration changes in `hdfs-site.xml`:

```
<property>
        <name>dfs.webhdfs.enabled</name>
        <value>true</value>
</property>
```

More details on WebHDFS REST API can be found at `http://hadoop.apache.org/docs/current/hadoop-project-dist/hadoop-hdfs/WebHDFS.html`.

MapReduce

MapReduce is similar to HDFS. The Hadoop MapReduce framework is inspired and built on Google's MapReduce framework. It is a distributed computing framework that facilitates processing gigantic amounts of data in parallel across clusters and has built-in fault tolerance mechanisms. It works on operating and processing the local data paradigm, where the processing logic is moved to the data instead of data moved to the processing logic.

MapReduce architecture

The MapReduce framework is also based on Master-slave architecture. The master job is called JobTracker, and the slave jobs are called TaskTrackers. Unlike NameNode and DataNodes, these are not physical nodes, but are daemon processors that are responsible for running the processing logic across the DataNodes:

- **JobTracker**: JobTracker schedules the execution of a job that comprises of multiple tasks. It is responsible for running the tasks or jobs on the task trackers and in parallel, monitors the status of processing. In the case of any failures, it is responsible for rerunning the failed tasks on the task tracker.
- **TaskTracker**: TaskTracker executes the tasks scheduled by the JobTracker and constantly communicates with JobTracker, working in cohesion.

Now, let's draw the analogy between the Master-slave architecture on the HDFS and MapReduce. The NameNode runs the JobTracker and DataNodes run TaskTrackers.

In a typical multi-node cluster, the NameNode and DataNodes are separate physical nodes, but in the case of a single node cluster, where the NameNode and DataNode are infrastructure wise the same, JobTracker and TaskTracker functions run on the same node. Single node clusters are used in the development environment.

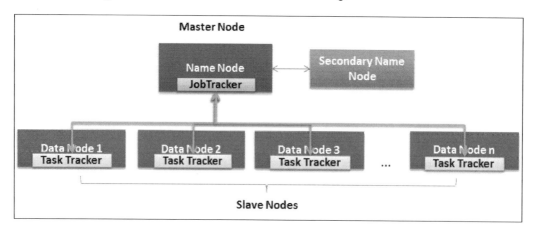

There are two functions in a MapReduce process—Map and Reduce.

- **Mapper**: Mapper job splits the file into multiple chunks in parallel, and runs some basic functions such as sorting, filtering, and any other specific business or analytics functions as needed. The output of the Mapper function is input to the Reducer function.

- **Reducer**: Reducer job is used to consolidate the results across Mappers, and is additionally used to perform any business or analytics function as needed. The intermediate output from the Mapper and Reducer jobs are stored on the file system as key-value pairs. Both the input and output of the map and reduce jobs are stored in HDFS. Overall, the MapReduce framework takes care of scheduling the tasks, monitoring the status, and handling failures (if any). The following diagram depicts how the `Map` and the `Reduce` functions work and operate on the data held in HDFS:

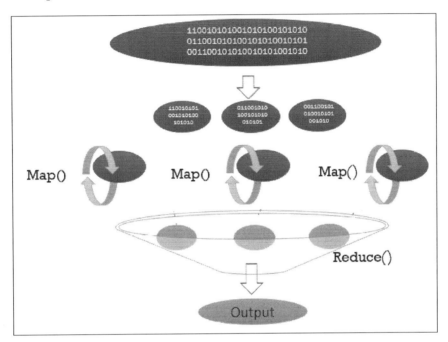

What makes MapReduce cater to the needs of large datasets?

Some of the advantages of MapReduce programming framework are listed as follows:

- **Parallel execution**: MapReduce programs are, by default, meant to be executed in parallel that can be executed on a cluster of nodes. Development teams need not focus on the internals of distributed computing and can just use the framework directly.

- **Fault Tolerance**: MapReduce framework works on Master-slave Architecture where, in case any node goes down, corrective actions are taken automatically by the framework.

- **Scalability**: MapReduce framework, having the ability to work distributed and with the ability to scale-out (horizontal scalability), with growing volumes new nodes, can be added to the cluster whenever needed.

- **Data Locality**: One of the core premises that the MapReduce framework does is to take the program to the data as opposed to the traditional way of bringing data to the code. So to be precise, MapReduce always has local data to it, and this is one of the most important reasons for the performance.

MapReduce execution flow and components

In this section, we will a take a deep dive into the execution flow of MapReduce and how each of the components function:

1. A new job is submitted by the client to JobTracker (a MapReduce job) along with the input and the output file paths and required configurations. The job gets queued for execution and gets picked by the job scheduler.

2. JobTracker gets the data at the place where the required data in context resides, and creates an execution plan that triggers TaskTrackers for the execution.

3. JobTracker submits the job to the identified TaskTrackers.

4. TaskTrackers execute the task using the data that is local to them. If the data is not available on the local Data Node, it communicates with other DataNodes.

5. TaskTrackers reports the status back to JobTracker by the means of heartbeat signals. JobTracker is capable of handling any failure cases inherently.

6. Finally, JobTracker reports the output to the Job client on the completion of the job.

The steps just described are depicted in the following figure. There are two parts to the flow: the HDFS and the MapReduce with the Nodes and the Trackers respectively.

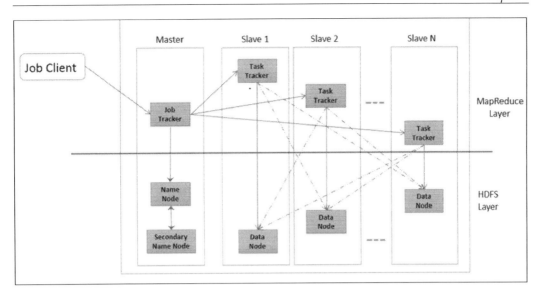

Let us focus on some core components of the MapReduce program and learn how to code it up. The following flow diagram details how the flow starts from the input data to the output data, and how each component or function of MapReduce framework kicks in to execute. The blocks in dotted red boxes are the components, and the blue boxes represent data being transitioned through the process.

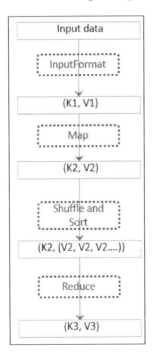

Developing MapReduce components

The MapReduce framework of Hadoop comprises a set of Java APIs that need to be extended or implemented to incorporate a specific function that is targeted to be executed in parallel over the Hadoop cluster. Following are some API implementations that need to be done:

- Input and output data format interfaces
- Mapper implementation
- Reducer implementation
- Partitioner
- Combiner
- Driver
- Context

InputFormat

The InputFormat class is responsible for reading data from a file and making it available as input to the map function. Two core functions are performed by this process; one is splitting the input data into logical fragments called InputSplits, and the second is the reading of these splits as key value pairs to feed into the map function. There are two distinct interfaces to perform these two functions:

- InputSplit
- RecordReader

Splitting of the input file is not an essential function. In case we need to consider a complete file for processing, we will need to override the isSplittable() function and set the flag to false.

OutputFormat

The OutputFormat API is responsible for validating that Hadoop has output data formats against output specification of the job. The RecordWriter implementation is responsible for writing the final output key value pairs to the file system. Every InputFormat API has a corresponding OutputFormat API. The following table lists some of the input and output format APIs of the MapReduce framework:

Input Format API	Corresponding Output Format API
TextInputFormat	TextOutputFormat
SequenceFileInputFormat	SequenceFileOutputFormat

Input Format API	Corresponding Output Format API
DBInputFormat	DBOutputFormat

Mapper implementation

All the Mapper implementations need to extend the Mapper<KeyIn, ValueIn, KeyOut, ValueOut> base class and importantly override the map() method to implement the specific business function. The Mapper implementation class takes key-value pairs as input and returns a set of key-value pairs as output. Any other interim output subsequently is taken by the shuffle and sort function.

There is one Mapper instance for each InputSplit generated by the InputFormat for a given MapReduce job.

Overall, there are four methods that the Mapper implementation class needs to extend from the base class. Following are the methods that are briefly described, along with the purpose of each method:

Method name and Syntax	Purpose
setup(Context)	This is the first method that is called back when a mapper is initiated for execution. It is not mandatory to override this method unless any specific initializations need to be done or any specific configuration setup needs to be done.
map(Object, Object, Context)	Overriding this method is the key to mapper implementation as this method would be invoked as a part of executing the mapper logic. It takes key-value pairs as input, and the response can be a collection of key-value pairs
clean (Context)	This method is called at the end of the mapper function execution in the lifecycle and facilitates clearing any resources utilized by the mapper.
run (Context)	Overriding this method provides additional capability to run multi-threaded mappers.

Let's take an example from a given file; we want to find out how many times a word is repeated. In this case, TextInputFormat is used. In fact, this is the default InputFormat. The following diagram shows what the InputSplit function does. It splits every row and builds a key-value pair.

The diagram shows how the text is stored in multiple blocks on DataNode. `TextInputFormat` then reads these blocks and multiple InputSplits (we can see that there are two InputSplits, and hence there are two mappers). Each mapper picks an InputSplit and generates a key value pair for each occurrence of the word followed by the number 1.

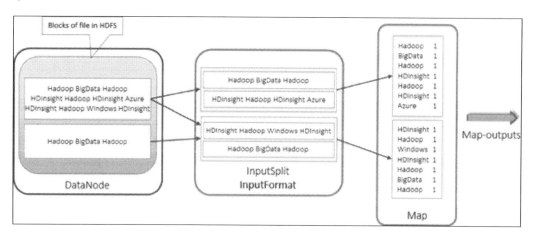

The output of the mapper function is written onto the disk at the end of the processing, and none of the intermediate results are written to the file system. They are held in the memory. This helps in optimizing performance. It's possible because the key space is partitioned and each mapper only gets a fragment of the total dataset. Now, in terms of how much memory should be assigned for this purpose, by default, 100 MB is allocated and for any changes to this value, the `io.sort.mb` property will have to be set. There is usually a threshold set to this limit and, in case it exceeds this, there is a background process that starts writing onto the disk. The following program snippet demonstrates how to implement a mapper class.

```
public static class VowelMapper extends Mapper<Object, Text, Text,
IntWritable>
{
private final static IntWritable one = new IntWritable(1);
private Text word = new Text();
public void map(Object key, Text value, Context context) throws
IOException, InterruptedException
{
StringTokenizer itr = new StringTokenizer(value.toString());
while (itr.hasMoreTokens())
{
word.set(itr.nextToken());
context.write(word, one);
}
}
}
```

Hadoop 2.x

Until Hadoop 2.x, all the distributions were focused on addressing the limitations in Hadoop 1.x but did not deviate from the core architecture. Hadoop 2.x really changed the underlying architecture assumptions and turned out to be a real breakthrough; most importantly, the introduction of YARN. YARN was a new framework for managing Hadoop cluster, which introduced the ability to handle real-time processing needs in addition to the batch. Some important issues that were addressed are listed as follows:

- Single NameNode issues
- Dramatic increase in the number of nodes in the cluster
- Extension to the number of tasks that can be successfully addressed with Hadoop

The following figure depicts the difference between the Hadoop 1.x and 2.x architectures and how YARN wires MapReduce and HDFS:

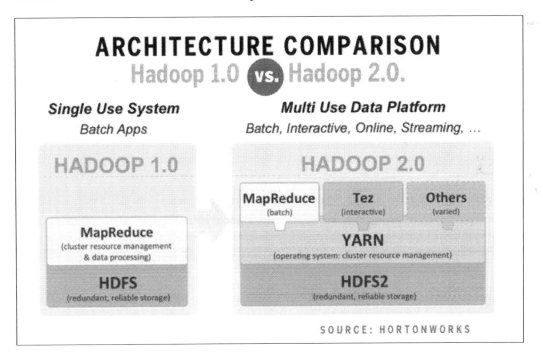

Hadoop ecosystem components

Hadoop has spawned a bunch of auxiliary and supporting frameworks. The following figure depicts the gamut of supporting frameworks contributed by the open source developer groups:

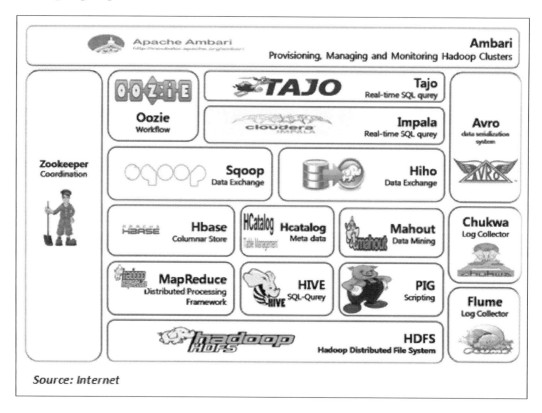

Source: Internet

The following table lists all the frameworks and purposes of each framework. These frameworks work with the Apache distribution of Hadoop. There are many frameworks built by Vendors, who are commercially positioned and are not in the scope of this book:

Framework	URL	Purpose (in brief)
HDFS (Hadoop Distributed File System)	`http://hadoop.apache.org/docs/current/hadoop-project-dist/hadoop-hdfs/HdfsUserGuide.html`	Hadoop File storage system is a core component of Hadoop, which has a built-in fault tolerance (refer to HDFS section for more details on the architecture and implementation specifics).

Framework	URL	Purpose (in brief)
MapReduce	`http://hadoop. apache.org/docs/ current/hadoop- mapreduce-client/ hadoop-mapreduce- client-core/ MapReduceTutorial. html`	MapReduce is a programming model and framework for processing large volumes of data on a distributed platform such as Hadoop. The latest version of Apache MapReduce extends another framework Apache YARN.

YARN: MapReduce has gone through a complete overhaul in Hadoop 2.0 and now it is called MapReduce 2. but the MapReduce programming model has not changed. YARN provides a new resource management and job scheduling model, along with its implementation to execute MapReduce jobs. In most cases, your existing MapReduce jobs run without any changes. In some instances, minor updates and recompilation might be needed. |
Pig	`https://pig.apache. org/`	Pig is a framework to execute data flows in parallel. It comes with a scripting language, Pig Latin, that helps in developing the data flows. Pig Latin comes with a bunch of internal operations for data such as join, split, sort, and so on. Pig runs on Hadoop and utilizes both HDFS and MapReduce. The compiled Pig Latin scripts run their functions in parallel and internally.
Hive	`https://hive.apache. org/`	Hive is a data warehouse framework for Hadoop. It supports querying and handling big datasets held in distributed stores. An SQL-like querying language called HiveQL can be used that allows plugging in the mapper and reducer programs.
Flume	`http://flume.apache. org/`	The Flume framework is more of an efficient transport framework that facilitates aggregating, analyzing, processing, and moving huge volumes of log data. It comes with an extensible data model and supports online analytics.

Framework	URL	Purpose (in brief)
Chukwa	`https://chukwa.apache.org/`	The Chukwa framework comes with an API that helps in easily collecting, analyzing, and monitoring prominent collections of data. Chukwa runs at the top of the HDFS and MapReduce framework, thus inheriting Hadoop's ability to scale.
HBase	`http://hbase.apache.org/`	HBase is inspired from Google BigTable. It is a NoSQL, columnar data store built to complement the Hadoop platform, and supports real-time operations on the data. HBase is a Hadoop database that is responsible for backing MapReduce job outputs.
HCatalog	`https://cwiki.apache.org/confluence/display/Hive/HCatalog`	HCatalog is like a relational view of the data in HDFS. It doesn't matter where and how or what format the underlying data is stored. It is currently a part of Hive, and there are no separate distributions for the current distributions.
Avro	`http://avro.apache.org/`	The Apache Avro framework is more of an interface to data. It supports modeling, serializing, and making **Remote Procedure Calls** (**RPC**). Every schema representation in Avro, also called the metadata definition, resides close to the data and on the same file, thus making the file self-describing.
HIHO	`https://github.com/sonalgoyal/hiho/wiki/About-HIHO`	HIHO stands for Hadoop-in Hadoop-out. This framework helps connecting multiple data stores with the Hadoop system and facilitate interoperability. HIHO supports several RDBMS and file systems, providing internal functions to load and off-load data between RDBMS and HDFS in parallel.

Framework	URL	Purpose (in brief)
Sqoop	`http://sqoop.apache.org/`	Sqoop is a widely adopted framework for data transfer between HDFS and RDBMS in bulk or batch. It is very similar to Flume but operates with RDBMS. Sqoop is one of the **ETL** (**Extract-Transform-Load**) tools for Hadoop.
Tajo	`http://tajo.apache.org/`	Tajo is a distributed data warehouse system for Apache Hadoop that is relational in nature. Tajo supports ad-hoc querying and online integration, and extract-transform-load functions on large datasets stored in HDFS or other data stores.
Oozie	`http://oozie.apache.org/`	Oozie is a framework that facilitates workflow management. It acts as a scheduler system for MapReduce jobs using **DAG** (**Direct Acyclical Graph**). Oozie can either be data aware or time aware while it schedules and executes jobs.
ZooKeeper	`http://zookeeper.apache.org/`	Zookeeper, as the name says it all, is more like an orchestration and coordination service for Hadoop. It provides tools to build, manage, and provide high availability for distributed applications.
Ambari	`http://ambari.apache.org/`	Ambari is an intuitive web UI for Hadoop management with RESTful APIs. Apache Ambari was a contribution from Hortonworks. It serves as an interface to many other Hadoop frameworks in the ecosystem.
Mahout	`http://mahout.apache.org/`	Apache Mahout is an open source library for Machine learning algorithms. The design focus for Mahout is to provide a scalable library for huge data sets distributed across multiple systems. Apache Mahout is a tool to derive useful information from raw data.

Hadoop installation and setup

There are three different ways to setup Hadoop:

- **Standalone operation**: In this operation, Hadoop runs in a non-distributed mode. All the daemons run within a single Java process and help in easy debugging. This setup is also called single node installation.

- **Pseudo-Distributed Operation**: In this operation, Hadoop is configured to run on a single node, but in a pseudo-distributed mode that can run different daemon processes on different JVMs.

- **Fully-Distributed Operation**: In this operation, Hadoop is configured to run on multiple nodes in a fully-distributed mode, and all Hadoop daemons such as NameNode, Secondary Namenode, and JobTracker in the Master node; and DataNode and TaskTracker in slave nodes (in short, run on a cluster of nodes).

The Ubuntu-based Hadoop Installation prerequisites are as follows:

- Java v1.7
- Creating dedicated Hadoop user
- Configuring SSH access
- Disable IPv6

Installing Jdk 1.7

1. Download Java using this command:

   ```
   wget https://edelivery.oracle.com/otn-pub/java/jdk/7u45-b18/jdk-
   7u45-linux-x64.tar.gz
   ```

```
HTTP request sent, awaiting response... 200 OK
Length: 96316511 (92M) [application/x-gzip]
Saving to: `jdk-7u25-linux-x64.tar.gz'

100%[===================================>] 96,316,511    311K/s   in 5m 3s

2013-10-24 14:34:22 (311 KB/s) - `jdk-7u25-linux-x64.tar.gz' saved [9631
6511/96316511]
```

2. Unpack the binaries using this:

```
sudo tar xvzf jdk-7u45-linux-x64.tar.gz
```

3. Create a directory to install Java with the help of the following command:

```
mkdir -P /usr/local/Java
cd /usr/local/Java
```

4. Copy the binaries into the newly created directory:

```
sudo cp -r jdk-1.7.0_45 /usr/local/java
```

5. Configure the PATH parameters:

```
sudo nano /etc/profile
```

Or else, use this command:

```
sudo gedit /etc/profile
```

6. Include the following content at the end of the file:

```
JAVA_HOME=/usr/local/Java/jdk1.7.0_45
PATH=$PATH:$HOME/bin:$JAVA_HOME/bin
export JAVA_HOME
export PATH
```

7. In Ubuntu, configure the path for Java:

```
sudo update-alternatives --install "/usr/bin/javac" "javac" "/usr/
local/java/jdk1.7.0_45/bin/javac" 1
sudo update-alternatives --set javac /usr/local/Java/jdk1.7.0_45/
bin/javac
```

8. Check for installation completion:

```
java -version
```

```
master@Hadoopupgrade:~$ java -version
java version "1.7.0_45"
Java(TM) SE Runtime Environment (build 1.7.0_45-b18)
Java HotSpot(TM) 64-Bit Server VM (build 24.45-b08, mixed mode)
master@Hadoopupgrade:~$
```

Creating a system user for Hadoop (dedicated)

1. Create/add a new group:

   ```
   sudo addgroup hadoop
   ```

2. Create/add a new user and attach it to the group:

   ```
   sudo adduser -ingroup hadoop hduser
   ```

```
master@Hadoopupgrade:~$ sudo addgroup hadoop
Adding group 'hadoop' (GID 1001) ...
Done.
master@Hadoopupgrade:~$ sudo adduser --ingroup hadoop hduser
Adding user 'hduser' ...
Adding new user 'hduser' (1001) with group 'hadoop' ...
Creating home directory '/home/hduser' ...
Copying files from '/etc/skel' ...
Enter new UNIX password:
Retype new UNIX password:
passwd: password updated successfully
Changing the user information for hduser
Enter the new value, or press ENTER for the default
        Full Name []:
        Room Number []:
        Work Phone []:
        Home Phone []:
        Other []:
Is the information correct? [Y/n] Y
master@Hadoopupgrade:~$ 
```

3. Create/configure the SSH key access:

   ```
   ssh-keygen -t rsa -P ""
   cat $HOME/.ssh/id_rsa.pub >> $HOME/.ssh/authorized_keys
   ```

4. Verify the SSH setup:

   ```
   ssh hduser@localhost
   ```

Disable IPv6

Open sysctl.conf using the following command:

```
sudo gedit /etc/sysctl.conf
```

Downloading the example code

You can download the example code files for all Packt books you have purchased from your account at http://www.packtpub.com. If you purchased this book elsewhere, you can visit http://www.packtpub.com/support and register to have the files e-mailed directly to you.

Add the following lines at the end of the file. Reboot the machine to update the configurations correctly:

```
#disable ipv6
net.ipv6.conf.all.disable_ipv6 = 1
net.ipv6.conf.default.disable_ipv6 = 1
net.ipv6.conf.lo.disable_ipv6 = 1
```

Steps for installing Hadoop 2.6.0

1. Download Hadoop 2.6.0 using this:

   ```
   wget  http://apache.claz.org/hadoop/common/hadoop-2.6.0/hadoop-2.6.0.tar.gz
   ```

2. Unpack compressed Hadoop file using this:

   ```
   tar -xvzf hadoop-2.6.0.tar.gz
   ```

3. Move hadoop-2.6.0 directory (a new directory):

   ```
   mv hadoop-2.6.0 hadoop
   ```

4. Move Hadoop to a local folder (for convenience) with this command:

   ```
   sudo mv hadoop /usr/local/
   ```

5. Change the owner of the folder:

   ```
   sudo chown -R hduser:hadoop Hadoop
   ```

6. Next, update the configuration files.

   There are three site-specific configuration files and one environment setup configuration file to communicate with the Master node (NameNode) and slave nodes (DataNodes):

   ○ core-site.xml
   ○ hdfs-site.xml
   ○ mapred-site.xml
   ○ yarn-site.xml

Navigate to the path that has the configuration files:

`cd /usr/local/Hadoop/etc/Hadoop`

```
<configuration>

<!-- Site specific YARN configuration properties -->
<property>
    <name>yarn.nodemanager.aux-services</name>
    <value>mapreduce_shuffle</value>
</property>
 <property>
    <name>yarn.nodemanager.aux-services.mapreduce.shuffle.class</name>
    <value>org.apache.hadoop.mapred.ShuffleHandler</value>
 </property>

</configuration>
```

yarn-site.xml

Th `core-site.XML` file has the details of the Master node IP or the hostname, Hadoop temporary directory path, and so on.

```
<configuration>
<property>
    <name>fs.default.name</name>
    <value>hdfs://localhost:9000</value>
</property>
</configuration>
```

core-site.xml

The `hdfs-site.xml` file has the details of the following:

- Local file system path where NameNode stores namespace and transactions logs
- A list of local file system paths to store the blocks
- Block size
- Number of replications

```
<configuration>
<property>
    <name>dfs.replication</name>
    <value>1</value>
 </property>
 <property>
    <name>dfs.namenode.name.dir</name>
    <value>file:/usr/local/hadoop/yarn_data/hdfs/namenode</value>
 </property>
<property>
    <name>dfs.datanode.data.dir</name>
    <value>file:/usr/local/hadoop/yarn_data/hdfs/datanode</value>
</property>
</configuration>
```

hdfs-site.xml

The `mapred-site.xml` file has the details of the following:

- The host or IP and port where the JobTracker runs
- The path on the HDFS where Map/Reduce stores the files
- A list of paths on the local file system to store the intermediate MapReduce data
- The maximum limit of Map/Reduce tasks for every task tracker
- A list of DataNodes that need to be included or excluded
- A list of TaskTrackers that need to be included or excluded

```
<configuration>
<property>
    <name>mapreduce.framework.name</name>
    <value>yarn</value>
</property>
</configuration>
```

mapred-site.xml

Edit the `.bashrc` file as shown in the following screenshot:

```
# Set Hadoop related environment variables
export HADOOP_PREFIX='/usr/local/hadoop'
export HADOOP_HOME='/usr/local/hadoop'
export HADOOP_MAPRED_HOME=${HADOOP_HOME}
export HADOOP_COMMON_HOME=${HADOOP_HOME}
export HADOOP_HDFS_HOME=${HADOOP_HOME}
export YARN_HOME=${HADOOP_HOME}
export HADOOP_CONF_DIR=${HADOOP_HOME}/etc/hadoop
# Native Path
export HADOOP_COMMON_LIB_NATIVE_DIR=${HADOOP_PREFIX}/lib/native
export HADOOP_OPTS="-Djava.library.path=$HADOOP_PREFIX/lib"
#Java path
export JAVA_HOME='/usr/local/Java/jdk1.7.0_45'
# Add Hadoop bin/ directory to PATH
export PATH=$PATH:$HADOOP_HOME/bin:$JAVA_HOME/bin:$HADOOP_HOME/sbin
```

Starting Hadoop

- To start the NameNode:

  ```
  $ Hadoop-daemon.sh start namenode
  $ jps
  ```

- To start the DataNode:

  ```
  $ Hadoop-daemon.sh start datanode
  $ jps
  ```

- To start ResourceManager, use the following command:

  ```
  $ yarn-daemon.sh start resourcemanager
  $ jps
  ```

```
hduser@Hadoopupgrade:~$ hadoop-daemon.sh start namenode
starting namenode, logging to /usr/local/hadoop/logs/hadoop-hduser-namenode-Hado
opupgrade.out
hduser@Hadoopupgrade:~$ jps
1244 NameNode
1280 Jps
hduser@Hadoopupgrade:~$ hadoop-daemon.sh start datanode
starting datanode, logging to /usr/local/hadoop/logs/hadoop-hduser-datanode-Hado
opupgrade.out
hduser@Hadoopupgrade:~$ jps
1400 Jps
1244 NameNode
1332 DataNode
hduser@Hadoopupgrade:~$ yarn-daemon.sh start resourcemanager
starting resourcemanager, logging to /usr/local/hadoop/logs/yarn-hduser-resource
manager-Hadoopupgrade.out
hduser@Hadoopupgrade:~$ jps
1474 Jps
1244 NameNode
1433 ResourceManager
1332 DataNode
```

- To start NodeManager:

  ```
  $ yarn-daemon.sh start nodemanager
  ```

- Check Hadoop Web interfaces:

  NameNode: http://localhost:50070

  Secondary Namenode: http://localhost:50090

- To stop Hadoop, use this:

  ```
  stop-dfs.sh
  stop-yarn.sh
  ```

Hadoop distributions and vendors

With the Apache distribution for Hadoop being the open source and core version that the big data community is adopting, several vendors have their distributions of the open source adoption of Apache Hadoop. Some of them have purely added support while others have wrapped and extended the capabilities of Apache Hadoop and its ecosystem components. In many cases, they have their frameworks or libraries built over the core frameworks to add new functionality or features to the underlying core component.

In this section, let us cover some of the distributions of Apache Hadoop and some differentiating data facts that help the development teams or organizations to take a decision about the distribution that works best for their requirements.

Let us now consider the following vendors:

- Cloudera
- Hortonworks
- MapR
- Pivotal / EMC
- IBM

Category	Function/ Framework	Cloudera	Hortonworks	MapR	Pivotal	IBM
Performance and Scalability	Data Ingestion	Batch	Batch	Batch and Streaming	Batch and Streaming	Batch and Streaming
	Metadata architecture	Centralized	Centralized	Distributed	Centralized	Centralized
	HBase performance	Spikes in latency	Spikes in latency	Low latency	Low latency	Spikes in latency
	NoSQL Support	Mainly batch applications	Mainly batch applications	Batch and online systems	Batch and online systems	Batch and online systems
Reliability	High Availability	Single failure recovery	Single failure recovery	Self healing across multiple failures	Self healing across multiple failures	Single failure recovery
	Disaster Recovery	File copy	N/A	Mirroring	Mirroring	File copy
	Replication	Data	Data	Data and metadata	Data and metadata	Data
	Snapshots	Consistent with closed files	Consistent with closed files	Point in time consistency	Consistent with closed files	Consistent with closed files

Category	Function/ Framework	Cloudera	Hortonworks	MapR	Pivotal	IBM
	Upgrading	Rolling upgrades	Planned	Rolling upgrades	Planned	Planned
Manageability	Volume Support	No	No	Yes	Yes	Yes
	Management Tools	Cloudera Manager	Ambari	MapR Control system	Proprietary console	Proprietary console
	Integration with REST API	Yes	Yes	Yes	Yes	Yes
	Job replacement control	No	No	Yes	Yes	No
Data Access & Processing	File System	HDFS, Read-only NFS	HDFS, read-only NFS	HDFS, read/write NFS and POSIX	HDFS, read/write NFS	HDFS, read-only NFS
	File I/O	Append-only	Append-only	Read/write	Append-only	Append-only
	Security ACLs	Yes	Yes	Yes	Yes	Yes
	Authentication	Kerberos	Kerberos	Kerberos and Native	Kerberos and Native	Kerberos and Native

Summary

In this chapter, we covered all about Hadoop, starting from core frameworks to ecosystem components. At the end of this chapter, readers should be able to set up Hadoop and run some MapReduce functions. Users should be able to run and manage a Hadoop environment and understand the command line usage using one or more ecosystem component.

In the next chapter, our focus is on the key Machine learning frameworks such as Mahout, Python, R, Spark, and Julia; these either have inherent support on the Hadoop platform, or need direct integration with the Hadoop platform for supporting large datasets.

4
Machine Learning Tools, Libraries, and Frameworks

In the previous chapter, we covered the Machine learning solution architecture and the implementation aspects of a technology platform—Hadoop. In this chapter, we will look at some of the highly adopted and upcoming Machine learning tools, libraries, and frameworks. This chapter is a primer for the following chapters as it covers how to implement a specific Machine learning algorithm using out-of-box functions of an identified Machine learning framework.

We will first cover the landscape of open source and commercial Machine learning libraries or tools that are available in the market, and pick the top five open source options. For each of the identified options, starting from installation steps, learning the syntax, implementing a complex Machine learning algorithm, to plotting graphs, we will cover it all. This chapter is mandatory for the readers in the order of occurrence as it is a foundation for all the example implementations in the chapters that follow.

Each of the identified frameworks can operate as standalone libraries and can run on Hadoop as well. In addition to learning how to program and implement a Machine learning algorithm, we will also cover how each of the identified frameworks integrate and run on Hadoop; this is what differentiates these tutorials from the mainstream ones found on the web.

The topics listed here are covered in depth in this chapter:

- A brief list of commercial and open source Machine learning libraries.
- Top libraries or frameworks covered are R, Mahout, Julia, Python (Machine learning libraries, in particular), and Spark.

- Apache Mahout is a framework used for running Machine learning algorithms built over Hadoop and is a Java-based open source Machine learning option. This framework can also work standalone. It is known for running Machine learning algorithms to heavy volumes of data. This framework is a part of Hadoop ecosystem components and has its distribution.

- R is an open source Machine learning and a data mining tool that is adopted very widely in the Machine learning community. This framework library can either work standalone or can be run on Hadoop using the Hadoop runtime R extensions.

- Julia is an open source high-performance programming language that supports running numeric and statistical computing functions in a distributed and parallel way.

- Python is an interpreted, high-level programming language that is designed to try out different things and it is something that does not fall into the traditional waterfall way of development. We will explore the basic Python libraries—**NumPy** and **SciPy** and use scikit-learn to execute our first Machine learning program. Also, we will explore how to write a Hadoop MapReduce program in Python.

- Apache Spark and its Machine learning core libraries: Spark is a cluster computing system with API for Java, Python, and Scala. We will explore the **MLlib API** for Machine learning and use a version for Apache Hadoop. The focus will be to explore the Spark Java APIs.

- A brief introduction to Spring XD and the related Machine learning libraries.

- For each of the identified Machine learning frameworks, integration with Hadoop will be a primary focus.

Machine learning tools – A landscape

There are several open source and commercial Machine learning frameworks and tools in the market that have evolved over the last few decades. While the field of Machine learning itself is evolving in building powerful algorithms for diverse requirements across domains, we now see a surge of open source options for large-scale Machine learning that have reached a significant level of maturity and are being widely adopted by the data science and Machine learning communities.

The model has changed significantly in the recent past, and researchers are encouraged to publish their software under an open source model. Since there are problems that authors face while publishing their work in using algorithmic implementations for Machine learning, any work that is reviewed and improvised through usage by the data science community is considered to be of more value.

The following figure shows a concept model of some important commercial and open source Machine learning frameworks and tools in the market. The highlighted ones will be covered in depth in this chapter.

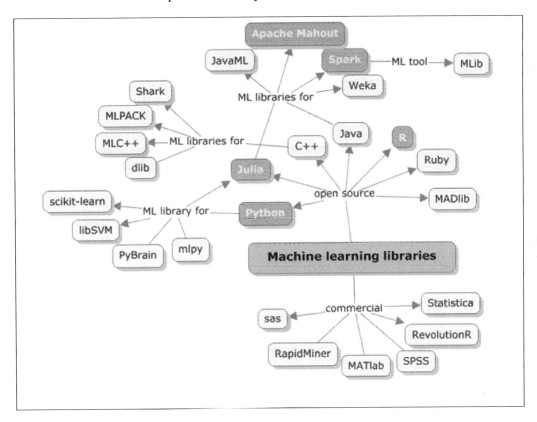

Some of these libraries are around specific programming languages such as Java, Python, C++, Scala, and so on. Some of these libraries, like Julia, Spark, and Mahout already support distributed, and parallel processing and others such as R and Python can run as MapReduce functions on Hadoop.

In the following sections, for each of the highlighted Machine learning libraries, the following will be covered:

- An overview of the library or tool with the details of out-of-box Machine learning functions supported

- Installation, setup, and configuration guide

- Introduction to syntax and basic data processing functions, and then the Advanced Machine learning functions example implementations

- Samples for visualizations and plotting (wherever applicable)
- Integration and execution on the Hadoop platform

Apache Mahout

Apache Mahout is a Machine learning library that comes packaged with Apache Hadoop and forms an important part of the Hadoop ecosystem.

Mahout came into existence in 2008 as a subproject of Apache Lucene (an open source search engine). Lucene is an API that has an implementation of search, text mining, and information-retrieval techniques. Most of these search and text analytics internally apply Machine learning techniques. The recommendation engines that were built for the search engines started off under a new subproject called Mahout. Mahout means the *rider of an elephant*, signifying the running of Machine learning algorithms over Hadoop. It is a scalable Machine learning implementation that can run in a standalone mode (does not tightly integrate with Hadoop) as well.

Mahout is a set of some basic Machine learning Java libraries used for classification, clustering, pattern mining, and so on. Though Mahout today provides support for a subset of Machine learning algorithms, it still ranks among the most adopted frameworks as it inherently supports analytics on large datasets to the degree of hundreds of millions of rows, which can be unstructured in nature as well.

How does Mahout work?

Mahout implements Hadoop MapReduce, and the most important aspect is that it works on top of Hadoop and applies a distributed computing paradigm.

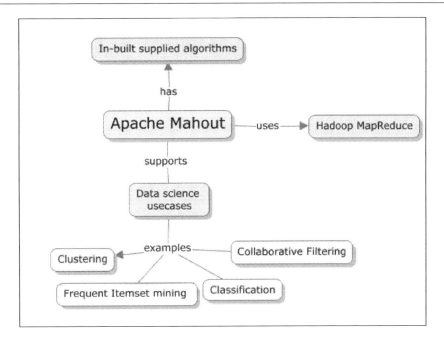

Following are some of the specific Machine learning tasks that Mahout currently implements:

- **Collaborative Filtering / Recommendation**: This takes a user input and finds items that the users might like
- **Clustering**: This takes a bunch of documents as input and groups them based on the topics they refer/belong to
- **Classification**: This takes a bunch of documents and, based on the existing categorization of the documents, learns what category a given document might belong to, and maps the document to that category
- **Frequent itemset mining**: This takes a bunch of items as input and, based on the learning from the real occurrences, identifies which items occur or appear together

There are certain algorithms, for example, logistic regression and SVM (more about these algorithms will be covered in the chapters to follow), which cannot be parallelized and run in a standalone mode.

Installing and setting up Apache Mahout

In this chapter, we will look at how to run Mahout in a standalone mode and on Hadoop. Though there was the new 1.0 version of Apache Mahout available at the time of writing this book, we will use version 0.9 (the latest stable version) in all the examples. The operating system used is Ubuntu 12.04 desktop 32-bit version.

Following are the dependencies and key requirements for installing Apache Mahout:

- JDK (1.6 or above; we will use 1.7 u9 version for the examples throughout this book)
- Maven (2.2 or above; we will use 3.0.4 for the examples throughout this book)
- Apache Hadoop (2.0; not mandatory as Mahout can be run locally)
- Apache Mahout (0.9 distribution)
- Development environment—Eclipse IDE (Luna)

In *Chapter 3, An Introduction to Hadoop's Architecture and Ecosystem*, we have seen how Apache Hadoop 2.0 single node installation is done along with the required prerequisites like Java.

In this chapter, we will cover the setting up of Maven, Eclipse for the development environment, and configuring Apache Mahout to run on and off Hadoop. As the considered platform and related frameworks are open sources, we will use the VirtualBox machine emulator hosted by the Windows 7 Professional edition.

As you may recollect, Hadoop cannot run as a root user, and hence we have a user created for this purpose—`practical-ml` to install and run everything.

Setting up Maven

It is recommended that Maven is used to get the required Mahout jars, and it gets easy to switch to any newer versions easily with Mahout. In the absence of Maven, downloading the dependencies will get more complicated. For more details on specific features of Maven and its utility in application development, refer to `https://www.packtpub.com/application-development/apache-maven-3-cookbook`.

Maven version 3.0.4 can be downloaded from one of the mirrors of the Apache website. The following command can be used for this purpose:

```
wget http://it.apache.contactlab.it/maven/maven-3/3.0.4/binaries/
apachemaven-3.0.4-bin.tar.gz
```

To manually install Maven, perform the following instructions:

1. Extract the distribution archive that is, `apache-maven-3.0.4-bin.tar.gz` to the directory you wish to install Maven 3.0.4.

2. With these instructions, the `/usr/local/apache-maven` path will be chosen. An `apache-maven-3.0.4` subdirectory will be created from the archive.

3. The following lines need to be appended to the `.bashrc` file:

    ```
    export M2_HOME=/usr/local/apache-maven-3.0.4
    export M2=$M2_HOME/bin
    export PATH=$M2:$PATH
    export JAVA_HOME=$HOME/programs/jdk
    ```

`JAVA_HOME` should point to a location where the JDK is installed. For example, export `JAVA_HOME=/usr/java/jdk1.7`. `$JAVA_HOME/bin` is in your `PATH` environment variable. The `PATH` variable is set during the Java installation. This should be verified.

We can now check for the successful installation of Maven by running the following command:

```
mvn -version
```

In case there are any proxy settings, we will have to explicitly update the proxy settings in the `settings.xml` file, which is in the `conf` folder of Maven installation.

Setting-up Apache Mahout using Eclipse IDE

The procedure detailed next covers the steps to set up the Mahout environment, code base, accessing of examples, running, debugging, and testing them using Eclipse IDE. This is the recommended way to set up and is the simplest way to set up Apache Mahout for the development teams.

Execute the following steps to get the Apache Mahout tar, untar it and navigate to the installation.

1. Set up Eclipse IDE.

    The latest version of Eclipse can be downloaded from the following link:

    ```
    https://www.eclipse.org/downloads/
    ```

2. Download Mahout Distribution from the direct link using the command here:

    ```
    $ wget -c http://archive.apache.org/dist/mahout/0.9/mahout-
    distribution-0.9.tar.gz
    ```

3. Extract the archive from it using the following command:

    ```
    $ tar zxf mahout-distribution-0.9.tar.gz
    ```

4. Convert the project into an Eclipse project:

    ```
    $ cd mahout-distribution-0.9
    $ mvn eclipse: eclipse
    ```

    The earlier command builds the Eclipse project.

5. Set the M2_REPO classpath variable to point to the local repository path. The following command adds all the Maven jars to the Eclipse classpath:

    ```
    mvn -Declipse.workspace= eclipse:add-maven-repo
    ```

6. Now, let's import the Eclipse Mahout projects.

    Navigate from the menu, **File | Import | General | Existing Projects** into **Workspace**.

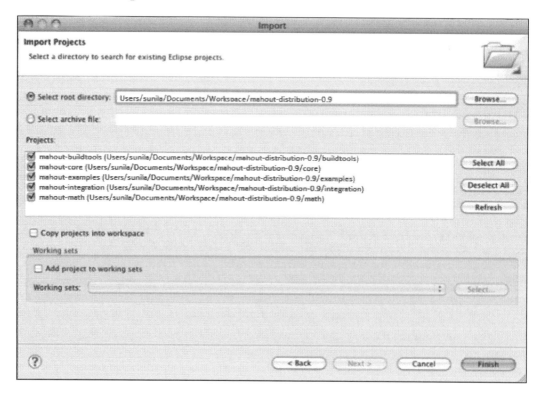

Setting up Apache Mahout without Eclipse

1. Download Mahout Distribution from the direct link using the command here:

```
$ wget -c http://archive.apache.org/dist/mahout/0.9/mahout-
distribution-0.9.tar.gz
```

2. Extract the Mahout distribution to the `/usr/local` folder:

```
$ cd /usr/local
$ sudo tar xzf mahout-distribution-0.9.tar.gz
$ sudo mv mahout-distribution-0.9.tar.gz mahout
$ sudo chown -R practical-ml:hadoop mahout
```

3. Set the Java, Maven, and Mahout paths in the `.bashrc` file.

   Open the `.bashrc` file using the command here:

   ```
   gedit ~/.bashrc
   ```

   Add the following content to the file:

   ```
   export MAHOUT_HOME = /usr/local/mahout
   path=$path:$MAHOUT HOME/bin
   export M2_HOME=/usr/local/maven
   export PATH=$M2:$PATH
   export M2=$M2_HOME/bin
   PATH=$PATH:$JAVA_HOME/bin;$M2_HOME/bin
   ```

4. To run Mahout in the local mode (this means in the standalone mode where there is no need for Hadoop, and the algorithms will not run in parallel or MapReduce mode).

   Set the local mode to true using the following command:

   ```
   $MAHOUT_LOCAL=true
   ```

   This will force Mahout to not look for the Hadoop configurations in `$HADOOP_CONF_DIR`.

   `MAHOUT_LOCAL` is set, so we don't add `HADOOP_CONF_DIR` to the classpath.

There is an alternative to run Mahout on Hadoop. Firstly, ensure Hadoop 2.x is installed and configured successfully. Then, follow these instructions:

1. Set `$HADOOP_HOME`, `$HADOOP_CONF_DIR` are set and added to `$PATH`.

   ```
   export HADOOP_CONF_DIR=$HADOOP_HOME/conf
   ```

   The above sets the mode in which Hadoop is run (for example, in `core-site.xml`, `hdfs-site.xml`, `mapred-site.xml`, and so on.)

2. Now, launch the Hadoop instance using the command here:

   `$HADOOP_HOME/bin/start-all.sh`

3. Check `http://localhost:50030`, and `http://localhost:50070` URLs to confirm whether Hadoop is up and running.

4. Build Apache Mahout using Maven by running the following Maven command from the Mahout directory:

   `/usr/local/mahout$ mvn install`

The following output is seen on a successful install:

Mahout Packages

The following figure depicts different packages in Mahout that provide some out-of-box support for several Machine learning algorithms. At the core, the modules are the utilities, math vectors, collections, and Hadoop with MapReduce for the parallel processing and the file system for distributed storage.

Moreover, over the core modules are the Machine learning packages as listed here:

- Classification
- Clustering
- Evolutionary Algorithms
- Recommenders
- Regression
- FPM
- Dimension Reduction

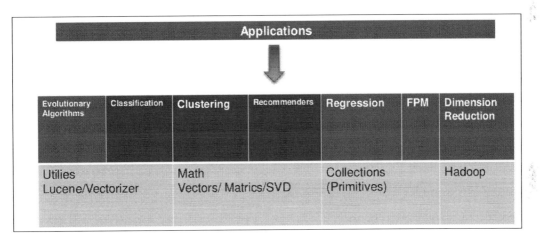

More details are covered on the previous packages in detail in the chapters to follow, with example implementations using each of the packages for an identified problem.

Implementing vectors in Mahout

As we understand, to demonstrate most of the Machine learning algorithm implementations in Mahout, we need the data in classic Mahout dataset format. At the core, the code for this is primary to use some Mahout ready-to-use scripts with some minor changes in the settings. Given below is the standard process:

1. Create sequence files from the raw text files.

   Sequence files are predominantly a binary encoding of the key/value pair representation of data. The attributes given next are the key header elements that represent metadata details:

   - Version
   - Key name
   - Value name
   - Compression

2. Generate vectors from the sequence files. More on the actual commands to generate sequence files is covered in the following chapters while demonstrating the implementation for each of the identified Machine learning algorithms.

3. Running functions on these working vectors

There are different types of vector implementations in Mahout, and the definitions hold good in general as well.

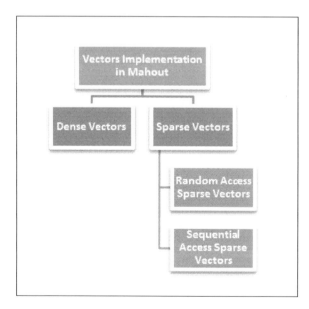

- **Dense Vectors**: These vectors are usually an array of doubles, and the size of this vector is the same as the number of features in the dataset. Since all the entries are preallocated irrespective of a zero value, these vectors are called dense vectors.

- **Sparse Vectors**: These vectors are arrays of vectors and are represented only with non-zero or null values. With sparse vectors, there are two subcategories: the random-access and sequential-access sparse vectors.

   ◦ **Random Access Sparse Vectors**: Random access sparse vectors are the HashMap representations where the key is an integer value, and the value is a double value. At any given point in time, a value can be accessed by passing in the given key.

   ◦ **Sequential Access Sparse Vectors**: These vectors are nothing but a set of two arrays where the first array is the array of keys (the integers), and the second array is an array of values (the doubles). These vectors are optimized for linear reads, unlike the random access sparse vectors. Again, the storage is done for only non-zero values.

 For a detailed understanding of working with Apache Mahout, refer to the Packt Publication for Apache Mahout titled *Apache Mahout Cookbook*.

While this section covers a framework that is built to work with Hadoop with small configuration changes, in the next section, we cover the powerful and highly adopted option in the market — R. Hadoop provides explicit adapters to have the R programs work in the MapReduce model, which is covered next.

R

R is a language for data analysis and is used as an environment that is a primary driver in the field of Machine learning, statistical computing, and data mining and provides a comprehensive platform for basic and advanced visualizations or graphics. Today, R is a basic skill that almost all data scientists or would-be data scientists have or *must* learn.

R is primarily a GNU project known to be similar to the S language that was initially developed at Bell Laboratories (formerly known as AT&T and now, Lucent Technologies) by John Chambers and team. The initial goal for S was to support all statistical functions and was widely used by hard-core statisticians.

R comes with a wide range of open source packages that can be downloaded and configured free of cost, and are installed or loaded on a need basis into the R environment. These packages provide out-of-box support for a wide variety of statistical techniques that include linear and non-linear modeling, time-series analysis, classification, clustering, and so on.

Along with these, the highly extensible graphical functions are available. The support for these advanced graphical functions has been a primary differentiator for R as the output is known for its publication quality plots. In addition to these, R also supports many open source graphical libraries and visualization tools that are both open source and commercial in nature.

Though, at the core, R is not meant to work in a distributed environment or run the algorithms in a parallel mode, there are several extensions available (both open source and commercial) that make R more scalable and support large dataset. In this chapter, we will cover how R can be integrated with Apache Hadoop, and thus can run and leverage the MapReduce capabilities.

Most importantly, R is free software that is widely adopted and has many committers and support groups constantly working on retaining its high relevance in the field of data science.

Some of the key capabilities that R supports today are listed here:

- The ability to effectively manage and store data that the models operate on
- Facilitating some core suite of functions for calculations on arrays, vectors, and matrices among others
- Several out-of-box Machine learning functions that can be loaded on demand and help implement data science projects with ease
- Advanced and sophisticated graphical functions that can be used with ease and help to produce valuable dashboards for business owners
- A wide and active community of adopters and committers that has developed rapidly with extensions via a large collection of packages
- R is considered as a platform that supports newly developing methods of interactive data analysis

Installing and setting up R

For all the examples in this book, we will use the stable version 2.15.1 of R and the CRAN references for all the latest R packages.

Refer to the `https://cran.r-project.org/bin/windows/base/old/2.15.1/` link to download R for Windows.

A detailed installation process is covered at `https://cran.r-project.org/doc/manuals/R-admin.html#Top`.

We can use R with the R GUI or the IDE RStudio. Following are the screenshots of the R interface that the users can see post a successful installation of the R GUI and R IDE, and the RStudio.

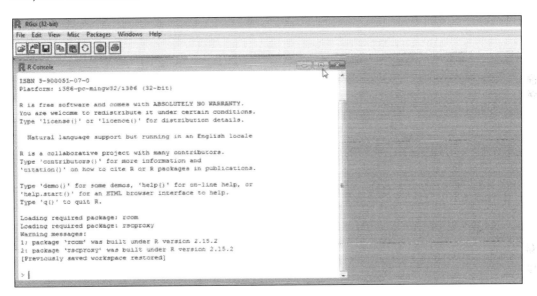

We will need to set the CRAN mirror path to be able to access and load the required R packages by navigating from the menu path **Packages | Set CRAN mirror**

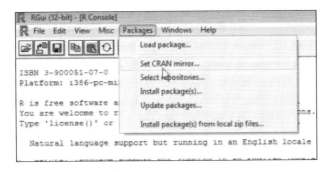

The following screenshot shows a list of mirror sites from which the developer can choose the most appropriate one:

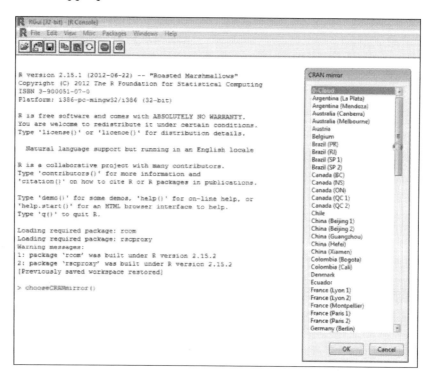

The R Editor can be used to write any advanced operations, and the results can be seen on the console as shown here:

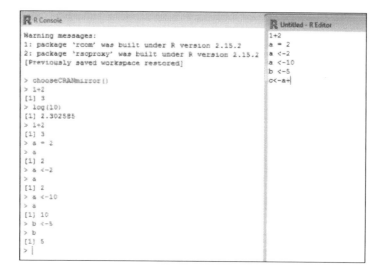

Following is a screenshot of a graphical plot:

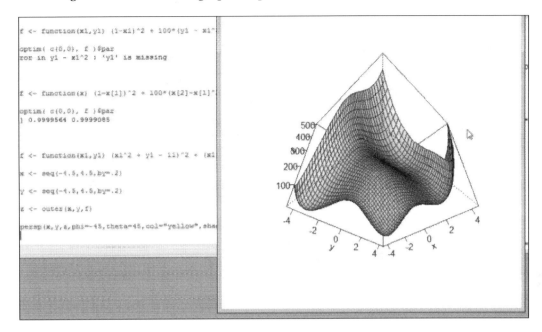

Integrating R with Apache Hadoop

So far, we have seen Apache Hadoop and its core components, HDFS and YARN (MapReduce 2.0), and R. There are three different ways in which we can look at integrating R with Hadoop, and hence the support for large-scale Machine learning.

Approach 1 – Using R and Streaming APIs in Hadoop

To integrate an R function with Hadoop and see it running in a MapReduce mode, Hadoop supports Streaming APIs for R. These Streaming APIs primarily help in running any script that can access and operate with standard I/O in a MapReduce mode. So in the case of R, there wouldn't be any explicit client side integration done with R. The following is an example of R and streaming:

```
$ ${HADOOP_HOME}/bin/Hadoop jar
${HADOOP_HOME}/contrib/streaming/*.jar \
-inputformat
org.apache.hadoop.mapred.TextInputFormat \
-input input_data.txt \
-output \
```

```
-mapper /home/tst/src/map.R \
-reducer /home/tst/src/reduce.R \
-file /home/tst/src/map.R \
-file /home/tst/src/reduce.R
```

Approach 2 – Using the Rhipe package of R

There is a package in R called Rhipe that allows running a MapReduce job within R. To use this way of implementing R on Hadoop; there are some prerequisites:

- R needs to be installed on each DataNode in the Hadoop Cluster

- Protocol Buffers will be installed and available on each DataNode (for more information on Protocol Buffers refer to `http://wiki.apache.org/hadoop/ProtocolBuffers`)

- Rhipe should be available on each data node

The following is a sample format for using the `Rhipe` library in R to implement MapReduce:

```
library(Rhipe)
rhinit(TRUE, TRUE);
map<-expression ( {lapply (map.values, function(mapper)…)})
reduce<-expression(
pre = {…},
reduce = {…},
post = {…},
)
x <- rhmr(map=map, reduce=reduce,
 ifolder=inputPath,
 ofolder=outputPath,
 inout=c('text', 'text'),
 jobname='test name'))
rhex(x)
```

Approach 3 – Using RHadoop

RHadoop, very similar to Rhipe, facilitates running R functions in a MapReduce mode. It is an open source library built by Revolution Analytics. Following are some packages, which are a part of the RHadoop library:

- **plyrmr**: This is a package that provides functions for common data manipulation requirements for large datasets running on Hadoop

- **rmr**: This is a package that has a collection of functions that integrate R and Hadoop
- **rdfs**: This is a package with functions that help interface R and HDFS
- **rhbase**: This is a package with functions that help interface R and HBase

The following is an example that uses the rmr package and demonstrates steps to integrate R and Hadoop using the functions from this package:

```
library(rmr)
maplogic<-function(k,v) { …}
reducelogic<-function(k,vv) { …}
mapreduce( input ="data.txt",
output="output",
textinputformat =rawtextinputformat,
map = maplogic,
reduce=reducelogic
)
```

Summary of R/Hadoop integration approaches

In summary, all of the previous three approaches yield results and facilitate integrating R and Hadoop. They help in scaling R to operate on the large-scale data that will help with HDFS. Each of these approaches has pros and cons. Here is a summary of conclusions:

- Hadoop Streaming API is the simplest of all the approaches as there are no complications regarding installation and setup requirements
- Both Rhipe and RHadoop require some effort to setup R and related packages on the Hadoop cluster
- Regarding implementation approach, Streaming API is more of a command line map, and reduce functions are inputs to the function, whereas both Rhipe and RHadoop allow developers to define and call custom MapReduce functions within R
- In case of Hadoop Streaming API, there is no client side integration required, whereas both Rhipe and RHadoop require the client side integration
- The alternatives to scaling Machine learning are Apache Mahout, Apache Hive, and some commercial versions of R from Revolution Analytics, Segue framework, and others

Implementing in R (using examples)

In this section, we will briefly cover some implementation aspects of R, and focus on learning the syntax and understanding some core functions and its usage.

R Expressions

R can be used as a simple math calculator; here are some basic ways of using it. Here is a trace of what is seen on the R console:

```
> 1+1
[1] 2
> "Welcome to R!"
[1] "Welcome to R!"
> 6*7
[1] 42
> 10<22
[1] TRUE
> 2+7==5
[1] FALSE
```

Assignments

This is used to assign value to a variable and apply some operations to this variable:

Case 1: Assigning a numeric value:

```
> x<-24
> x/2
[1] 12
```

Case 2: Assigning a string literal:

```
> x <- "Try R!"
[1] "Try R!"
> x
[1] " Try R!"
```

Case 3: Assigning a logical value:

```
> x <- TRUE
[1] TRUE
```

Functions

There are many out-of-box functions and to invoke a function in R, we should provide the function name and pass required arguments. Here are some examples of functions and the results, as seen in the R Console:

```
> sum(4,3,5,7)
[1] 19
> rep("Fun!", times=3)
[1] " Fun!" "Fun!" "Fun!"
> sqrt(81)
[1] 9
```

Here is the command to get help for a function in R:

```
> help(sum)
sum package: base R Documentation


Sum of Vector Elements


Description:


     'sum' returns the sum of all the values present in its arguments.


Usage:


     sum(..., na.rm = FALSE)
```

R Vectors

A vector is a simple list of values by definition that forms the core of R data types. Many of the Machine learning functions leverage these.

Here are some key functions with their usage context:

Function/Syntax	Purpose	Example	Output on R Console
m:n	Outputs numbers from m to n increment by 1	> 5:9	[1] 5 6 7 8 9
seq(m,n)	Outputs numbers from m to n increment by 1	> seq(5,9)	[1] 5 6 7 8 9
seq(m,n, i)	Outputs numbers from m to n increment by i	> seq(1,3,0.5)	[1] 1 1.5 2 2.5 3

Assigning, accessing, and manipulating vectors

The following table has examples for creating, accessing, and manipulating matrices in R:

Purpose	Example
Creating a vector of literals	`> sentence <- c('practical', 'machine', 'learning')`
Accessing the third value of the vectors	`> sentence[3]` `[1] "learning."`
Updating a value in the vector	`> sentence[1] <- "implementing"`
Adding a new value to the vector	`> sentence[4] <- "algorithms"`
Getting values for the given indices	`> sentence[c(1,3)]` `[1] "implementing" "learning"`
Getting values for range of indices	`> sentence[2:4]` `[1] "machine" "learning" "algorithms"`
Adding a range of new values	`> sentence[5:7] <- c('for','large','datasets')`

Incrementing vector values by 1	`> a <- c(1, 2, 3)`
	`> a + 1`
	`[1] 2 3 4`

Dividing each value in vector by a value	`> a / 2` `[1] 0.5 1.0 1.5`
Multiplying each value of the vector by a value	`> a*2` `[1] 2 4 6`

Adding two vectors	`> b <- c(4, 5, 6)`
	`> a + b`
	`[1] 5 7 9`

Comparing two vectors	`> a == c(1, 99, 3)` `[1]    TRUE FALSE    TRUE`
Applying a function on each value of the vector	`> sqrt(a)` `[1] 1.000000 1.414214 1.732051`

R Matrices

Matrices are two-dimensional vectors that have rows and columns. The following table has examples for creating, accessing, and manipulating matrices in R:

Purpose	Example
Creating a 3 X 4 matrix with values defaulted to zero	```> matrix(0, 3, 4) [,1] [,2] [,3] [,4] [1,] 0 0 0 0 [2,] 0 0 0 0 [3,] 0 0 0 0```
Initializing a matrix with a range of values	```> a <- 1:12 > m <- matrix(a, 3, 4) [,1] [,2] [,3] [,4] [1,] 1 4 7 10 [2,] 2 5 8 11 [3,] 3 6 9 12```
Accessing a value from the matrix	```> m[2, 3] [1] 8```
Assigning a value to a position of choice in a matrix	```> m[1, 4] <- 0```
Retrieving an array of the entire row or a column of choice	```> m[2,] [1] 2 5 8 11 > m[3,] [1] 7 8 9```
Retrieving a subset of the bigger matrix	```> m[, 2:4] [,1] [,2] [,3] [1,] 4 7 10 [2,] 5 8 11```

R Factors

In data analytics and Machine learning, it is common to group or categorize data. For example, a good or a bad customer. R's `factor` data type is used to track the categorized data. All that needs to be done is defining a vector of categories and passing it as a parameter to the `factor` function.

The following example demonstrates creation and assignment of categories using factors:

```
> ornaments <- c('ring', 'chain', 'bangle', 'anklet', 'nosepin',
'earring', 'ring', 'anklet')
> ornamenttypes <- factor(ornaments)
> print(ornamenttypes)
[1] ring chain bangle anklet nosepin earring
Levels: anklet bangle chain earring nosepin ring
```

Each of the defined categories usually has an integer value associated with the literal. Passing the factor to the as.integer function will give the integer equivalents, as shown here:

```
> as.integer(ornamenttypes)
[1] 6 3 2 1 5 4 6 1
```

R Data Frames

Data frames relate to the concept of database tables. This data type is very powerful in R, and it helps tie different related attributes of a dataset together. For example, the number of items purchased has a relationship with the total bill value and the overall applicable discount. There should be a way to link these attributes, and data frames help to do so:

Purpose	Example

Creating a data frame and checking the values	```> purchase <- data.frame(totalbill, noitems, discount```
	
	```> print(purchase)```
	
	``` totalbill noitems discount```
	
	```1 300 5 10```
	
	```2 200 3 7.5```
	
	```3 100 1 5```
	
	```)```

Accessing the data of the data frame using indexes or labels	```> purchase[[2]]```
	
	```[1] 5 3 1```
	
	```> purchase[["totalbill"]]```
	
	```[1] 300 200 100```
	
	```> purchase$discount```
	
	```[1] 10 7.5 5```

Purpose	Example
Loading data frames with the data from CSV files	``` > list.files() [1] "monthlypurchases.csv" > read.csv("monthlypurchases.csv") Amount Items Discount 1 2500 35 15 2 5464 42 25 3 1245 8 6 ```

R Statistical frameworks

R supports a bunch of statistical out-of-box functions that help statisticians explain the data. Some of the functions with examples are shown in the following table:

Function	Example
Mean	``` limbs <- c(4, 3, 4, 3, 2, 4, 4, 4) names(limbs) <- c('One-Eye', 'Peg-Leg', 'Smitty', 'Hook', 'Scooter', 'Dan', 'Mikey', 'Blackbeard') > mean(limbs) [1] 3.5 ```
Median	``` > median(limbs) [1] 4 ```
Standard deviation	``` > pounds <- c(45000, 50000, 35000, 40000, 35000, 45000, 10000, 15000) > deviation <- sd(pounds) ```

Each piece of the contained R code is saved for a run in a file with the .R extension.

In this section, we have seen how R can be set up and how some basic functions and data types can be used. There are many Machine learning specific packages that we will be exploring in the following chapters.

 For a detailed understanding of working with R for Machine learning, refer to the Packt Publication for R titled *Machine learning with R*.

Julia

Julia, in recent times, has gained much popularity and adoption in the Machine learning and data science fields as a high-performance alternative to Python. Julia is a dynamic programming language that is built to support distributed and parallel computing, thus known to be convenient and fast.

Performance in Julia is a result of the JIT compiler and type interfacing feature. Also, unlike other numeric programming languages, Julia does not enforce vectorization of values. Similar to R, MATLAB, and Python, Julia provides ease and expressiveness for high-level numerical computing.

Following are some key characteristics of Julia:

- The core APIs and mathematical primitive operations are written in Julia
- It consists rich types for constructing and describing objects
- Julia supports for multiple dispatch that enable using functions across many combinations of arguments
- It facilitates the automation of specialized code generation for different argument types
- Proven performance is on par with statically compiled languages like C
- It is a free and open source programming language (MIT licensed)
- User-defined types are as fast and compact as built-ins
- It does not enforce or require vectorization code for performance
- It is designed for distributed and parallel computation
- Julia comes with co-routines and lightweight threading
- Julia supports the ability to invoke the C functions directly
- Shell-like capabilities for managing processes
- It provides Lisp-like macros

Installing and setting up Julia

We will be using Julia's latest version that was available at the time of writing this book—v 0.3.4.

Julia programs can be built and executed by:

- Using Julia command line
- Using Juno—an IDE for Julia
- Using a ready-to-use environment at `https://juliabox.org/`, where the Julia environment can be accessed using a browser

Downloading and using the command line version of Julia

Use the link http://julialang.org/downloads/ to download the required Julia version.

1. Download the appropriate executable and run it.

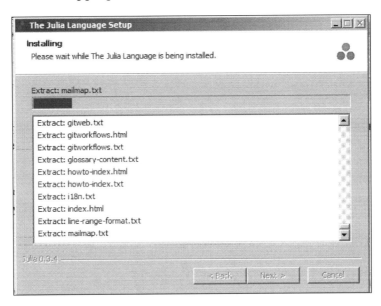

2. After the successful installation, open the Julia console and Julia is ready to use.

Using Juno IDE for running Julia

Juno IDE makes developing Julia code easy. Download the latest Juno IDE version from `http://junolab.org/docs/install.html`.

Juno has Julia's core APIs and functions that help in simplifying the development process. Following is a screenshot of how Juno can be used:

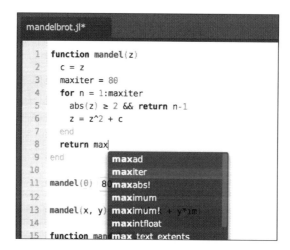

Using Julia via the browser

Using this option does not require any installation of Julia. Follow these steps to access the Julia environment online:

1. Access `https://juliabox.org/` from the browser

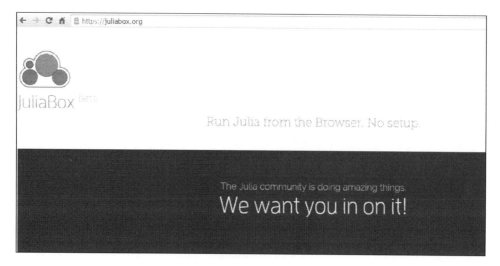

2. Log in using the Google account. This will create a unique instance of Julia for the logged-in user. This will give access to the Julia console and the IJulia instances.

With one of the three approaches that we have seen previously, we have access to the Julia console from where the Julia code can be executed. Each piece of the contained Julia code is built in a file with a `.jl` extension.

Running the Julia code from the command line

Julia compiles the code at runtime and translates each method into a machine code using **just-in-time** (**JIT**) compilers. Internally, it utilizes **Low-Level Virtual Machine** (**LLVM**) for optimization and code generation. LLVM is a full-fledged project that is a collection of standard compiler technologies. This is used as a part of iOS.

From the shell of choice, run the following:

```
<</path/to/Julia>>/myjuliascript.jl
```

Alternatively, open the Julia console from the Julia command line installation and run the following command:

```
julia> include("<<path/to/juliascript>>/myjuliascript.jl")
```

Implementing in Julia (with examples)

In this section, we will cover some basic topics under coding Julia and understanding the syntax. At the end of this section, readers should be able to easily write their Julia script and run the same. Regarding syntax, Julia programming language is very similar to MATLAB.

Using variables and assignments

Variables in Julia, like any other programming language, are used for storing and manipulating data. Following is an example of defining, assigning, and manipulating variables and values:

```
# Assign a numeric value to a variable
julia> x = 10
10

# Perform a simple mathematical manipulation of variables
julia> x + 1
11
```

```
# Assigning or reassigning values to variables.
julia> x = 1 + 1
2

# Assigning a string literal to a variable
julia> x = "Hello World!"
"Hello, World!"
```

Julia, being a mathematical programming language, provides several fundamental constants. Here is an example that can be directly used in the code. Additionally, we can define our constants and reassign values:

```
julia> pi
π = 3.1415926535897...
```

Numeric primitives

For any mathematical programming language that supports numeric-based computing, Integers and floating-point values form the basic building blocks and are called numeric primitives.

Julia comes with a support for large set numeric primitives that are extensive and very well-complimented mathematical functions.

Data structures

Julia supports several data structures in addition to all the primitive data types such as Vectors, Matrices, Tuples, Dictionaries, Sets and so on. Following are some example representations with the usage:

```
# Vector
b = [4, 5, 6]
b[1] # => 4
b[end] # => 6

# Matrix
matrix = [1 2; 3 4]

# Tuple
tup = (1, 2, 3)
tup[1] # => 1
tup[1] = 3 # => ERROR #since tuples are immutable, assigning a value
results in an error

# Dictionary
```

```
dict = ["one"=> 1, "two"=> 2, "three"=> 3]
dict["one"] # => 1

# Set
filled_set = Set(1,2,2,3,4)
```

Working with Strings and String manipulations

Here are some examples of operating with Strings in Julia:

```
split("I love learning Julia ! ")
# => 5-element Array{SubString{ASCIIString},1}:
"I"
"love."
"learning."
"Julia"
"!"

join(["It seems to be interesting", "to see",
"how it works"], ", ")
# => "It seems interesting, to see, how it works."
```

Packages

Julia comes with several packages that have inbuilt functions and support many out-of-box features for implementing Machine learning algorithms as well. Following is the list:

- Images.jl
- Graphs.jl
- DataFrames.jl
- DimensionalityReduction.jl
- Distributions.jl
- NLOpt.jl
- ArgParse.jl
- Logging.jl
- FactCheck.jl
- METADATA.jl

More details on Julia packages can be accessed at https://github.com/JuliaLang/.

Interoperability

This following section covers the integration aspects of Julia with various other programming languages.

Integrating with C

Julia is flexible and without any wrappers, supports invoking C functions directly. Following is an example that demonstrates how this is done:

```
julia> ccall(:clock, Int32, ())
2292761
julia> ccall(:getenv, Ptr{Uint8int8}, (Ptr{Uint8},), "SHELL")
Ptr{Uint8} @0x00007fff5fbffc45
julia> bytestring(ans)
"/bin/bash"
```

Integrating with Python

Similar to the C function calls, Julia supports invoking Python functions directly. It is important that we have the `PyCall` package installed to be able to do so. `PyCall.jl` offers automatic type conversion between Julia and Python. For example, Julia arrays are converted to NumPy arrays.

Following is an example that demonstrates invoking Python functions from the Julia code:

```
julia> using PyCall # Installed with Pkg.add("PyCall")
julia> @pyimport math
julia> math.sin(math.pi / 4) - sin(pi / 4)
0.0
julia> @pyimport pylab
julia> x = linspace(0,2*pi,1000); y = sin(3*x + 4*cos(2*x));
julia> pylab.plot(x, y; color="red", linewidth=2.0, linestyle="--")
julia> pylab.show()
```

Integrating with MATLAB

Following example demonstrates integrating Julia to invoke MATLAB functions:

```
using MATLAB

function sampleFunction(bmap::BitMatrix)
@mput bmap
@matlab bmapthin = bwmorph(bmap, "thin", inf)
convert(BitArray, @mget bmapthin)
end
```

Graphics and plotting

Julia has several packages that help produce graphs and plots. Some of them are listed here:

- `Gadfly.jl`: This is very similar to ggplot2
- `Winston.jl`: This is very similar to Matplotlib
- `Gaston.jl`: This interfaces with gnuplot

The example here demonstrates using `PyPlot`:

```
using PyPlot
x = linspace(-2pi, 2pi)
y = sin(x)
plot(x, y, "--b")
```

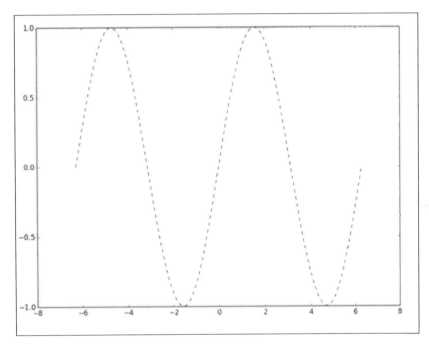

Benefits of adopting Julia

Here are some of the direct benefits that one can look forward to for adopting Julia in the Machine learning implementations:

- Julia facilitates fast prototyping without compromising on performance
- It inherently supports the parallelization of code
- It provides a simpler way of expressing algorithms with special Julia types
- Julia can easily invoke or integrate with C, Python, MATLAB, and C++
- Julia is facilitated by an enthusiastic, friendly, and supportive community
- It works with Hadoop and leverages Hive-based querying

Integrating Julia and Hadoop

Integrating any programming language with Hadoop typically means the data stored in Hadoop should be accessible, and the program should be able to execute a specific logic on the data. This can happen either by retrieving the data from Hadoop and bringing it closer to the program or by moving the program to the data and to execute in a MapReduce or parallel processing mode. Obviously, in the first case where the data is fetched from Hadoop and brought to the code for executing the logic, there needs to be sufficient RAM to be able to hold and process this data in the memory, and this could restrict the ability to run on really large volumes. In the second case, where the code is taken to the data that is distributed across the data nodes, the logic should be parallelizable, and the Map and Reduce logics should be built.

The Julia integration with the Hadoop platform is slightly in its initial stages, and the current approach that is detailed is the first approach described previously where the connection to Hadoop/HDFS is made from the Julia code using a standard ODBC connectivity. The data is fetched into the RAM for further processing. Now, this code can run directly on the DataNode and can update the HDFS data.

We will use ODBC.jl that can be obtained from GitHub using the following link:

https://github.com/quinnj/ODBC.jl

This is a simple low-level ODBC interface for Julia. It can be installed through the Julia package manager using the following commands:

Following command creates a Julia package repository (only runs once for all packages)

```
julia> Pkg.init()
```

Following command creates the ODBC repo folder and downloads the ODBC package and dependency (if needed)

```
julia> Pkg.add("ODBC")
```

Following command loads the ODBC module for use (needs to be run with each new Julia instance)

```
julia> using ODBC
```

Following are some important functions that can be used to work with Hadoop/HDFS:

- To connect using an ODBC datasource, user and password use — co = ODBC. connect("mydatasource",usr="johndoe",pwd="12345").

- To disconnect use disconnect(connection::Connection=conn).

- To connect using a connection string use advancedconnect(conn_string::String).

- To ask a query and fetch a subset of data on the datasource, this query string is a Hive query that will be run on HDFS — query(connecti on Connection=conn, querystring; fi le=: DataFrame,delim='\t').

An example implementation is given here:

Use following command to load ODBC module:

```
using ODBC
```

To connect to Hadoop cluster via Hive use this:

```
hiveconn = ODBC.connect("servername"; usr="your-user-name", pwd="your-password-here")
```

To write a Hive query and store it as a Julia string, use the following command:

```
hive_query_string = "select …;"
```

To run a query, save results directly to file use the following command:

```
query(hive_query_string, hiveconn;output="C:\\sample.csv",delim=',')
```

The Julia program can now access the data from this file to execute Machine learning algorithms.

Python

Python is one of the highly adopted programming or scripting languages in the field of Machine learning and data science. Python is always known for its ease of learning, implementation, and maintenance. Python is highly portable and can run on the Unix-based, Windows and Mac platforms. With the availability of libraries such as Pydoop and SciPy, its relevance in the world of big data analytics has tremendously increased.

Some of the key reasons for the popularity of Python in solving Machine learning problems are listed here:

- Python is known to be well suited for data analysis

- It is a versatile scripting language that can be used for writing some basic quick and dirty scripts for testing some basic functions, or it can be used in real-time applications leveraging its full-featured toolkits

- Python comes with complete Machine learning packages (refer to `http://mloss.org/software/`) and can be used in a plug-and-play manner

Toolkit options in Python

Before we go deeper into what toolkit options we have in Python, let's first understand the toolkit options trade-offs that should be considered before choosing one.

Some of the questions that we should evaluate for the appropriate toolkit can be as follows:

- What are my performance priorities? Do I need offline or real-time processing implementations?

- How transparent are the toolkits? Can I customize the library myself?

- What is the community status? How fast are bugs fixed and how is the community support and expert communication availability?

There are three options in Python:

- Use Python external bindings. These are the interfaces to popular packages in markets such as Matlab, R, Octave, and so on. This option will work well, in case we already have some implementations existing in the previously mentioned frameworks that we are looking at seamlessly migrating into Python.

- Use Python-based toolkits. There are some toolkits written in Python that come with a bunch algorithms. Some of the Python toolkits will be covered in the next section.
- Write your logic/toolkit.

Implementation of Python (using examples)

Python has two core toolkits, which are more of building blocks and almost all the specialized toolkits that are listed here use these core toolkits. These are as follows:

- **NumPy**: NumPy is about fast and efficient arrays built in Python
- **SciPy**: This is a bunch of algorithms for standard operations built in NumPy

There are a bunch of C/C++ based implementations such as LIBLINEAR, LIBSVM, OpenCV, and others

Let's now see some of the popular Python toolkits and also those that have been updated within a span of a year of writing this book:

- **NLTK**: This stands for natural language toolkit. This focuses on the **Natural language processing (NLP)**.
- **mlpy**: This is Machine learning algorithms toolkit that comes with support for some key Machine learning algorithms such as classifications, regression, and clustering among others.
- **PyML**: This toolkit focuses on **Support Vector Machine (SVM)**. We will cover more on this in the coming chapters.
- **PyBrain**: This toolkit focuses on Neural networks and related functions.
- **mdp-toolkit**: The focus of this toolkit is data processing and it supports scheduling and parallelizing the processing.
- **scikit-learn**: This is one of the most popular toolkits and is being highly adopted by data scientists in the recent past. It has support for supervised, and unsupervised learning, some special support for feature selection, and visualizations as well. There is a large team that is actively building this toolkit and is known for its excellent documentation.
- **Pydoop**: This is the Python integration with the Hadoop platform.

Pydoop and **SciPy** are heavily deployed in big data analytics.

In this chapter, we will explore the scikit-learn toolkit, and demonstrate all our examples in the upcoming chapters using this toolkit.

For a Python programmer, using scikit-learn can help bring Machine learning into a production system very easily.

Installing Python and setting up scikit-learn

Following are the core Python toolkit versions and dependencies for installing Python and scikit-learn:

- Python (>= 2.6 or >= 3.3)
- NumPy (>= 1.6.1)
- SciPy (>= 0.9).
- A working C++ compiler

We will be using the wheel packages (.whl files) for scikit-learn from PyPI, and install it using the pip utility.

To install in your home directory, use the following:

```
python setup.py install --home
```

For using the git repo directly from the GitHub to install scikit-learn on the local disk, use the following command:

```
% git clone git://github.com/scikit-learn/scikit-learn/
% cd scikit-learn
```

Loading data

Scikit-learn comes with a few standard datasets, for instance, the `iris` and `digits` datasets that can be used for building and running Machine learning algorithms.

Here are some steps to follow to load the standard datasets shipped with scikit-learn:

```
>>> from sklearn import datasets
>>> iris = datasets.load_iris()
>>> digits = datasets.load_digits()
>>> print digits.data
[[  0.   0.   5. ...,   0.   0.   0.]
 [  0.   0.   0. ...,  10.   0.   0.]
 [  0.   0.   0. ...,  16.   9.   0.]
 ...,
 [  0.   0.   1. ...,   6.   0.   0.]
 [  0.   0.   2. ...,  12.   0.   0.]
 [  0.   0.  10. ...,  12.   1.   0.]]
>>> digits.target
array([0, 1, 2, ..., 8, 9, 8])
```

Apache Spark

Apache Spark is an open-source framework for fast, big data or large-scale processing with the support for streaming, SQL, Machine learning, and graph processing. This framework is implemented in Scala and supports programming languages such as Java, Scala, and Python. The magnitude of performance is up to 10X to 20X is the traditional Hadoop stack. Spark is a general purpose framework and allows interactive programming along with the support for streaming. Spark can work with Hadoop supporting Hadoop formats like SequenceFiles or InputFormats in a standalone mode. It includes local file systems, Hive, HBase, Cassandra, and Amazon S3 among others.

We will use Spark 1.2.0 for all the examples throughout this book.

The following figure depicts the core modules of Apache Spark:

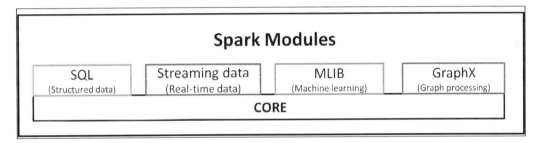

Some of the basic functions of Spark framework include task scheduling, interaction with storage systems, fault tolerance, and memory management. Spark follows a programming paradigm called **Resilient Distributed Dataset (RDD)**. This is primarily related to managing distributed data storage and parallel computing.

- **Spark SQL** is Spark's package for querying and processing structured and unstructured data. The core functions of this package are:
    - To facilitate loading the data from varied structured sources such as Hive, JSON, and others
    - To provide integration between SQL and regular Python or Java or Scala code, and provide the capability to build custom functions that can execute on distributed data and in parallel
    - To support the SQL-based querying from external tools through standard database connections (JDBC/ODBC) including **Tableau**

- **Spark Streaming** module is used for processing real-time, large-scale streams of data. This API is different from the Streaming I/O API of Hadoop.

- **MLib** module provides out-of-box Machine learning algorithm functions that are scalable and can run on a cluster.
- **GraphX** module provides functions for graph manipulations.

In this chapter, we will learn how to use Spark in conjunction with the Scala programming language. Let's now have a quick overview of Scala and learn how to code in Scala.

Scala

Scala is a strongly typed programming language that requires **JVM (Java Virtual Machine)** to run. It is an independent platform and can leverage Java APIs. We will use interpretive prompt to run Scala with Spark. The command prompt here shows how Scala can be run with Spark using the interpretive prompt.

Let's look at some Scala examples.

The following code can be pasted directly into the command prompt:

```
//Default variables are assigned to any expressions
scala>8 * 5 + 2
Res0: Int = 42
Scala>0.5 * res0
Res1= Double = 21.0
//All simple data types are objects
scala>"Hello, " + res0
Res2: java.lang.String = Hello, 42
scala>10.toString()
Res2: String = 10
scala>a.+(b)
Res1: Int = 200              //So you can consider , the operator as a
method
A method b as a shorthand for a.method(b)
scala>val myVal: String = "Foo"
keyword "val" this means that a variable cannot change value
(immutable variable)
scala>var myVar:String = "Foo"
the keyword var means that it is a variable that can be changed
(mutable variable)
scala> def cube(a: Int): Int = a * a * a
cube: (a: Int)Int
scala> myNumbers.map(x => cube(x))
res8: List[Int] = List(1, 8, 27, 64, 125, 64, 27)
scala> myNumbers.map(x => x * x * x)
res9: List[Int] = List(1, 8, 27, 64, 125, 64, 27)
scala> val myNumbers = List(1,2,3,4,5,4,3)
myNumbers: List[Int] = List(1, 2, 3, 4, 5, 4, 3)
scala> def factorial(n:Int):Int = if (n==0) 1 else n * factorial(n-1)
factorial: (n: Int)Int
scala> myNumbers.map(factorial)
res18: List[Int] = List(1, 2, 6, 24, 120, 24, 6)
scala> myNumbers.map(factorial).sum
res19: Int = 183
scala> var factor = 3
factor: Int = 3
scala> val multiplier = (i:Int) => i * factor
multiplier: Int => Int = <function1>
scala> val l1 = List(1,2,3,4,5) map multiplier
l1: List[Int] = List(3, 6, 9, 12, 15)
scala> factor = 5
factor: Int = 5
```

Programming with Resilient Distributed Datasets (RDD)

RDDs are Spark's core abstraction for working with data. They are immutable distributed collections of elements. All functions in Spark only work on RDDs.

Spark automatically distributes the data contained in RDDs across the nodes within a cluster as partitions and supports parallel processing to be performed on them. RDDs can be created by importing from external datasets or distributing collections in the driver program. The following command demonstrates this function:

```
scala> val c = file.filter(line => line.contains("and"))
```

The `collect()` method will write the output to the console:

```
scala>c.collect()
```

The output of the results is usually saved to the external storage system. The `count()` function gives the number of output lines. The following will print out the lines:

```
scala>println("input had " + c.count() + " lines")
```

The `take()` function will fetch *n* records from the result:

```
scala>c.take(10).foreach(println)
```

RDDs process in a lazy manner by Spark to bring in the efficiency while handling large datasets.

To reuse RDD in multiple actions, you can ask Spark to persist it using `RDD.persist()`.

We can ask Spark to persist our data in some different places. After computing it the first time, Spark will store the RDD contents in the memory (partitioned across the machines in your cluster) and reuse them for future actions.

Hence, following are the basic steps to process RDDs:

1. Create input RDDs from external data.
2. Transforming them to define new RDDs using transformations, for example `filter()`.
3. Storing intermediate RDDs for reuse using `persist()`.
4. Invoking any required function (for example, `count()`) to start a parallel computation process.

Following is an example of RDD using Pi Estimation with Scala:

```
scala>var NUM_SAMPLES=5
scala> val count = sc.parallelize(1 to NUM_SAMPLES).map{i =>
    | val x = Math.random()
    | val y = Math.random()
    |   if (x*x + y*y < 1) 1 else 0
    | }.reduce(_ + _)
scala>println("Pi is roughly " + 4.0 * count / NUM_SAMPLES)
```

Spring XD

Though this book does not include Spring XD framework to demonstrate the Machine learning algorithm, a small introduction is given here as this is found to be fast emerging for adoption in the Machine learning world.

XD stands for eXtreme Data. This open source framework is built by the Pivotal team (earlier the SpringSource) as the one-stop-shop for developing and deploying big data applications.

Spring XD is a distributed and extensible framework that unifies data ingestion, analytics functions in real-time, batch, and supports data export. Spring XD is built on Spring Integration and Spring Batch frameworks.

Following are some key features:

* Spring XD is a unified platform for batch and stream workloads. It is an open and extensible runtime.

* Scalable and high-performance, it is a distributed data ingestion framework that can ingest data from a variety of sources that include HDFS, NOSQL, or Splunk.

* It supports for real-time analytics at ingestion time, for example, gathering metrics and counting values.

* It has workflow management through batch jobs that include interactions with standard RDBMS and Hadoop systems.

* It is a scalable and high-performance data export, for example, from HDFS to an RDBMS or NoSQL database.

Spring XD is known to implement Lambda Architecture that in theory is defined to support both batch and real-time processing. More information on evolutionary architectures such as Lambda Architecture is covered in *Chapter 14, New generation data architectures for Machine learning*.

Spring XD architecture primarily has three architecture layers to help facilitate the previous features:

1. **Speed Layer**: This is about accessing and processing data in real time. This process keeps the system more up-to-date.

2. **Batch Layer**: The Batch layer has access to the complete master dataset also called the data lake meaning *source of truth*.

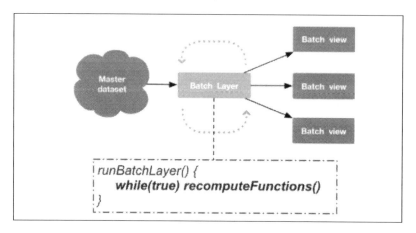

3. **Serving Layer**: The Service layer is more of a query layer that is responsible for exposing the data post processing to an unsubscribed consumer. This layer makes batch data queryable and is usually known for high throughput driven responses.

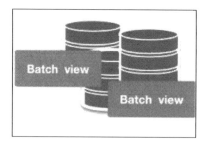

Spring XD Runtime architecture is shown here (source Pivotal):

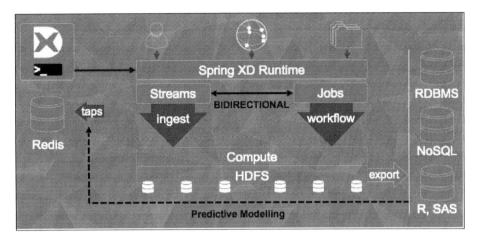

Summary

In this chapter, we learned about the open source options for implementing Machine learning, and covered installation, implementation, and execution of libraries, tools, and frameworks such as Apache Mahout, Python, R, Julia, and Apache Spark's MLib. Importantly, we covered the integration of these frameworks with the big data platform—Apache Hadoop. This chapter is more of a foundation for the coming chapters where we will learn how to use these frameworks in implementing specific Machine learning algorithms.

5
Decision Tree based learning

Starting this chapter, we will take a deep dive into each of the Machine learning algorithms. We begin with a non-parametric supervised learning method, Decision trees, and advanced techniques, used for classification and regression. We will outline a business problem that can be addressed by building a Decision tree-based model and learn how it can be implemented in Apache Mahout, R, Julia, Apache Spark, and Python.

The following topics are covered in depth in this chapter:

- Decision trees: definition, terminology, the need, advantages, and limitations.

- The basics of constructing and understanding Decision trees and some key aspects such as Information gain and Entropy. You will also learn to build regression, the classification of trees and measuring errors.

- Understanding some common problems with Decision trees, need for pruning Decision trees, and techniques for pruning.

- You will learn Decision tree algorithms such as CART, C4.5, C5.0 and so on; and specialized trees such as Random forests, Oblique trees, Evolutionary and Hellinger trees.

- Understanding a business use case for classification and regression trees, and an implementation of the same using Apache Mahout, R, Apache Spark, and Julia and Python (scikit-learn) libraries and modules.

Decision trees

Decision trees are known to be one of the most powerful and widely used modeling techniques in the field of Machine learning.

Decision trees naturally induce rules that can be used in data classification and prediction. Following is an example of a rule definition derived from building a Decision tree:

If (laptop model is *x*) and (manufactured by *y*) and (is *z* years old) and (with some owners being *k*) then (the battery life is *n* hours).

When closely observed, these rules are expressed in simple, human readable, and comprehensible formats. Additionally, these rules can be stored for later reference in a data store. The following concept map depicts various characteristics and attributes of Decision trees that will be covered in the following sections.

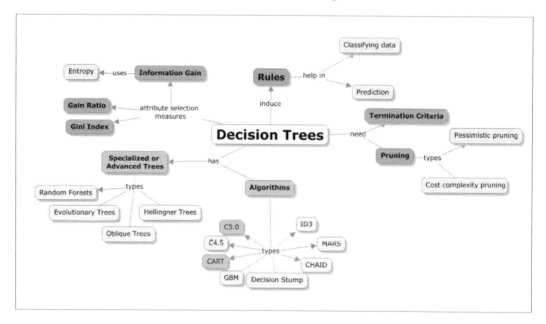

Terminology

Decision trees classify instances by representing in a tree structure starting from the root to a leaf. Most importantly, at a high level, there are two representations of a Decision tree—a node and an arc that connects nodes. To make a decision, the flow starts at the root nodes, navigates to the arcs until it has reached a leaf node, and then makes a decision. Each node of the tree denotes testing of an attribute, and the branches denote the possible values that the attribute can take.

Following are some of the characteristics of a Decision tree representation:

- Every non-leaf node (for example, a decision node) denotes a representation of the attribute value
- Every branch denotes the rest of the value representation
- Every leaf (or terminal) node represents the value of the target attribute
- The starting node is called the root node

The following figure is a representation of the same:

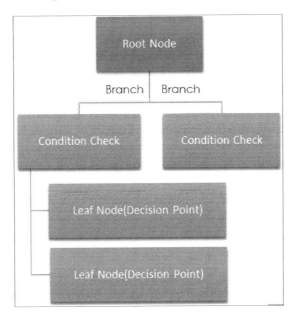

Purpose and uses

Decision trees are used for classification and regression. Two types of trees are used in this context:

- Classification trees
- Regression trees

Classification trees are used to classify the given data set into categories. To use classification trees, the response of the target variable needs to be a categorical value such as yes/no, true/false. On the other hand, regression trees are used to address prediction requirements and are always used when the target or response variable is a numeric or discrete value such as stock value, commodity price, and so on.

The next figure depicts the purpose of the Decision tree and relevant tree category as the classification or regression tree:

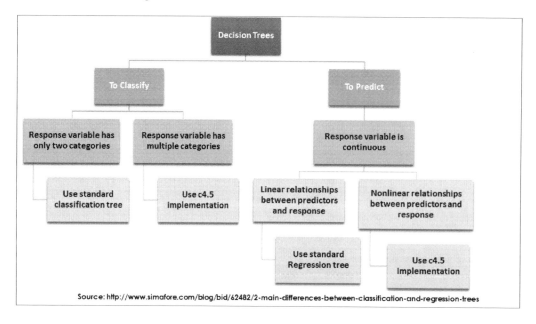

Source: http://www.simafore.com/blog/bid/62482/2-main-differences-between-classification-and-regression-trees

Constructing a Decision tree

Decision trees can be learned best by taking a simple example and constructing a Decision tree by hand. In this section, let's look at a simple example; the following table shows the dataset on hand. Our target is to predict whether a customer will accept a loan or not, given their demographics. Clearly, it will be most useful for the business user if we can come out with a rule as a model for this dataset.

ID	Age	Experience	Income	Family	CCAvg	Personal Loan
1	25	1	49	4	1.60	0
2	45	19	34	3	1.50	0
3	39	15	11	1	1.00	0
4	35	9	100	1	2.70	0
5	35	8	45	4	1.00	0
6	37	13	29	4	0.40	0
10	34	9	180	1	8.90	1
17	38	14	130	4	4.70	1
19	46	21	193	2	8.10	1
30	38	13	119	1	3.30	1
39	42	18	141	3	5.00	1
43	32	7	132	4	1.10	1
48	37	12	194	4	0.20	1

From the previous table, since age and experience are highly correlated, we can choose to ignore one of the attributes. This aids the feature selection implicitly.

Case 1: Let's start building the Decision tree. To start with, we will choose to split by CCAvg (the average credit card balance).

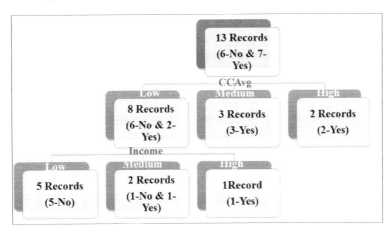

With this Decision tree, we now have two very explicit rules:

If CCAvg is medium then loan = accept or if CCAvg is high then loan = accept

For more clarity in the rules, let's add the income attribute. We have two more rules:

If CCAvg is low and income is low, then loan is not accept

If CCAvg is low and income is high, then loan is accept

By combining the second rule here and the first two rules, we can derive the following rule:

If (CCAvg is medium) or (CCAvg is high) or (CCAvg is low, and income is high) then loan = accept

Case 2: Let's start building the Decision tree using Family:

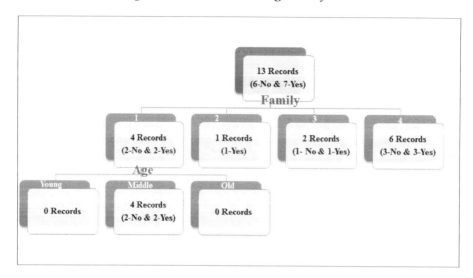

In this case, there is just one rule that it is not giving an accurate result as it has only two data points.

So, choosing a valid attribute to start the tree makes a difference to the accuracy of the model. From the previous example, let's list out some core rules for building Decision trees:

- We usually start building Decision trees with one attribute, split the data based on the attribute, and continue with the same process for other attributes.
- There can be many Decision trees for the given problem.
- The depth of the tree is directly proportional to the number of attributes chosen.
- There needs to be a Termination Criteria that will determine when to stop further building the tree. In the case of no termination criteria, the model will result in the over-fitting of the data.
- Finally, the output is always in the form of simple rule(s) that can be stored and applied to different datasets for classification and/or prediction.

One of the reasons why Decision trees are preferred in the field of Machine learning is because of their robustness to errors; they can be used when there are some unknown values in the training datasets too (for example, the data for income is not available for all the records).

Handling missing values

One of the interesting ways of assigning values to some unknowns is to see that the most common value in terms of occurrence is assigned and in some cases they can belong to the same class, if possible we should bring it closer to accuracy.

There is another probabilistic way of doing this where the prediction is distributed proportionately:

Assign a probability pi for every value vi of x.

Now, assign the fraction pi of x to each of the descendants. These probabilities can be estimated again based on the observed frequencies of the various values for A, among the examples at node n.

For example, let's consider a Boolean attribute A. Let there be 10 values for A out of which three have a value of True and the rest 7 have a value of False. So, the probability of $A(x) - True$ is 0.3, and the probability that $A(x) = False$ is 0.7.

A fractional 0.3 of this is distributed down the branch for $A = True$, and a fractional 0.7 is distributed down the other. These probability values are used for computing the information gain, and can be used if a second missing attribute value needs to be tested. The same methodology can be applied in the case of learning when we need to fill any unknowns for the new branches. The C4.5 algorithm uses this mechanism for filling the missing values.

Considerations for constructing Decision trees

The key to constructing Decision trees is knowing where to split them. To do this, we need to be clear on the following:

- Which attribute to start and which attribute to apply subsequently?
- When do we stop building the Decision tree (that is avoid over-fitting)?

Choosing the appropriate attribute(s)

There are three different ways to identify the best-suited attributes:

- Information Gain and Entropy
- Gini index
- Gain ratio

Information gain and Entropy

This entity is used in an algorithm known as C4.5. Entropy is a measure of uncertainty in the data. Let us take an intuitive approach to understand the concepts of Information gain and Entropy.

For example, consider a coin is being tossed, and there are five coins with a probability for heads as 0, 0.25, 0.5, 0.75, and 1 respectively. So, if we think which one has the highest and which one has the lowest uncertainty, then the case of 0 or 1 will be the lowest certain one and highest would be when it is 0.5. The following figure depicts the representation of the same:

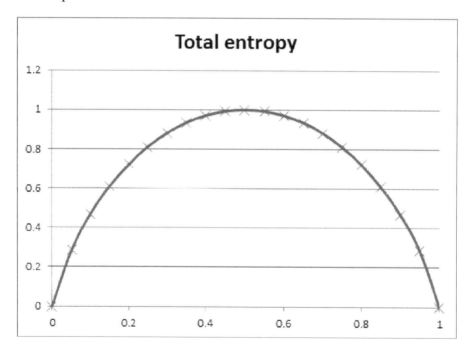

A mathematical representation is shown here:

$$H = -\sum p_i \log 2 p_i$$

Here, p_i is the probability of a specific state.

If a system has four events with probabilities 1/2, 1/4, 1/5, and 1/8 indicate the total Entropy of the system as shown here:

$$H = -1/2 \log_2(1/2) - 1/4\log_2(1/4) - 1/5\log_2(1/5) - 1/8\log_2(1/8)$$

In the original version of the C5.0 and C4.5 algorithms (ID3), a root node was chosen on the basis of how much of the total Entropy was reduced if this node was chosen. This is called information gain.

Information gain = Entropy of the system before split - Entropy of the system after split

Entropy in the system before split is shown as follows:

$$E = -\sum_{i=1}^{m} p_i log_2(p_i)$$

Entropy after using A to split D into v partitions to classify D:

$$E_A = \sum_{i=1}^{v} \frac{D_i}{D} E(D_i)$$

Information gained by branching on an attribute is:

Let's now compute the information gained from our data:

ID	Age	Income	Family	CCAvg	Personal Loan
1	Young	Low	4	Low	0
2	Old	Low	3	Low	0
3	Middle	Low	1	Low	0
4	Middle	Medium	1	Low	0
5	Middle	Low	4	Low	0
6	Middle	Low	4	Low	0
10	Middle	High	1	High	1
17	Middle	Medium	4	Medium	1
19	Old	High	2	High	1
30	Middle	Medium	1	Medium	1
39	Old	Medium	3	Medium	1
43	Young	Medium	4	Low	1
48	Middle	High	4	Low	1

Class P accepts the loan = yes/ 1. Class N accepts the loan = no / 0

Entropy before split is as follows:

$$-\frac{6}{13}log_2\left(\frac{6}{13}\right) - \frac{7}{13}log_2(\frac{7}{13}) = 0.995727$$

This is obvious and expected as we have almost a fifty-fifty split of the data. Let's now see which attribute gives the best information gain.

In case the split is based on CCAvg and Family, the Entropy computations can be shown as follows. The total Entropy is weighted as the sum of the Entropies of each of the nodes that were created.

		CCAvg		
	Fraction	Loan=No	Loan=Yes	Entropy
Low	0.615385	0.25	0.75	0.81
Medium	0.230769	0.00	1.00	0.00
High	0.153846	0.00	1.00	0.00
Entropy	0.499248			

The Entropy after its split is shown here:

$$Entropy_{CCAvg} = \frac{8}{13}E(6,2) + \frac{3}{13}E(0,3) + \frac{2}{13}E(0,2) = 0.499248$$

The information gain is as follows:

$$I_{CCAvg} = 0.995727 - 0.499248 = 0.496479$$
$$I_{Family} = 0.995727 - 0.923077 = 0.07265$$

This methodology is applied to compute the information gain for all other attributes. It chooses the one with the highest information gain. This is tested at each node to select the best node.

Gini index

Gini index is a general splitting criterion. It is named after an Italian statistician and economist—Corrado Gini. Gini Index is used to measure the probability of two random items belonging to the same class. In the case of a real dataset, this probability value is 1. The Gini measure of a node is the sum of the squares of the proportions of the classes. A node with two classes each has a score of *0.52 + 0.52 = 0.5*. This is because the probability of picking the same class at random is 1 out of 2. Now, if we apply Gini index for the data set we get the following:

The original Gini Index = $\left(\frac{6}{13}\right)^2 + \left(\frac{7}{13}\right)^2 = 0.502959$

When split with CCAvg and Family, the Gini Index changes to the following:

	CCAvg			
	Fraction	Loan=No	Loan=Yes	Gini
Low	0.615385	0.250000	0.750000	0.625
Medium	0.230769	0.000000	1.000000	1.000
High	0.153846	0.000000	1.000000	1.000
Gini Index			0.769231	

		Family		
	Fraction	Loan=No	Loan=Yes	Entropy
1	0.307692	0.5	0.5	0.5
2	0.076923	0	1	1
3	0.153846	0.50	0.50	0.5
4	0.461538	0.50	0.50	0.5
Gini Index			0.538462	

Gain ratio

Another improvement in C4.5 compared to ID3 is that the factor that decides the attribute is the gain ratio. The gain ratio is the ratio of information gain and information content. The attribute that gives the maximum amount of gain ratio is the attribute that is used to split it.

Let's do some calculations with an extremely simple example to highlight why the gain ratio is a better attribute than the information gain:

Men				Female			
Number	Age	Married		Number	Age	Married	
Man 1	1	No		Woman 1	41	Yes	
Man 2	2	No		Woman 2	42	Yes	
...	...	...		...	...	...	
Man 40	40	No		Woman 59	99	Yes	
				Woman 60	99	No	

The dependent variable is whether they are married under a specific circumstance. Let's assume that in this case, no man is married. Whereas all women, except the last one (60 women), are married.

So, intuitively the rule has to be as follows:

- If it is a man, then he is unmarried
- If it is a woman then she is married (the only isolated case where she is not married must be noise).

Let's systematically solve this problem to gain insights into various parameters. First let's split the data into two halves as training and testing data. So, our training set consists of the last 20 males (all insensible and aged between 21-40), and the last 30 females (all married and aged between 71-99, except the last one). Testing contains the other half where all the women are married.

The gain ratio requires measure for **Information content**.

Information content is defined as $-f_i \log_2 f_i$. Note that here, we do not take the value of the dependent variable into account. We only want to know the fraction of the members in a state divided by the total members.

The information content of gender is that it has only two states; males are 20 and females are 30. So, the information content for the gender is $2/5*LOG(2/5,2)-3/5*LOG(3/5,2)=0.9709$.

The information content of age is that there is a total of 49 states for the age. For the states that have only one data point, the information content is $-(1/50)*log(1/50,2)$ = 0.1129.

There are 48 such states with a single data point. So, their information content is (0.1129*48), 5.4192. In the last state, there are two data points. So, its information content is $-(2/50 * LOG(2/50,2))$ = 0.1857. The total information content for the age is 5.6039.

The gain ratio for the gender = Information gain for gender / Information content for gender = 0.8549/0.9709 = 0.8805.

The gain ratio for the age = 0.1680

So, if we consider the gain ratio, we get that the gender is a more suitable measure. This aligns with the intuition. Let's now say that we used the gain ratio and built the tree. Our rule is if the gender is male, the person is unmarried and if it is female, the person is married.

Termination Criteria / Pruning Decision trees

Each branch is grown deeply enough to classify the training examples perfectly by the Decision tree algorithm. This can turn out to be an acceptable approach and most of the times results in problems when there is some noise in the data. In case the training dataset is too small and cannot represent the true picture of the actual data set the Decision tree might end up over-fitting the training examples.

There are many ways of avoiding over-fitting in Decision tree learning. Following are the two different cases:

- One case where the Decision tree is terminated for growth way before a perfect classification of the training data is done
- Another case where the over-fitting of data is done and then the tree is pruned to recover

Though the first case might seem to be more direct, the second case of post-pruning the over-fitting trees is more successful in reality. The reason is the difficulty to know when to stop growing the tree. Irrespective of the approach taken, it is more important to identify the criterion to determine the final, appropriate tree size.

Following are a couple of approaches to find the correct tree size:

1. Identify a separate and different dataset to that of the target training data set to be used, and evaluate the correctness of post-pruning nodes in the tree. This is a common approach and is called training and validation set approach.

2. Instead of having a subset of data in the training set, use up all the data in the training set, and apply probabilistic methods to check if pruning a particular node has any likelihood to produce any improvement over and above the training dataset. Use all the available data for training. For example, the chi-square test can be used to check this probability.

Reduced-Error-Pruning (D): We prune at a node by removing the subtree that is rooted at the node. We make that node a leaf (with the majority label of associated examples); algorithm is shown as follows:

> *Partition D into D$_{train}$ (training / "growing"), D$_{validation}$(validation / "pruning")*
>
> *Build complete tree T on D$_{train}$*
>
> *UNTIL accuracy on D$_{validation}$ decreases DO*
>
> *FOR each non-leaf node candidate in T*
>
> *Temp[candidate] ←Prune (T, candidate)*
>
> *Accuracy[candidate] ←Test (Temp[candidate], D$_{validation}$)*
>
> *T←T" ∈Temp with best value of Accuracy (best increase; greedy)*
>
> *RETURN (pruned)*

Rule post-pruning is a more commonly used method and is a highly accurate hypotheses technique. A variation of this pruning method is used in C4.5.

Following are the steps of the Rule Post-Pruning process:

1. Construct a Decision tree from the training set by growing it until there is an obvious over-fitting seen.

2. Generate rules from the constructed Decision tree with every path, starting from the root node to a particular leaf node mapping to a rule.

3. Apply pruning to each rule for removing identified preconditions and help improve the probabilistic accuracy.

4. Next, use the pruned rules in the order of their increased accuracy on the subsequent instances.

Following are the advantages of rule-based pruning and its need for converting into rules:

- Improving the readability of the rules

- A consistent testing can be done at both the root and leaf level nodes

- There is a clear decision that can be made of either removing the decision node or retaining it

Decision trees in a graphical representation

Until now, we have seen how Decision trees are described by dividing the data at the node and comparing the value with a constant. Another way of representing Decision trees is to visualize and have graphical representation. For example, we can choose two input attributes in two dimensions, then compare the value of one attribute with constant and show the split on the data to a parallel axis. We can also compare two attributes with one another along with a linear combination of attributes, instead of a hyperplane that is not parallel to an axis.

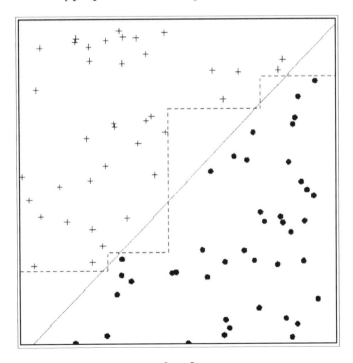

Constructing multiple Decision trees for the given data is possible. The process of identifying the smallest and a perfect tree is called a minimum consistent hypothesis. Let's use two arguments to see why this is the best Decision tree:

Occam's Razor is simple; when there are two ways to solve a problem and both give the same result, the simplest of them prevails.

In data mining analysis, one is likely to fall into the trap of complex methods and large computations. So, it is essential to internalize the line of reasoning adopted by Occam. Always choose a Decision tree that has an optimum combination of size and errors.

Inducing Decision trees – Decision tree algorithms

There are many Decision tree inducing methods. Among all the methods, C4.5 and CART are the most adopted or popular ones. In this section, we will cover these methods in depth and list a brief on other methods.

CART

CART stands for Classification and Regression Trees (Breiman et al., 1984). CART creates binary trees. This means there are always two branches that can emerge from a given node. The philosophy of the CART algorithm is to follow a *goodness* criterion, which is all about choosing the best possible partition. Moreover, as the tree grows, a cost-complexity pruning mechanism is adopted. CART uses the Gini index to select appropriate attributes or the splitting criteria.

Using CART, the prior probability distribution can be provided. We can generate Regression trees using CART that in turn help in predicting real numbers against a class. The prediction is done by applying the weighted mean for the node. CART identifies splits that minimize the prediction squared error (that is, the least-squared deviation).

The depiction in the following figure of CART is for the same example referred in the previous section, where Decision tree construction is demonstrated:

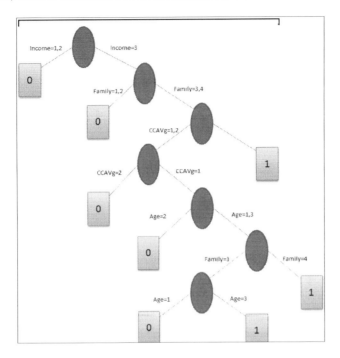

C4.5

Similar to CART, C4.5 is a Decision tree algorithm with a primary difference that it can generate more than binary trees, which means support for multiway splits. For attribute selection, C4.5 uses the information gain measure. As explained in the previous section, an attribute with the largest information gain (or the lowest Entropy reduction) value helps to achieve closer to accurate classification with the least quantity of data. One of the key drawbacks of C4.5 is the need for large memory and CPU capacity for generating rules. The C5.0 algorithm is a commercial version of C4.5 that was presented in 1997.

C4.5 is an evolution of the ID3 algorithm. The gain ratio measure is used for identifying the splitting criteria. The splitting process stops when the number of splits reaches a boundary condition definition that acts as a threshold. Post this growing phase of the tree, pruning is done, and an error-based pruning method is followed.

Here is a representation of the C4.5 way of constructing the Decision tree for the same example used in the previous section:

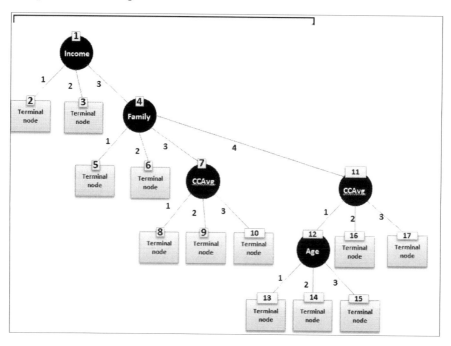

Tree Induction method	How does it work?
ID3	The ID3 (**Iterative Dichotomiser 3**) algorithm is considered the simplest among the Decision tree algorithms. The information gain method is used as splitting criteria; the splitting is done until the best information gain is not greater than zero. There is no specific pruning done with ID3. It cannot handle numeric attributes and missing values.
CHAID	**CHAID (Chi-squared Automatic Interaction Detection)** was built to support only nominal attributes. For every attribute, a value is chosen in such a way that it is the closest to the target attribute. There is an additional statistical measure, depending on the type of the target attribute that differentiates this algorithm. F test for a continuous target attribute, Pearson chi-squared test for nominal target attribute, and likelihood–ratio test for an ordinal target attribute is used. CHAID checks a condition to merge that can have a threshold and moves for a next check for merging. This process is repeated until no matching pairs are found. CHAID addresses missing values in a simple way, and it operates on the assumption that all values belong to a single valid category. No pruning is done in this process.

Tree Induction method	How does it work?
QUEST	The acronym QUEST stands for Quick, Unbiased, Efficient, and Statistical Tree. This algorithm supports univariate and linear combination splits. ANOVA F-test or Pearson's chi-square or two-means clustering methods are used to compute the relationship between each input attribute and the target attribute, depending on the type of the attribute. Splitting is applied on attributes that have stronger association with the target attribute. To ensure that there is an optimal splitting point achieved, **Quadratic Discriminant Analysis (QDA)** is applied. Again, QUEST achieves binary trees and for pruning 10-fold cross-validation is used.
CAL5	This works with numerical attributes.
FACT	This algorithm is an earlier version of QUEST that uses statistical methods followed by discriminant analysis for attribute selection.
LMDT	This uses a multivariate testing mechanism to build Decision trees.
MARS	A multiple regression function is approximated using linear splines and their tensor products.

Greedy Decision trees

A vital characteristic of Decision trees is that they are *Greedy!* A greedy algorithm targets achieving optimal solutions globally by achieving local optimums at every stage. Though the global optimum is not always guaranteed, the local optimums help in achieving global optimum to a maximum extent.

Every node is greedily searched to reach the local optimum, and the possibility of getting stuck at achieving local optima is high. Most of the time, targeting local optima might help in providing a good enough solution.

Benefits of Decision trees

Some of the advantages of using Decision trees are listed here:

- Decision trees are fast and easy to build and require little experimentation
- They are robust
- They are easy to understand and interpret
- Decision trees do not require complex data preparation
- They can handle both categorical and numerical data

- They are supported using statistical models for validation
- They can handle highly dimensional data and also operate large datasets

Specialized trees

In this section, we will explore some important special situations we face and special types of Decision trees. These become handy while solving special kinds of problems.

Oblique trees

Oblique trees are used in cases where the data is extremely complex. If the attributes are *x1, x2, AND x3...xn*, then the C4.5 and CART tests the criteria as *x1>some value* or *x2< some other value*, and so on. The goal in such cases is to find an attribute to test at each node. These are graphically parallel axis splits as shown in the following figure:

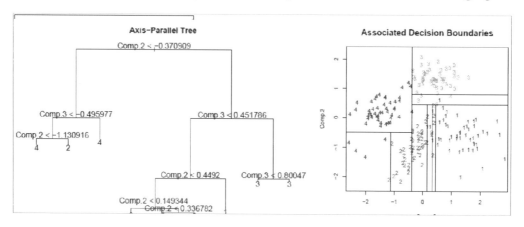

Clearly, we need to construct enormous trees. At this point, let's learn a data mining jargon called hyperplanes.

In a **1 D** problem, a point classifies the space. In **2 D**, a line (straight or curved) classifies the space. In a **3 D** problem, a plane (linear or curved) classifies the space. In higher dimensional space, we imagine a plane like a thing splitting and classifying the space, calling it **hyperplane**. This is shown in the following figure:

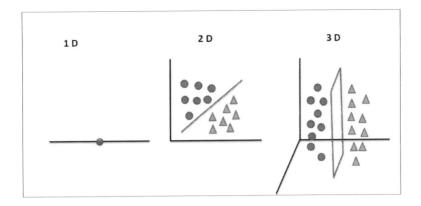

So, the traditional Decision tree algorithms produce axis parallel hyperplanes that split the data. These can be cumbersome if the data is complex. If we can construct oblique planes, the explicability may come down, but we might reduce the tree size substantially. So, the idea is to change the testing conditions from the following:

$$x_i > K \text{ or} < K \text{ to } a_1x_1 + a_2x_2 + \ldots + c > K \text{ or} < K$$

These oblique hyperplanes can at times drastically reduce the length of the tree. The same data shown in figure 2 is classified using oblique planes in the figure here:

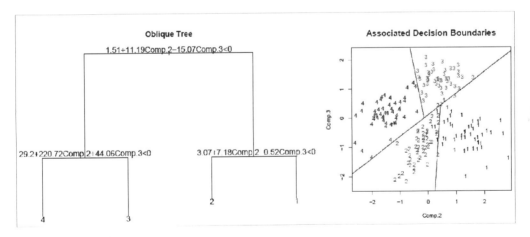

Random forests

These specialized trees are used when there are too many dimensions. We have learned about curse of dimensionality in the Machine learning introduction chapter. The basic premise of the curse of dimensionality is that high dimensional data brings in complexity. With more dimensions and features, the possibility of errors is also high. Before we take a deep dive into Random forests, let's understand the concept of Boosting. More details on boosting methods are covered as a part of *Chapter 13, Ensemble learning*. In the case of Random forests, the application of boosting is about how single tree methods are brought together to see a boost in the result regarding accuracy.

A Random forest extends Decision trees by including more number of Decision trees. These Decision trees are built by a combination of random selection of data (samples) and a random selection of a subset of attributes. The following diagram depicts the random selection of datasets to build each of the Decision trees:

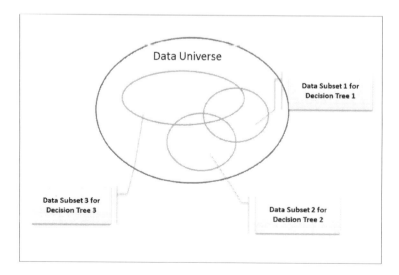

Another variable input required for the making of multiple Decision trees are random subsets of the attributes, which is represented in the diagram here:

S No	Variable
1	X1
2	X2
3	X3
4	X4
5	X5
...	...
N	Xn

X1, X2, X3 variable set for Decision Tree 1

X3, X4, X5 variable set for Decision Tree 2

Xa, Xb, Xn variable set for Decision Tree 3

Since each tree is built using random dataset and random variable set, these trees are called Random trees. Moreover, many such Random trees define a Random forest.

The result of a Random tree is based on two radical beliefs. One is that each of the trees make an accurate prediction for maximum part of the data. Second, mistakes are encountered at different places. So, on an average, a poll of results is taken across the Decision trees to conclude a result.

There are not enough observations to get good estimates, which leads to sparsity issues. There are two important causes for exponential increase on spatial density, one, is increase in dimensionality and the other is increase in the equidistant points in data. Most of the data is in the tails.

To estimate the density of a given accuracy, the following table shows how the sample size increases with dimensionality. The subsequent computations table shows how the mean square error of an estimate of multivariate normal distribution increases with an increase in dimensionality (as demonstrated by Silverman and computed by the formula given here):

$$\text{MSE}\left[\hat{f}_m(p)\right] = O\left(\frac{1}{m^{4/(D+4)}}\right)$$

Dimensionality	Required Sample Size
1	4
2	19
5	786
7	10,700
10	842,000

Random forests are a vital extension of the Decision trees that are very simple to understand and are extremely efficient, particularly when one is dealing with high dimensional spaces. When the original data has many dimensions, we randomly pick a small subset of the dimensions (columns) and construct a tree. We let it grow all the way without pruning. Now, we iterate this process and construct hundreds of trees with a different set of attributes each time.

For prediction, a new sample is pushed down the tree. A new label of the training sample is assigned to the terminal node, where it ends up. This procedure is iterated over all the trees in the group, and the average vote of all trees is reported as the Random forest prediction.

Evolutionary trees

When achieving the global optima seems almost impossible, Evolutionary trees are used. As you learned, Decision trees are greedy. So sometimes, we may be constructing much bigger trees just because we are stuck in local optima. So, if your tree length is just too much, try oblique trees or evolutionary trees.

The concept of evolutionary trees is originated from a very exciting concept called genetic algorithms. You will learn about it in detail in a different course. Let us only look at the essence.

Instead of mathematically computing the best attribute at every node, an Evolutionary tree randomly picks a node at each point and creates a tree. It then iterates and creates a collection of trees (forest). Now, it identifies the best trees in the forest for the data. It then creates the next generation of the forest by combining these trees randomly.

Evolutionary trees, on the other hand, choose a radically different top node and produce a much shorter tree, which has the same efficiency. Evolutionary algorithms take more time to compute.

Hellinger trees

There have been attempts to identify impurity measures that are less sensitive to the distribution of dependent variable values than Entropy or Gini index. A very recent paper suggested Hellinger distance as a measure of impurity that does not depend on the distribution of the target variable.

$$d_H\left(P\left(Y_+\right), P\left(Y_-\right)\right) = \sqrt{\sum_{i \in V}\left(\sqrt{P\left(Y_+ \mid X_i\right)} - \sqrt{P\left(Y_- \mid X_i\right)}\right)^2}$$

Essentially, $P(Y+ \mid X)$ is the probability of finding $Y+$ for each attribute and similarly, $P(Y- \mid X)$ for each attribute is computed.

High	Low	0
High	High	1

From the previous image, for a **High** value of the first attribute, only a **High** value of the second attribute results in a probability value of 1. This brings the total distance value to *sqrt(2)*.

Implementing Decision trees

Refer to the source code provided for this chapter for implementing Decision Trees and Random Forests (source code path . . . /chapter5/. . . under each of the folder for the technology).

Using Mahout

Refer to the folder .../mahout/chapter5/decisiontreeexample/.

Refer to the folder.../mahout/chapter5/randomforestexample/.

Using R

Refer to the folder .../r/chapter5/decisiontreeexample/.

Refer to the folder .../r/chapter5/randomforestexample/.

Using Spark

Refer to the folder .../spark/chapter5/decisiontreeexample/.

Refer to the folder .../spark/chapter5/randomforestexample/.

Using Python (scikit-learn)

Refer to the folder .../python scikit-learn/chapter5/decisiontreeexample/.

Refer to the folder .../python scikit-learn/chapter5/randomforestexample/.

Using Julia

Refer to the folder .../julia/chapter5/decisiontreeexample/.

Refer to the folder .../julia/chapter5/randomforestexample/.

Summary

In this chapter, you learned a supervised learning technique with Decision trees to solve classification and regression problems. We also covered methods to select attributes, split the tree, and prune the tree. Among all other Decision tree algorithms, we have explored the CART and C4.5 algorithms. For a special requirement or a problem, you have also learned how to implement Decision tree-based models using MLib of Spark, R, and Julia. In the next chapter, we will cover **Nearest Neighbour** and **SVM (Support Vector Machines)** to solve supervised and unsupervised learning problems.

6
Instance and Kernel Methods Based Learning

We have covered Decision tree models for solving classification and regression problems in the previous chapter. In this chapter, we will cover two important models of supervised and unsupervised learning techniques which are the Nearest Neighbors method, which uses the instance-based learning model, and the **Support Vector Machines (SVM)** model, which uses kernel methods based learning model. For both methods, we will learn the basics of the technique and see how it can be implemented in Apache Mahout, R, Julia, Apache Spark, and Python. The following figure depicts different learning models covered in this book and the techniques highlighted will be dealt in covered in this chapter.

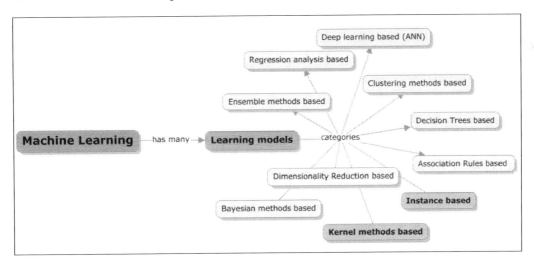

The following topics are covered in-depth in this chapter:

- Instance-based learning models
- Introduction to instance-based learning
- Lazy and eager learning
- A brief look at different algorithms/approaches of instance-based learning techniques Nearest Neighbor method, Case-based reasoning, Locally weighed regression, and Radial basis functions
- A deep dive into KNN (k-Nearest Neighbor) algorithm with a real-world use case example; mechanisms to speed up KNN
- Sample implementation of Apache Mahout, R, Apache Spark, Julia and Python (scikit-learn) libraries and modules
- Kernel-based learning models
  - Introduction to kernel-based learning
  - A brief look at different algorithms/approaches of Kernel-based learning techniques, Support Vector Machines (SVM), Linear Discriminate Analysis (LDA), and more
  - A deep dive into SVM algorithm with a real-world use case example

Instance-based learning (IBL)

The IBL technique approaches learning by simply storing the provided training data and using it as a reference for predicting/determining the behavior of a new query. As learned in *Chapter 1, Introduction to Machine learning*, instances are nothing but subsets of datasets. The instance-based learning model works on an identified instance or groups of instances that are critical to the problem. The results across instances are compared and can include an instance of new data as well. This comparison uses a particular similarity measure to find the best match and predict. Since it uses historical data stored in memory, this learning technique is also called memory-based or case-based learning. Here, the focus is on the representation of the instances and similarity measures for comparison between them.

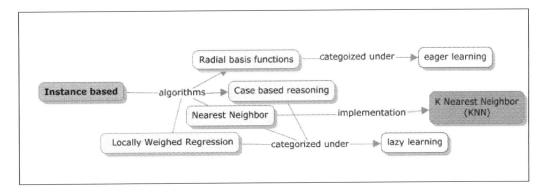

Every time a new query instance is received for processing, a set of similar, related instances are retrieved from memory, and then this data is used to classify the new query instance.

Instance-based learners are also called lazy learners. Overall, the entire database is used to predict behavior. A set of data points referred to as **neighbors** are identified, having a history of agreeing with the target attribute. Once a neighborhood of data points is formed, the preferences of neighbors are combined to produce a prediction or **top-K recommendation** for the active target attribute.

These methods are applicable for complex target functions that can be expressed using less complex local approximations. Unfortunately, with these methods, the cost of classifying a new instance is always high and in cases where there is a curse of dimensionality, these methods might end up with a bigger footprint as all the attributes of all the instances are considered. Classifiers and regressions are what we will cover in this and the next chapters that are to come. With classifiers, we try to predict a category and, with regression, we predict a real number. We will first look at the Nearest Neighbor algorithm that can be used both for classification and regression problems.

Rote Learner is one of the instance-based classifiers and focuses on memorizing the entire training data. Classification is primarily done only if the target attribute value exactly matches with the attribute value in the training example. The other classifier is the Nearest Neighbor, which classifies based on the closest neighbor(s). In the next section, let's dive deeply into the Nearest Neighbor algorithm.

Nearest Neighbors

Before we start understanding what the Nearest Neighbor algorithm is all about, let's start with an example; the following graph shows the plotting of data points X and Y that have two classes: stars and triangles. Let's not really worry about what is the exact data representation or the data points. If we had to solve intuitively the problem of finding what that particular red square box data point is, then the answer would obviously be a green triangle. This is an intuition and, without actually understanding or analyzing the data points, we can arrive at this conclusion. But what actually happened here is that we have seen the traits of the neighbors of the data point in context and have predicted the class to which the new data point could possibly belong to. Overall, the basis for the learning algorithm is actually the behavior of the nearby or neighboring points.

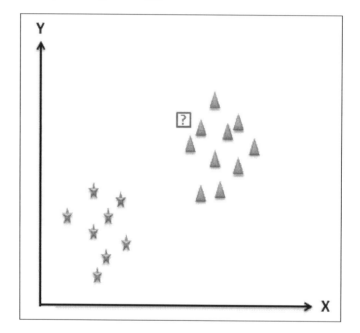

Nearest Neighbor is an algorithm that uses this basic technique of intuition. This algorithm finds the Nearest Neighbor using some distance measurement techniques that will be discussed in the following sections. Let's now extend this to another example data set; and again, the new data point with a question mark (?) will be needed for classification.

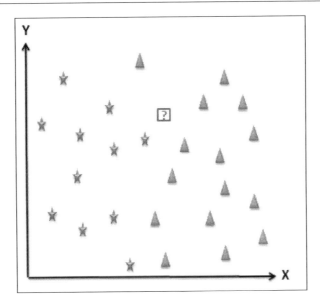

Let's now assume that the class the new data point belongs to is the yellow star. An important aspect of the distance measure is that the Nearest Neighbor is never just a single point but is usually a region. The following figure shows a region and all the data points that fall in this region belong to the class yellow star. This region is called the **Voronoi cell**. This region is usually a polygon with straight lines in case the distance measure used is the **Euclidean** distance measure.

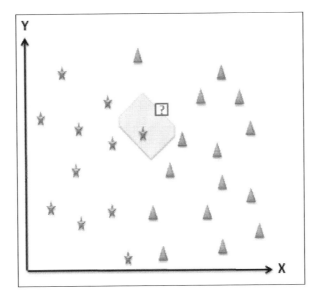

For each training example if the Voronoi cells are computed, we can see the Voronoi tessellation as shown next. This tessellation represents the partition of space into the non-overlapping region and typically each region has one example.

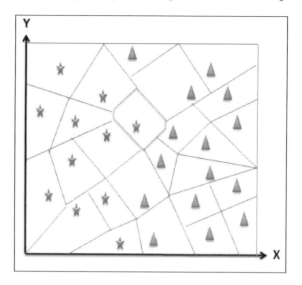

The size of the cell is determined by the number of examples available. The more the examples, the less the size of the regions. Another interesting aspect of the Voronoi tessellation is that there can be boundaries carved that form a separation for the classes, as shown in the following figure. The right side of the bold line belongs to the triangle class, and the left side belongs to the star class.

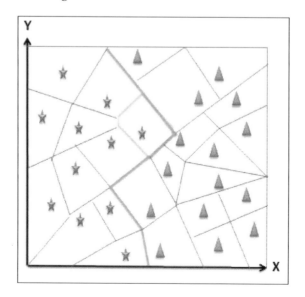

One of the major complications with the Nearest Neighbor approach is its insensitivity to the outliers, thus really messing up the boundaries, and one way of solving this problem is to consider more than one neighbor, which this would make the model more stable and smooth. Hence, a consideration of k-Neighbors signifies the k-Nearest Neighbor algorithm.

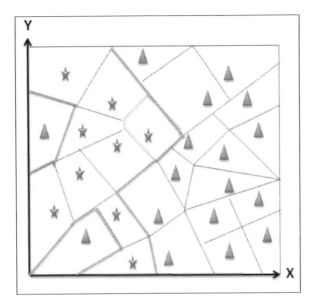

Let's now look at how the KNN classification algorithm works:

Given the $\{x_i, y_i\}$ training examples, where x_i represents attribute values, y_i represents class labels, and there is a new test point X that needs to be classified, the following steps are performed in a KNN classification algorithm:

1. Distance is computed between x and x_i for every given value of x_i.
2. Choose k nearest neighbors *xi1, ... xik* and the respective class labels *yi1, ... yik*.
3. Return a *y* that is the most frequent in the list of labels *yi1, ... yik*.

Let's now see how different the KNN regression algorithm is among the important differences. Instead of outputting a class, we will output real numbers like ratings or age, and so on. The algorithm is identical, but the only variation is in the return value, Step 3, and instead of a most frequent value, we take the mean of *y*'s.

Value of k in KNN

The value of *k* has a tremendous effect on the KNN performance. If the value of *k* is too large, the KNN algorithm uses the previous value and thus might result in inaccuracies. And in the case where the *k* value is too small, the model would become too sensitive to outliers as we saw in the previous section. Hence, an accurate *k* value usually lies midway through the smallest and largest value. The approach is to choose a value in this range and measure the error on the training data and pick a *k* that gives the best generalization performance.

The following figure depicts 1, 2, and 3 Nearest Neighbors for the point *x*:

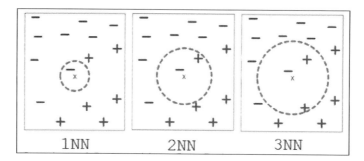

k-Nearest Neighbors for the point *x* are all the data points that have the k smallest distance from *x*.

Distance measures in KNN

This is one of the attributes of the Nearest Neighbor algorithm and possibly the only area that one can experiment or try alternatives in. There are many distance measurement options and in this section, we will discuss some of the commonly used measures. The primary purpose of distance measure is to identify the examples that are similar or dissimilar. Similar to the k value, distance measure determines the performance of KNN.

Euclidean distance

The Euclidean distance is the default option for numeric attributes. The distance measure formula is given here:

$$D\left(x, x'\right) = \sqrt{\sum \left| x_d - x_d' \right|^2}$$

The Euclidean distance measure is symmetrical and spherical and treats all the dimensions equally. One of the drawbacks of this measure is its sensitivity to the extreme values within a single attribute. This is similar to the mean squared error.

Hamming distance

The Hamming distance measure is a default option if we need to deal with categorical attributes. The primary function of a Hamming distance measure is to check whether the two attributes are equal or not. When they are equal, the distance is 0, otherwise it is 1; in effect, we check the number of attributes between two instances. The formula for the Hamming distance measure is as given here:

$$D\left(x, x'\right) = \sum_d 1_{x_d \neq x_d'}$$

Different attributes are measured on different scales, and there is a need to normalize the attributes.

Minkowski distance

We will now look at the *p*-norm distance measures family that is a generalization of the Euclidean distance measures. These measures are relatively quite flexible.

The Minkowski distance formula looks similar to Euclidean and is as follows:

$$D\left(x, x'\right) = \sqrt[p]{\sum \left| x_d - x_d' \right|^p}$$

If *p=0*, the distance measure is the Hamming measure.

If *p=1*, the distance measure is the Manhattan measure.

If $p=2$, the distance measure is the Euclidean measure.

Case-based reasoning (CBR)

CBR is an advanced instance-based learning method used with more complex instance objects. In addition to having a fixed database of past cases, CBR accumulates and stores the new data that is classified. Like all other instance-based learning methods, CBR matches new cases to find similar past cases. Semantic nets-based distance measures for matching the data is applied in this case. This is a diagrammatic matching method unlike other methods such as the Euclidean distance measure.

Similar to the other instance-based learning methods, CBR is a lazy learner, and the power comes from the organization and content of the cases.

Reusing past cases is one of the key factors in the way human problem solving and reasoning works. Since CBR is modeled on human problem solving, it is more understandable to humans. This means the way CBR works can be altered by experts or with the consultation of experts.

By the virtue of its ability to handle very complex instances, CBR is often used in medical diagnosis for detecting heart diseases, hearing defects, and other relatively complex conditions. The following figure depicts a typical CBR learning flow and is famously called the R4 Model.

Lazy learning in Machine learning is all about delaying the process of generalization beyond the training data until the time of the query. The advantage is that we can now perform parallel processing while the downside is higher memory requirements. The following diagram presents a process flow for a CBR function:

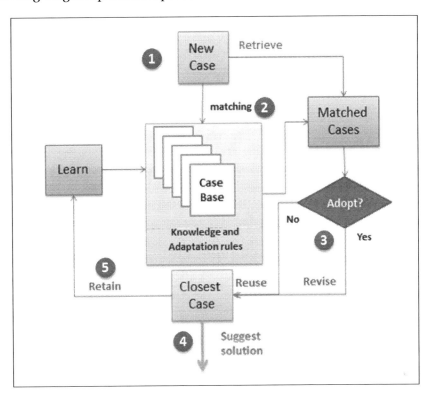

1. First, a New Case is received.

2. Then, a matching process is triggered where the received case is matched to the Case Base that has existing cases and already classified cases. This is the retrieval process.

3. Check if the Matched Cases perfectly fits the new case.

4. If yes, Reuse it, otherwise Revise it.

5. Output the final recommended solution.

6. At a later point in time, based on the facts, if the recommendation is in agreement, retain the learning and add to the case base. The learning phase may also add rules to the knowledge base that the eventual facts suggest.

Locally weighed regression (LWR)

LWR is a particular case of linear regression where, due to noise, the dataset is no more linear, and linear regression underfits the training data. The problem of non-linearity is solved by assigning weights to the Nearest Neighbors. The assigned weights are usually bigger for data points that are closer to the data that needs a prediction.

Implementing KNN

Refer to the source code provided for this chapter for implementing the k-Nearest Neighbor algorithm (source code path `.../chapter6/...` under each of the folders for the technology).

Using Mahout

Refer to the folder `.../mahout/chapter6/knnexample/`.

Using R

Refer to the folder `.../r/chapter6/knnexample/`.

Using Spark

Refer to the folder `.../spark/chapter6/knnexample/`.

Using Python (scikit-learn)

Refer to the folder `.../python scikit learn/ chapter6/knnexample/`.

Using Julia

Refer to the folder `.../julia/chapter6/knnexample/`.

Kernel methods-based learning

We have just seen what instance-based learning methods are, and we have taken a deep dive into the Nearest Neighbor algorithm and covered specific implementation aspects. In this section, we will look into kernels and the kernel-based Machine learning algorithms.

A kernel, in simple terms, is a similarity function that is fed into a Machine learning algorithm. It takes two inputs and suggests how similar they are. For example, if we are dawned with a task of classifying images, the input data is a key-value pair (image, label). So, in terms of the flow, the image data is taken, features are computed, and a vector of features are fed into the Machine learning algorithm. But, in the case of similarity functions, we can define a kernel function that internally computes the similarity between images, and feed this into the learning algorithm along with the images and label data. The outcome of this is a classifier.

The standard regression or SVM or Perceptron frameworks work with kernels and only use vectors. To address this requirement, we will have the Machine learning algorithms expressed as dot products so that kernel functions can be used.

Kernels are preferable to feature vectors. There are many advantages; one of the key reasons being the ease of computing. Also, feature vectors need more storage space in comparison to dot products. It is possible to write Machine learning algorithms to use dot products and later map them to use kernels. This way, the usage of feature vectors can be completely avoided. This will support us in working with highly complex, efficient-to-compute, and yet high performing kernels effortlessly, without really developing multi-dimensional vectors.

Kernel functions

Let's understand what exactly kernel functions are; the following figure represents a 1D function using a simple 1-Dimensional example. Assume that given points are as follows:

A general 1-Dimensional hyperplane, as depicted previously, will be a vertical line and no other vertical lines will separate the dataset. If we look at the 2-Dimensional representation, as shown next, there is a hyperplane (an arbitrary line in 2-Dimensions) that separates red and blue points, thus eligible for a separation using SVMs.

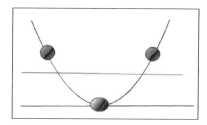

With the growing dimensional space, the need to be able to separate data increases. This mapping, $x \to (x, x2)$, is called the kernel function.

In case of growing dimensional space, the computations become more complex and **kernel trick** needs to be applied to address these computations cheaply.

Support Vector Machines (SVM)

SVMs are used in solving classification problems. Overall, as an approach, the goal is to find that hyperplane effectively divides the class representation of data. Hyperplane can be defined as a generalization of a line in 2-Dimensions and a plane in 3-Dimensions. Let's now take an example to understand how SVM works for linearly separable binary datasets. We will use the same example as we have in the Nearest Neighbor algorithms. The following diagram represents data with two features X and Y and available classes being triangles and stars.

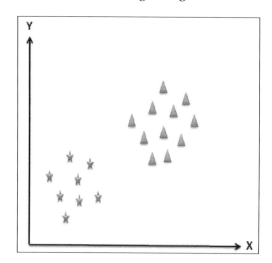

The goal of SVM is to find the hyperplane that separates these two classes. The following diagram depicts some of the possible hyperplanes that can divide the datasets. The choice of the best hyperplane is defined by the extent to which a maximum margin is left for both classes. The margin is the distance between the hyperplane and the closest point in the classification.

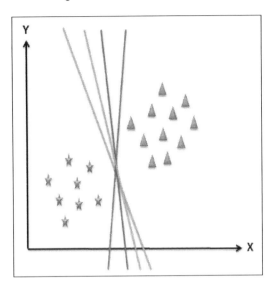

Let's take two hyperplanes among others and check the margins represented by **M1** and **M2**. It is very clear that margin **M1** > **M2**, so the choice of the hyperplane that separates best is the new plane between the green and blue planes.

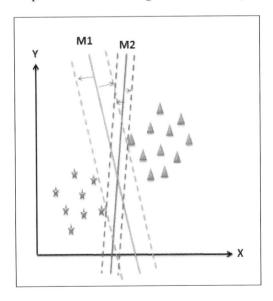

The new plane can be represented by a linear equation as:

$$f(x) = ax + b$$

Let's assume that this equation delivers all values ≥ 1 from the triangle class and ≤ -1 for the star class. The distance of this plane from the closest points in both the classes is at least one; the modulus is one.

$f(x) \geq 1$ for triangles and $f(x) \leq 1$ or $|f(x)| = 1$ for star

The distance between the hyperplane and the point can be computed using the following equation.

$$M1 = |f(x)| / ||a|| = 1 / ||a||$$

The total margin is $1 / ||a|| + 1 / ||a|| = 2 / ||a||$.

To maximize the separability, which is the goal of SVM, we will need to maximize the $||a||$ value. This value is referred to as a weight vector. This process of minimizing the a weight value is a non-linear optimization task. One method is to use the **Karush-Kuhn-Tucker (KKT)** condition, using the Lagrange multiplier λ_i.

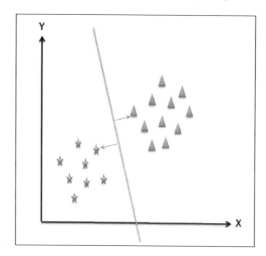

$$a' = \sum_{i=0}^{N} \lambda_i y_i \vec{x}_i$$

$$\sum_{i=0}^{N} \lambda_i y_i = 0$$

Let's take an example of two points between the two attributes X and Y. We need to find a point between these two points that has a maximum distance between these points. This requirement is represented in the graph depicted next. The optimal point is depicted using the red circle.

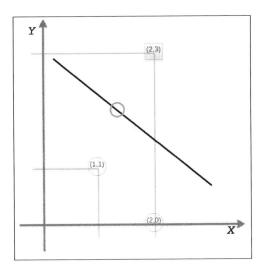

The maximum margin weight vector is parallel to the line from *(1, 1)* to *(2, 3)*. The weight vector is at *(1,2)*, and this becomes a decision boundary that is halfway between and in perpendicular, that passes through *(1.5, 2)*.

So, $y = x1 + 2x2 - 5.5$ and the geometric margin is computed as $\sqrt{5}$.

Following are the steps to compute SVMs:

With $w = (a, 2a)$ for a the functions of the points (1,1) and (2,3) can be represented as shown here:

$a + 2a + \omega_0 = -1$ for the point (1,1)

$2a + 6a + \omega_0 = 1$ for the point (2,3)

The weights can be computed as follows:

$$\omega_0 = 1 - 8a \quad 3a + 1 - 8a = -1$$
$$\therefore \quad 5a = 2$$
$$a = \frac{2}{5}$$

$$\omega_0 = 1 - 8\frac{2}{5} = \frac{5-16}{5}$$

$$\omega_0 = -\frac{11}{5}$$

These are the support vectors:

$$\vec{w} = \left(\frac{2}{5}, \frac{4}{5}\right)$$

Lastly, the final equation is as follows:

$$g(\vec{x}) = \frac{2}{5}x_1 + \frac{4}{5}x_2 - \frac{11}{5}$$
$$g(\vec{x}) = x_1 + 2x_2 - 5.5$$

Inseparable Data

SVMs can probably help you to find out a separating hyperplane if it exists. There might be cases where there is no possibility to define a hyperplane, which can happen due to noise in the data. In fact, another reason can be a non-linear boundary as well. The following first graph depicts noise and the second one shows a non-linear boundary.

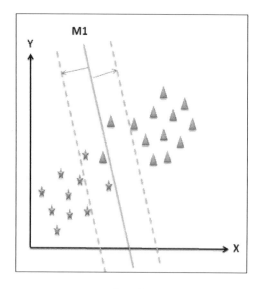

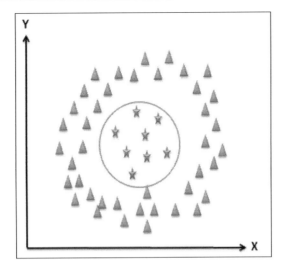

In the case of problems that arise due to noise in the data, the best way to look at it is to reduce the margin itself and introduce slack.

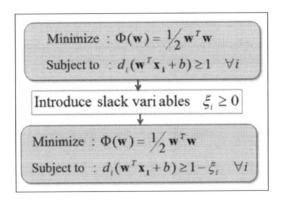

The non-linear boundary problem can be solved by introducing a kernel. Some of the kernel functions that can be introduced are depicted in the following diagram:

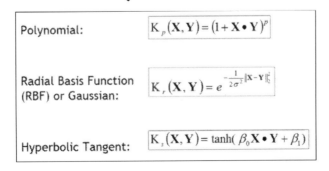

Polynomial:	$K_p(\mathbf{X}, \mathbf{Y}) = (1 + \mathbf{X} \bullet \mathbf{Y})^p$
Radial Basis Function (RBF) or Gaussian:	$K_r(\mathbf{X}, \mathbf{Y}) = e^{-\frac{1}{2\sigma^2}\|\mathbf{X}-\mathbf{Y}\|_2^2}$
Hyperbolic Tangent:	$K_s(\mathbf{X}, \mathbf{Y}) = \tanh(\beta_0 \mathbf{X} \bullet \mathbf{Y} + \beta_1)$

Implementing SVM

Refer to the source code provided for this chapter to implement the SVM algorithm (source code path .../chapter6/... under each of the folders for the technology).

Using Mahout

Refer to the folder .../mahout/chapter6/svmexample/.

Using R

Refer to the folder .../r/chapter6/svmexample/.

Using Spark

Refer to the folder .../spark/chapter6/svmexample/.

Using Python (Scikit-learn)

Refer to the folder .../python-scikit-learn/chapter6/svmexample/.

Using Julia

Refer to the folder .../julia/chapter6/svmexample/.

Summary

In this chapter, we have explored two learning algorithms, instance-based and kernel methods, and we have seen how they address the classification and prediction requirements. In the instance-based learning methods, we explored the Nearest Neighbor algorithm in detail and have seen how to implement this using our technology stack, Mahout, Spark, R, Julia, and Python. Similarly, in the kernel-based methods, we have explored SVM. In the next chapter, we will cover the Association Rule-based learning methods with a focus on Apriori and FP-growth algorithms.

7
Association Rules based learning

We have covered Decision tree, instance and kernel-based supervised and unsupervised learning methods in the previous chapters. We also explored the most commonly used algorithms across these learning algorithms in the previous chapters. In this chapter, we will cover association rule based learning and, in specific, Apriori and FP-Growth algorithms among others. We will learn the basics of this technique and get hands-on implementation guidance using Apache Mahout, R, Julia, Apache Spark, and Python. The following figure depicts different learning models covered in this book. The techniques highlighted in orange will be dealt with in detail in this chapter.

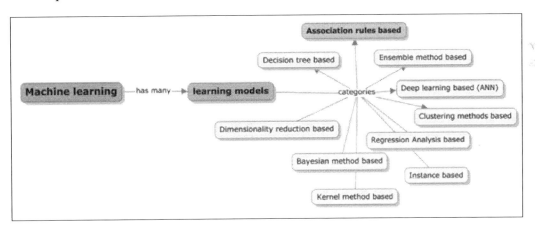

The following topics are covered in depth in this chapter:

- Understanding the basics and core principles of association rules based learning models

- Core use cases for association rule such as the Market Basket problem

- Key terms such as itemsets, lift, support, confidence and frequent itemsets, and rule generation techniques

- A deep dive into association rule based algorithms such as Apriori and FP-Growth; comparing and contrasting Apriori and FP-Growth in the context of large datasets

- Overview and purpose of some advanced association rules concepts such as correlation and sequential rules

- A sample implementation for Apache Mahout, R, Apache Spark, Julia and Python (scikit-learn) libraries and modules.

Association rules based learning

Association rule-based Machine learning deals with finding frequent patterns, associations, and transactions that can be used for classification and prediction requirements. The association rule based learning process is as follows: given a set of transactions, finding rules and using these rules to predict the occurrence of an item based on the occurrences of other items in the transaction is Association rule based learning. The following diagram represents the scope of Machine learning:

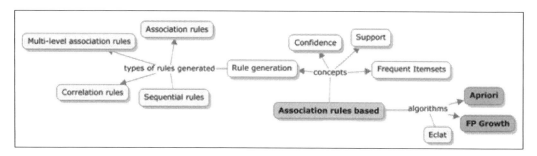

Association rule – a definition

An association rule is a representation of a pattern that describes the probability with which an event occurs, given the occurrence of another event. Usually, the syntax for association rules follows the *if...then* statements that relate two sets of unrelated data from the repository. In short, it helps find the relationship between objects that are frequently used together. The goal of association rules is to find all the sets of items that have greater support than minimum support using the large dataset to predict the rules that have confidence greater than the minimum confidence. One of the most common examples where association rule is used is the Market Basket example. To elaborate the Market basket example, if a customer buys an iPad, he or she is likely to buy an iPad case as well.

Two important criteria are used in association rules, **Support** and **Confidence**. Every association rule should have a minimum Confidence and minimum Support at the same time. This is usually user-defined.

Now, let's look at what Support, Confidence, and lift measures are. Let's consider the same example as explained previously, *If X then Y.* where X is buying an iPad and Y is buying an iPad case.

Then Support is defined as the frequency with which X and Y are purchased together over the total number of purchases or transactions.

$$Support = \frac{frq(X,Y)}{N}$$

Confidence can be defined as the frequency with which X and Y are purchased together over the frequency with which X is purchased in isolation.

$$Confidence = \frac{frq(X,Y)}{frq(X)}$$

Lift is defined as the Support over the Support for X times the Support for Y.

$$Lift = \frac{Support}{Supp(X) \times Supp(Y)}$$

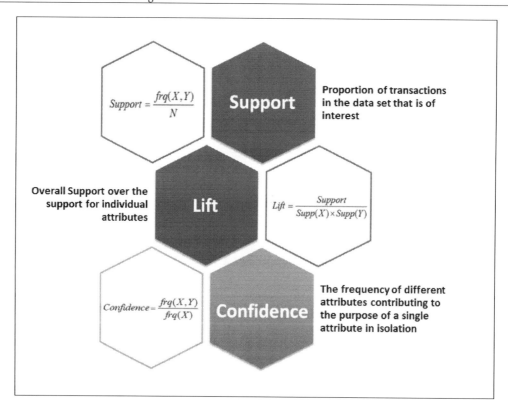

Before understanding the significance of these measures, let's look at the terms used in this context as an example. A collection of items in a warehouse called itemset are represented as $I = \{ i_1, i_2, \dots i_n\}$, a set of all transactions where each transaction consists of a subset of itemset is represented as $T = \{ t_1, t_2, \dots t_n\}$, where t_x is a subset of I with a **Unique Transaction Identifier (UTI)**.

Let's represent items, transactions, and measures using an example now.

Consider five items and five transactions as depicted here:

I = {iPad(A), iPad case(B), iPad scratch guard(C), Apple care (D), iPhone (E)}

$T = \{\{$ *iPad, iPad case, iPad scratch guard* $\}, \{$ *iPad, iPad scratch guard, Apple care* $\}, \{$ *iPad case, iPad scratch guard, Apple care* $\}, \{$ *iPad, Apple care, iPhone* $\}, \{$ *iPad case, iPad scratch guard, iPhone* $\}\}$

The table below shows the support, confidence and lift values for each of the identified rules.

#	Rule	Support	Confidence	Lift
1	If iPad (*A*) is purchased, iPhone (*D*) is also purchased	2/5	2/3	10/9
2	If iPad scratch guard(*C*) is purchased, iPad (*A*) is also purchased	2/5	2/4	5/6
3	If iPad (*A*) is purchased, iPad scratch guard (*C*) is also purchased	2/5	2/3	5/6
4	If iPad case(*B*) and iPad scratch guard (*C*) are purchased, then apple care (*D*) is also purchased	1/5	1/3	5/9

From these itemsets, based on the support and confidence computations, frequent itemset(s) can be determined. The goal of association rule mining is to find the rules that satisfy the criteria given here:

- support ≥ minsup (minimum support) threshold
- confidence ≥ minconf (minimum confidence) threshold

The following are the steps involved in frequent itemset generation and mining association rules:

1. List all the possible association rules.
2. Compute the support and confidence for each rule.
3. Prune the rules that fail to satisfy the minsup and minconf threshold values.

This approach is called the brute force approach and is usually known to be computationally prohibitive.

 Rules originating from the same itemset usually have the same support, but vary with confidence. The minimum support (minsup) and the minimum confidence (minconf) are the values that are agreed upon during the problem definition statement. For example, minimum support and confidence can take percentage values like 75% and 85% respectively.

To avoid all expensive computations, we can simplify this process into two steps:

- **Frequent itemset generation**: This requires generating all the itemsets with support ≥ minsup
- **Rule generation**: From the identified frequent itemsets, generate rules with the highest confidence

When there are five items, there are 32 candidate itemsets. The following figure depicts the itemset combination for five items: **A, B, C, D,** and **E**:

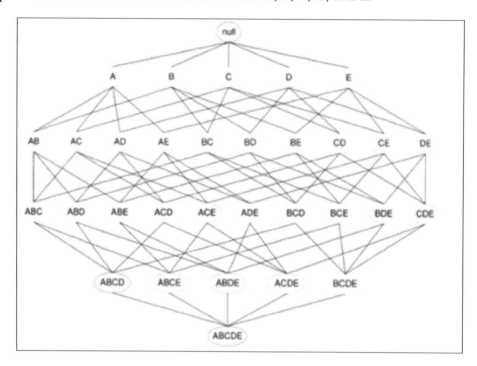

The possible number of itemsets and rules, given the number of items is defined here:

Given *d* unique items:

Total number of possible itemsets = 2^d

The standard formula for computing total possible association rules is defined here:

$$\sum_{k=1}^{d-1}\left[\binom{d}{k}\times\sum_{j=1}^{d-k}\binom{d-k}{j}\right]$$
$$= 3^d - 2^{d+1} + 1$$

For example, if d is equivalent to 6, then the *total number of possible itemsets* = 2^d = 64

Thus, the *total number of possible association rules* = *602 rules*

The following graph shows the relationship between the number of items and possible association rules.

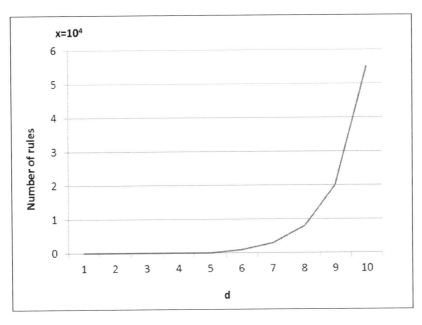

Efficient ways of generating frequent itemsets and association rules determine the efficiency of the association rule algorithms. In the next sections, we will cover the Apriori and FP-Growth algorithms in detail.

Apriori algorithm

In this section, we will cover the Apriori algorithm step-by-step using an example. The Apriori algorithm is as stated here:

C_k: Candidate itemset of size k
L_k : frequent itemset of size k

L_1 = {frequent items};
for (k = 1; L_k !=∅; k++) do begin
    C_{k+1} = candidates generated from L_k;
    for each transaction t in database do
        increment the count of all candidates in C_{k+1}
        that are contained in t
    L_{k+1} = candidates in C_{k+1} with min_support
    end
return ∪$_k$ L_k;

 Apriori principle—for all the frequent itemsets, the subsets must also be frequent.

Consider the five items (from the example in the previous section)

I = {*iPad(A), iPad case(B), iPad scratch guard(C), Apple care (D), iPhone (E)*}, and the following nine transactions. Let's assume that the minimum Support count is two:

TID	The purpose or meaning in the context of Machine learning
1	iPad(A), iPad case(B), and iPhone(E)
2	iPad case(B) and Apple care(D)
3	iPad case(B) and iPad scratch guard(C)
4	iPad(A), iPad case(B), and Apple care(D)
5	iPad(A) and Apple care(D)
6	iPad case(B) and iPad scratch guard(C)

TID	The purpose or meaning in the context of Machine learning
7	iPad(A) and Apple care(D)
8	iPad(A), iPad case(B), iPad scratch guard(C), and iPhone (E)
9	iPad(A), iPad case(B), and iPad scratch guard(C)

Let's debug the previous algorithm using the previous datasets:

1. Get the number of occurrences for each item from the previous transactions (C_1):

Itemset	Support count
{iPad(A)}	6
{iPad case(B)}	7
{iPad scratch guard(C)}	6
{Apple care(D)}	2
{iPhone(E)}	2

Determine Frequent $1-$Itemsets (L_1) from C_1:

Itemset	Support count
{iPad(A)}	6
{iPad case(B)}	7
{iPad scratch guard(C)}	6
{Apple care(D)}	2
{iPhone(E)}	2

2. Generate $2-$Itemset candidates (C_2) and scan the dataset for Support count:

Itemset	Support count
{iPad(A), iPad case(B)}	4
{iPad(A), iPad scratch guard(C)}	4
{iPad(A), Apple care(D)}	1
{iPad(A), iPhone(E)}	2

Itemset	Support count
{iPad case(B), iPad scratch guard(C)}	4
{iPad case(B), Apple care(D)}	2
{iPad case(B), iPhone(E)}	2
{iPad scratch guard(C), Apple care(D)}	0
{iPad scratch guard(C), iPhone(E)}	1
{Apple care(D), iPhone(E)}	0

3. Determine Frequent 2 — Itemsets (L_2) from C_2:

Itemset	Support count
{iPad(A), iPad case(B)}	4
{iPad(A), iPad scratch guard(C)}	4
{iPad(A), Apple care(D)}	2
{iPad case(B), iPad scratch guard(C)}	4
{iPad case(B), Apple care(D)}	2
{iPad case(B), iPhone(E)}	2

4. Generate 3 — Itemset candidates (C_3).

5. Finally, scan the dataset for Support count and frequent 3 — Itemset identification.

This is similar to the previously followed steps, but we will demonstrate how pruning can be applied to identify the frequent itemset, based on the Apriori principle effectively. First, we identify the possible subset itemsets. We then check whether there are any of the subset itemsets that do not belong to the frequent itemset list. If not found, we eliminate that 3 — Itemset possibility.

C_3	Itemset	Possible subset itemsets		
1✓	{A,B,C}	{A,B}✓	{A,C}✓	{B,C}✓
2✓	{A,B,D}	{A,B}✓	{A,D}✓	{B,D}✓
3✗	{A,C,D}	{A,C}✓	{A,D}✓	{C,D}✗
4✗	{B,C,D}	{B,C}✓	{B,D}✓	{C,D}✗
5✗	{B,C,E}	{B,C}✓	{B,E}✗	{C,E}✗
6✗	{B,D,E}	{B,D}✓	{B,E}✗	{D,E}✗

In the previous table, the × itemsets are pruned using the Apriori technique, and the data from step 4 (L_2) is used. The itemsets are represented using the item codes A, B, C, D, and E instead of the actual names for ease of understanding. The 3−itemset candidates can be identified as follows:

C_3	Itemset	Support Count
1	{iPad(A), iPad case (B), iPad scratch guard(C)}	2
2	{iPad(A), iPad case (B), Apple care(C)}	2

Thus, the Frequent 3−Itemsets are:

L_3	Itemset	Support Count
1	{iPad(A), iPad case (B), iPad scratch guard(C)}	2
2	{iPad(A), iPad case (B), Apple care(C)}	2

1. Generate 4− Itemset candidates (C_4).
2. Finally, scan the dataset for the Support count and frequent 3−Itemset identification (L_4).

As we can see, the pruning stops here, as there are no further C_3 options available.

The Apriori algorithm is not efficient as it requires multiple dataset scans. However, there are some techniques to improve the efficiency. Some of them are as follows:

- If a transaction does not contain any frequent item-sets, it is not useful and need not participate in the subsequent scans
- Any itemset that is frequent in the dataset should be frequent in at least one partition of the dataset
- Application of sampling, to include a subset of the whole data set with a lower support threshold, will yield more efficiency

Rule generation strategy

Let's say we have a frequent itemset {*A, B, C, D*}, and the possible candidate rules are:

ABC → D

ABD → C

ACD → B

BCD → A

AB → CD

AC → BD

AD → BC

BC → AD

BD → AC

CD → AB

A → BCD

B → ACD

C → ABD

D → ABC

The standard formula is, for every k items in the frequent itemset, *2k-2* possible candidate rules can be defined. Only the rules with high confidence can be retained. The following figure depicts marking the low confidence rules and knocking them off:

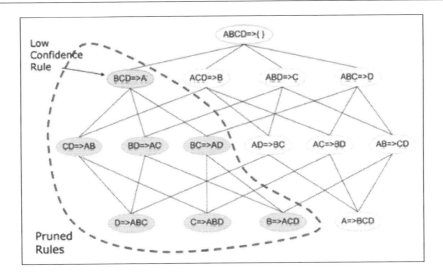

Rules for defining appropriate minsup

Some important guidelines to be followed for defining the minsup threshold for the association rule based mining are as follows:

- Too high minsup: This will lead to missing itemsets with rare items
- Too low minsup: This will result in computational expense as more scans will be needed

Apriori – the downside

It is now clear that in Apriori algorithm, for every k itemsets we will need to use $(k-1)$ frequent itemsets and when the database scans are done, the pattern matching approach is used. The primary bottlenecks are two huge candidate sets and multiple database scans. Let's see an example—if there are 10^4 frequent 1-itemsets, then this will result in 10^7 candidate 2-itemsets. And for every n itemsets, the longest pattern length, $n + 1$ scans are required.

The solution for this would be to avoid the candidate itemset generation completely, and one way of solving this is to compress a large dataset or database into a compact **frequent pattern tree (FP-tree)** that will avoid expensive scans.

There are several ways of optimizing the Apriori implementation and here are some of the important ones:

- **Approach 1—Has-based itemset counting**: There is a threshold value set for every k itemset bucket, and if the count of the itemset for that itemset is lower than the threshold, this bucket will not be processed. This in-turn reduces the itemset buckets that are to be considered for processing, thus improving the efficiency.

- **Approach 2—Transaction elimination / counting**: In case a transaction does not contain the target k itemset, this transaction does not add value or make sense for being processed. So, this approach is about identifying these transactions and eliminating them from being processed.

- **Approach 3—Partitioning**: Any itemset that is potentially frequent in the dataset will need to be frequent in the partitions of the dataset as well; in the absence of which, the itemset could potentially be excluded from being processed.

- **Approach 4—Sampling**: This is a simpler way to consider a sample or a subset of the bigger universe of data and run the mining process. This would reduce the k, and thus the frequent k-itemsets.

- **Approach 5—Dynamic itemset counting**: This is one of the most effective methods, and involves including a new itemset only if it is frequent in all its subset itemsets.

Although, there are optimization techniques for Apriori; it poses inefficiency as a result of expensive scans that are inherent, which will need to be addressed. This brings us to the next algorithm of association rule based learning, the **FP-growth** algorithm.

FP-growth algorithm

The FP-growth algorithm is an efficient and scalable alternative to mining frequent patterns, and thus association rule mining. It addresses most of the performance bottlenecks that an Apriori algorithm would undergo. It allows frequent itemset generation without having to actually generate the candidate itemsets. This algorithm has two steps primarily:

- Building a compact data structure from the database called FP-tree

- Extracting frequent itemsets directly from the FP-tree

Let's consider the same example we used in the Apriori algorithm. There is a total of five items (from the example in the previous section):

I is {iPad(A), iPad case(B), iPad scratch guard(C), Apple care (D), iPhone (E)}, and the following nine transactions. Let's assume that the minimum support count is two:

TID	Transaction Itemsets
1	iPad(A), iPad case(B), and iPhone(E)
2	iPad case(B), Apple care(D)
3	iPad case(B), iPad scratch guard(C)
4	iPad(A), iPad case(B), and Apple care(D)
5	iPad(A), Apple care(D)
6	iPad case(B), iPad scratch guard(C)
7	iPad(A), Apple care(D)
8	iPad(A), iPad case(B), iPad scratch guard(C), and iPhone (E)
9	iPad(A), iPad case(B), and iPad scratch guard(C)

We will now look at building an FP-tree for this database:

1. Identify/calculate the minimum support count. Since it needs to be 30%, the minimum support count is calculated as follows:

$$\text{Minimum support count} = 30/100 * 9 = 2.7 \sim 3$$

2. Calculate the frequency of occurrence for 1-itemset. Additionally, based on the support count, add priority:

Itemset	Support count	Priority
{iPad(A)}	6	2
{iPad case(B)}	7	1
{iPad scratch guard(C)}	6	3
{Apple care(D)}	2	4
{iPhone(E)}	2	5

3. Order the items for each transaction as per the priority:

TID	Transaction Itemsets	Re-ordered Itemsets based on priority
1	iPad(A), iPad case(B), and iPhone(E)	iPad case(B), iPad(A), and iPhone(E)
2	iPad case(B), Apple care(D)	iPad case(B), Apple care(D)
3	iPad case(B), iPad scratch guard(C)	iPad case(B), iPad scratch guard(C)
4	iPad(A), iPad case(B), and Apple care(D)	iPad case(B), iPad(A), and Apple care(D)
5	iPad(A), Apple care(D)	iPad(A), Apple care(D)
6	iPad case(B), iPad scratch guard(C)	iPad case(B), iPad scratch guard(C)
7	iPad(A), Apple care(D)	iPad(A), Apple care(D)
8	iPad(A), iPad case(B), iPad scratch guard(C), and iPhone (E)	iPad case(B), iPad(A), iPad scratch guard(C), and iPhone (E)
9	iPad(A), iPad case(B), and iPad scratch guard(C)	iPad case(B), iPad(A), and iPad scratch guard(C)

4. Create FP-tree for transaction for **TID = 1**, and the ordered itemset is iPad case(*B*), iPad(*A*), and iPhone(*E*).

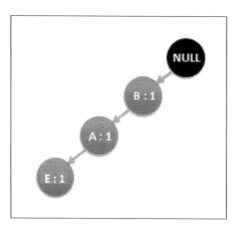

5. Now, scan the database for **TID = 2**, iPad case (*B*) and Apple care(*D*). The updated FP-tree will look like this:

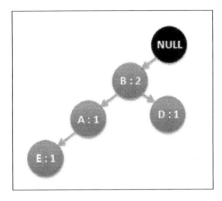

6. Scan all the transactions in the order of L and update the FP-tree accordingly. The final FP-tree will be as shown next. Note that every time an item is encountered again in the transaction, the count value on the node is incremented.

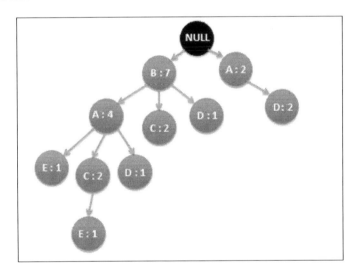

7. Generate a conditional FP-tree for each of the transactions and define the conditional pattern base.

8. Finally, generate the frequent patterns. The result for the given dataset is shown here:

    E: {B, E: 2}, {A, E: 2}, {B, A, E: 2}
    D: {B, D: 2}
    C: {B, C: 4}, {A, C: 4}, {B, A, C: 2}
    A: {B, A: 4}

Apriori versus FP-growth

The following graph shows the relationship between the algorithms with different minsup threshold values:

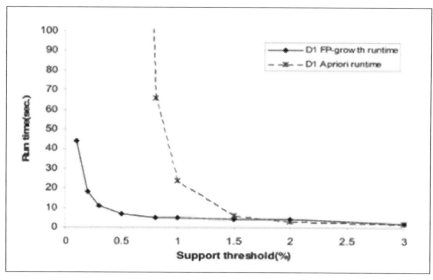

Image source: An article by Prof. Pier Luca Lanzi

The advantages of the FP-growth algorithm are detailed here:

- The complete information for frequent pattern mining is preserved, without breaking the pattern in a long transaction

- Data is compacted by eliminating irrelevant information as infrequent itemsets are avoided upfront

- The FP-growth algorithm works in a divide-and-conquer mode, where the dataset is decomposed as per the frequent itemset patterns uncovered so far. This reduces searches to the subset of datasets as against the complete database

- The candidate itemsets are not generated in this case and hence, will not need to be tested

Implementing Apriori and FP-growth

Refer to the source code provided for this chapter for implementing the Apriori classifier (source code path .../chapter7/... under each of the folders for the technology.)

Using Mahout

Refer to the code files folder .../mahout/chapter7/aprioriexample/.

Refer to the code files folder .../mahout/chapter7/fpgrowthexample/.

Using R

Refer to the code files folder .../r/chapter7/aprioriexample/.

Refer to the code files folder .../r/chapter7/fpgrowthexample/.

Using Spark

Refer to the code files folder .../spark/chapter7/aprioriexample/.

Refer to the code files folder .../spark/chapter7/fpgrowthexample/.

Using Python (Scikit-learn)

Refer to the code files folder .../python-scikit-learn/ chapter7/aprioriexample/.

Refer to the code files folder .../python-scikit-learn/chapter7/fpgrowthexample/.

Using Julia

Refer to the code files folder .../julia/chapter7/aprioriexample/.

Refer to the code files folder .../julia/chapter7/fpgrowthexample/.

Summary

In this chapter, you have learned the association rule based learning methods and, Apriori and FP-growth algorithms. With a common example, you learned how to do frequent pattern mining using Apriori and FP-growth algorithms with a step-by-step debugging of the algorithm. We also compared and contrasted the algorithms and their performance. We have example implementations for Apriori using Mahout, R, Python, Julia, and Spark. In the next chapter, we will cover the Bayesian methods and specifically, the Naïve-Bayes algorithm.

8
Clustering based learning

In this chapter, we will cover the clustering-based learning methods, and in specific the k-means clustering algorithm among others. Clustering-based learning is an unsupervised learning technique and thus works without a concrete definition of the target attribute. You will learn basics and the advanced concepts of this technique, and get hands-on implementation guidance in using Apache Mahout, R, Julia, Apache Spark, and Python to implement the k-means clustering algorithm.

The following figure depicts different learning models covered in this book, and the techniques highlighted in orange will be dealt in detail in this chapter:

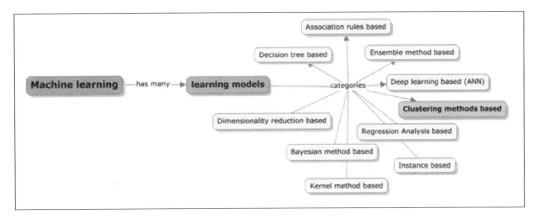

The topics listed next are covered in depth in this chapter:

- The core principles and objectives of the clustering-based learning methods
- How to represent clusters and understand the required distance measurement techniques

- Learning in depth, the k-means clustering and choosing the right clustering algorithm and the rules of cluster evaluation. More importantly, choosing the right number of clusters.

- An overview of hierarchical clustering, data standardization, discovering holes, and data regions.

- Sample implementation using the Apache Mahout, R, Apache Spark, Julia, and Python (scikit-learn) libraries and modules.

Clustering-based learning

The clustering-based learning method is identified as an unsupervised learning task wherein the learning starts from no specific target attribute in mind, and the data is explored with a goal of finding intrinsic structures in them.

The following diagram represents the scope of the clustering-based learning method that will be covered in this chapter:

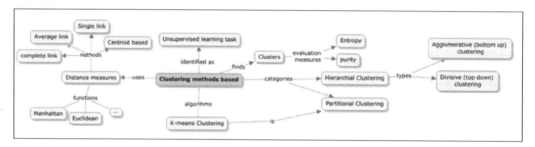

The primary goal of the clustering technique is finding similar or homogenous groups in data that are called **clusters**. The way this is done is — data instances that are similar or, in short, are near to each other are grouped in one cluster, and the instances that are different are grouped into a different cluster. The following diagram shows a depiction of data points on a graph, and how the clusters are marked (in here, it is by pure intuition) by the three natural clusters:

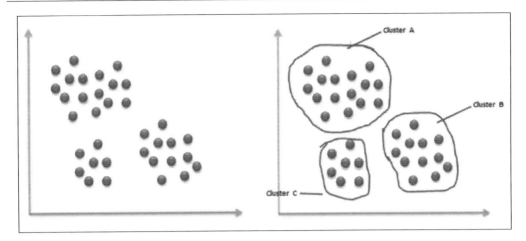

Thus, a cluster can be defined as a collection of objects that are similar to each other and dissimilar from the objects of another cluster. The following diagram depicts the clustering process:

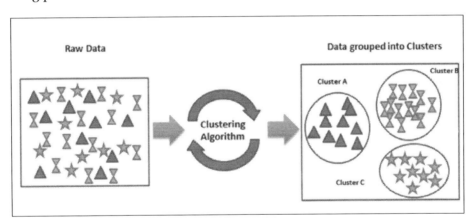

Some simple examples of clustering can be as follows:

- Shirts are grouped based on the sizes small (S), medium (M), large (L), extra large (XL), and so on

- Target Marketing: grouping customers according to their similarities

- Grouping text documents: The requirement here is to organize documents, and build a topic hierarchy based on their content similarities

In fact, clustering techniques are very heavily used in many domains such as archeology, biology, marketing, insurance, libraries, financial services, and many others.

Types of clustering

Cluster analysis is all about the kind of algorithms that can be used to find clusters automatically given the data. There are primarily two classes of clustering algorithm; they are as follows:

- The Hierarchical Clustering algorithms
- The Partitional Clustering algorithms

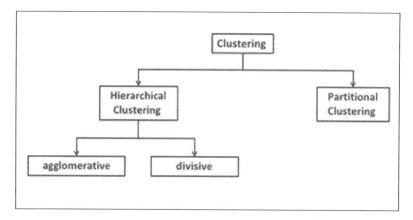

The Hierarchical clustering algorithms define clusters that have a hierarchy, while the partitional clustering algorithms define clusters that divide the dataset into mutually disjoint partitions.

Hierarchical clustering

The Hierarchical clustering is about defining clusters that have a hierarchy, and this is done either by iteratively merging smaller clusters into a larger cluster, or dividing a larger cluster into smaller clusters. This hierarchy of clusters that are produced by a clustering algorithm is called a **dendogram**. A dendogram is one of the ways in which the hierarchical clusters can be represented, and the user can realize different clustering based on the level at which the dendogram is defined. It uses a similarity scale that represents the distance between the clusters that were grouped from the larger cluster. The following diagram depicts a dendogram representation for the Hierarchical clusters:

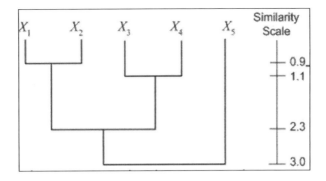

There is another simple way of representing the Hierarchical clusters; that is, the Venn diagram. In this representation, we circle the data points that are a part of the cluster. The following diagram depicts a Venn representation for five data points:

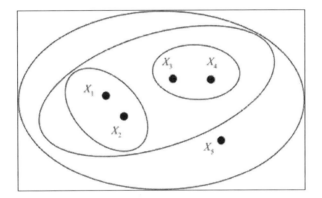

There are two clustering algorithms in the Hierarchical clustering: the Agglomerative and Divisive clustering algorithms.

The Agglomerative clustering algorithm uses the bottom-up approach and merges a set of clusters into a larger cluster. The Divisive clustering algorithm uses the top-down approach and splits a cluster into subclusters. The identification of which cluster will be considered for merging or splitting is decided using greedy methods, and distance measurement becomes critical here. Let's have a quick recap of the instance-based learning methods from *Chapter 6, Instance and Kernel Methods Based Learning*. We have covered the Euclidean distance, Manhattan distance, and cosine similarity as some of the most commonly used metrics of similarity for numeric data, and hamming distance for non-numeric data. For the Hierarchical clustering, the actual data points are not required? only the distance measure matrix is sufficient, as the grouping is done based on the distances.

The Hierarchical clustering algorithm steps can be defined as follows:

1. Start with clusters such as *S1={X1}, S2={X2} … Sm= {Xm}.*
2. Find a set of the nearest clusters and merge them into a single cluster.
3. Repeat the step 2 until the number of clusters formed is equal to a number defined.

Partitional clustering

Partitional clustering algorithms are different in comparison to the Hierarchical clustering algorithms as the clusters or partitions are generated and evaluated using a specific predefined criterion that is domain specific. Since each cluster formed is mutually exclusive, there can never be a hierarchical relationship between the clusters. In fact, every instance can be placed in one and only one of the *k* clusters. The number of clusters (*k*) to be formed is input to this algorithm, and this one set of *k* clusters is the output of the partitional cluster algorithms. One of the most commonly used partitional clustering algorithms that we will be covering in this chapter is the k-means clustering algorithm.

Before we take a deep dive into the k-means clustering algorithm, let's have a quick definition stated here. With an input of *k*, which denotes the number of expected clusters, *k* centers or centroids will be defined that will facilitate defining the *k* partitions. Based on these centers (centroids), the algorithm identifies the members and thus builds a partition followed by the recomputation of the new centers based on the identified members. This process is iterated until the clear, and optimal dissimilarities that make the partition really unique are exposed. Hence, the accuracy of the centroids is the key for the partition-based clustering algorithm to be successful. The following are the steps involved in the centroid-based partitional clustering algorithm:

Input: *k* (the number of clusters) and *d* (the data set with *n* objects)

Output: Set of *k* clusters that minimize the sum of dissimilarities of all the objects to the identified mediod (centroid)

1. Identify the *k* objects as the first set of centroids.
2. Assign the remaining objects that are nearest to the centroid.
3. Randomly select a non-centroid object and recompute the total points that will be swapped to form a new set of centroids, until you need no more swapping.

The Hierarchical and partitional clustering techniques inherently have key differences in many aspects, and some of them include some basic assumptions; execution time assumptions, input parameters, and resultant clusters. Typically, partitional clustering is faster than Hierarchical clustering. While the hierarchical clustering can work with similarity measure alone, partitional clustering requires number of clusters and details around the initial centers. The Hierarchical clustering does not require any input parameters while the partitional clustering algorithms require an input value that indicates the number of clusters required to start running. The cluster definition for hierarchical clustering technique is more subjective as against the partitional clustering results in a exact and precise "k" cluster.

The quality of clustering depends on the chosen algorithm, distance function, and the application. A cluster quality is said to be the best when the inter-cluster distance is *maximized,* and the intra-cluster distance is *minimized.*

The k-means clustering algorithm

In this section, we will cover the k-means clustering algorithm in depth. The k-means is a partitional clustering algorithm.

Let the set of data points (or instances) be as follows:

$D = \{x_1, x_2, \ldots, x_n\}$, where

$xi = (xi_1, xi_2, \ldots, xi_r)$, is a vector in a real-valued space $X \subseteq R_r$, and r is the number of attributes in the data.

The k-means algorithm partitions the given data into k clusters with each cluster having a center called a centroid.

k is specified by the user.

Given k, the k-means algorithm works as follows:

Algorithm k-means (k, D)

1. Identify the k data points as the initial centroids (cluster centers).
2. Repeat step 1.
3. For each data point $x \in D$ do.

4. Compute the distance from *x* to the centroid.

5. Assign *x* to the closest centroid (a centroid represents a cluster).

6. endfor

7. Re-compute the centroids using the current cluster memberships until the stopping criterion is met.

Convergence or stopping criteria for the k-means clustering

The following list describes the convergence criteria for the k-means clustering algorithm:

- There are zero or minimum number of reassignments for the data points to different clusters

- There are zero or minimum changes of centroids

- Otherwise, the decrease in the **sum of squared error of prediction (SSE)** is minimum

If C_j is the jth cluster, then m_j is the centroid of cluster C_j (the mean vector of all the data points in C_j), and if $dist(x, m_j)$ is the distance between the data point *x* and centroid m_j then the following example demonstrated using graphical representation explains the convergence criteria.

For example:

1. Identification of random k centers:

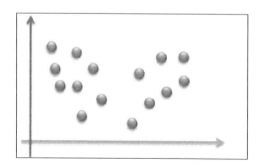

2. Iteration 1: Compute centroids and assign the clusters:

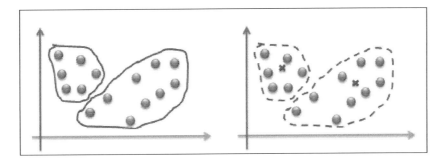

3. Iteration 2: Recompute centroids and reassign the clusters:

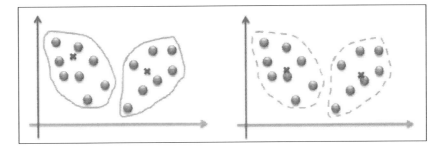

4. Iteration 3: Recompute centroids and reassign the clusters:

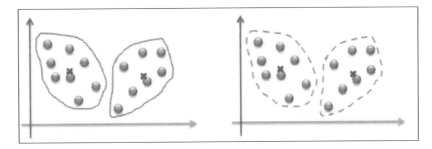

5. Terminate the process due to minimal changes to centroids or cluster reassignments.

K-means clustering on disk

The k-means clustering algorithm can also be implemented with data on disk. This approach is used with large datasets that cannot be accommodated in memory. The strategy used here is to compute centroids incrementally by scanning the dataset only once for each iteration. The performance of this algorithm is determined by how well the number of iterations can be controlled. It is recommended that a limited set of iterations, less than 50 should be run. Although this version helps scaling, it is not the best algorithm for scaling up; there are other alternative clustering algorithms that scale-up, for example, BIRCH is one of them. The following algorithm describes the steps in disk the k-means algorithm:

Algorithm disk k-means (k, D)

1. Choose the k data points as the initial centroids (cluster centers) m_j, where $j = 1,2,3....k$.

2. Repeat

3. Initialize $s_j=0$, where $j=1,2,3....k$; (a vector with all the zero values).

4. Initialize $n_j=0$, where $j=1,2,3....k$; (n_j is number points in the cluster),

5. For each data point $x \in D$ do.

6. $j = arg\ min\ dist(x, m_j)$.

7. Assign x to the cluster j.

8. $s_j = s_j + x$.

9. $n_j = n_j + 1$.

10. endfor.

11. $m_i = s_j/n_j$, where $i=1,2,...k$.

12. Until the stopping, the criterion is met.

Advantages of the k-means approach

The k-means way of unsupervised learning has many benefits; some of them are as follows:

- The k-means clustering is popular and widely adopted due to its simplicity and ease of implementation.

It is efficient and has optimal time complexity defined by $O(ikn)$, where n is the number of data points, k is the number of clusters, and i is the number of iterations. Since the l and k values are kept small, the k-means clustering can represent a linear expression too.

Disadvantages of the k-means algorithm

The following are the downsides or disadvantages of the k-means algorithm:

- The value of k is always a user input and is as good as the identified number k.

- This algorithm is applicable only when the means are available, and in the case of categorical data the centroids are none other than the frequent values.

- Clusters can never be elliptical and are always hyperspherical.

- The clusters identified are very sensitive to the initially identified seeds, and can be different when to run multiple times with different random seeds involved. The following figure depicts how two different centroids can change the clusters. This can be achieved by iterative processing:

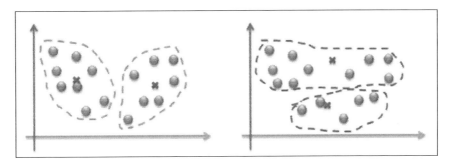

- Again, k-means is very sensitive to outliers. Outliers can be the errors in the data recording or some special data points with very different values. The following diagram depicts the skew that an outlier can bring into the cluster formation. The first representation shows the ideal cluster, and the second one shows the undesirable cluster:

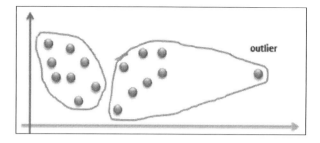

Many of the algorithms and learning techniques that we have seen until now are sensitive to outliers. There are some standard techniques that can be employed.

One way is to get the outliers filtered from evaluation, and this requires us to apply some techniques to handle the noise in the data. The noise reduction techniques will be covered in the next chapters. In the case of k-means clustering, the removal of outliers can be done after a few iterations just to make sure the identified data points are really the outliers. Or, another way is to stick to a smaller sample of data on which the algorithm will be run. This way, the possibility of choosing an outlier will be minimal.

Distance measures

The distance measure is important in clustering algorithms. Reassigning data points to the clusters is determined by redefining the centroids. The following are some ways of measuring distance between two clusters:

- **Single link**: This method refers to measuring the distance between the two closest data points that belong to two different clusters. There can be noise in the data that might be considered with seriousness too.

- **Complete link**: This method refers to measuring the distance between two farthest data points that belong to two different clusters. This method can make the clusters more sensitive to outliers.

- **Average link**: This method uses the average distance measure of all the pairs of distances between the two clusters.

- **Centroids**: This method refers to measuring the distance between the two clusters by measuring the distance between their centroids.

Complexity measures

Choosing the best clustering algorithm has always been a challenge. There are many algorithms available and both, accuracy and complexity measures are important for choosing the right algorithm. The single link method can help achieve *O(n2)*; complete and average links can be done in *O(n2logn)*. There are both advantages and limitations for each of the algorithms, and they work well in certain contexts of data distribution; no standard patterns in the data distribution make it a complex problem to solve. Hence, data preparation and standardization becomes an important aspect in Machine learning. Which distance measure would be an ideal choice can only be determined by implementing the different distance measures iteratively, and comparing the results across iterations. The clustering methods overall are highly dependent on the initial choices and can be subjective.

Implementing k-means clustering

Refer to the source code provided for this chapter for implementing the k-means clustering methods (only supervised learning techniques - source code path .../`chapter08/`... under each of the folders for the technology).

Using Mahout

Refer to the folder ...`/mahout/chapter8/k-meansexample/`.

Using R

Refer to the folder ...`/r/chapter8/k-meansexample/`.

Using Spark

Refer to the folder ...`/spark/chapter8/k-meansexample/`.

Using Python (scikit-learn)

Refer to the folder ...`/python-scikit-learn/chapter8/k-meansexample/`.

Using Julia

Refer to the folder ...`/julia/chapter8/k-meansexample/`.

Summary

In this chapter, we have covered the clustering-based learning methods. We have taken a deep dive into the k-means clustering algorithm using an example. You have learned to implement k-means clustering using Mahout, R, Python, Julia, and Spark. In the next chapter, we will cover the Bayesian methods and in specific, the Naïve-Bayes algorithm.

9
Bayesian learning

In this chapter, we will go back to covering an important, statistical-based method of learning called the Bayesian method learning, and in particular, the Naïve Bayes algorithm among others. The statistical models generally have an explicit probability model, which reveals the probability of an instance belonging to a particular class rather than just classification while solving a classification problem. Before taking a deep dive into the Bayesian learning, you will learn some important concepts under statistics such as probability distribution and the Bayes theorem which is the heart of Bayesian learning.

Bayesian learning is a supervised learning technique where the goal is to build a model of the distribution of class labels that have a concrete definition of the target attribute. Naïve Bayes is based on applying Bayes' theorem with the *naïve* assumption of independence between each and every pair of features.

You will learn the basics and advanced concepts of this technique and get hands-on implementation guidance in using Apache Mahout, R, Julia, Apache Spark, and Python to implement the means - clustering algorithm.

The following figure depicts different learning models covered in this book, and the technique highlighted will be dealt with in detail in this chapter:

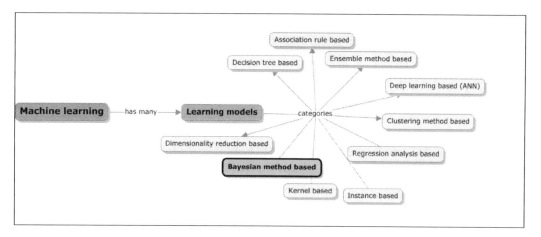

The topics listed here are covered in depth in this chapter:

- An overview of Bayesian statistics and core principles or concepts of probability, distribution, and other relevant statistical measures

- Bayes' theorem and its mechanics

- Deep dive into the Naïve Bayes algorithm and variations of Naïve Bayes classifiers like multinomial and Bernoulli classifiers

- A detailed explanation of some real-world problems or use cases that the Bayesian learning technique can address

- Sample implementation using Apache Mahout, R, Apache Spark, Julia, and Python (scikit-learn) libraries and modules

Bayesian learning

Under supervised learning techniques, the learning models that are categorized under statistical methods are instance-based learning methods and the Bayesian learning method. Before we understand the Bayesian learning method, we will first cover an overview of concepts of probabilistic modeling and Bayesian statistics that are relevant in the context of Machine learning. The core concepts of statistics are very deep, and what will be covered in the next few sections is primarily focused on equipping you with a basic understanding of the dynamic and diverse field of probabilistic Machine learning, which is sufficient to interpret the functioning of the Bayesian learning methods.

Statistician's thinking

The objective of statisticians is to answer questions asked by people from various domains using data. The typical engineering methods use some subjective/objective methods that do not require data to answer the questions. But, statisticians always look at the data to answer questions. They also incorporate variability (the probability that measurements taken on the exact quantity at two different times will slightly differ) in all their models.

Let's take an example: *was M.F. Hussain a good painter?* One method of answering this question measures the paintings based on some accepted norms (by the person or community) of the quality of paintings. The answer in such a case may be based on creative expression, color usage, form, and shape. *I believe M.F. Hussain is a good painter.* In this case, this response can be fairly subjective (which means that the response you get from one person can be very different from the response you get from another). The statistician's method of answering this is very different. They first collect the data from a sample of people who are considered experts in assessing the quality of paintings (university professors of art, other artists, art collectors, and more). Then, after analyzing the data, they will come up with a conclusion such as: "75% of the university professors of arts, 83% of the professional artists, and 96% of the art collectors from the data of 3000 participants of the survey (with equal number of participants from each category) opined that Mr. M.F. Hussain is a good painter". Hence, it can be stated that he is considered a good painter by most. Very obviously, this is a very objective measure.

Important terms and definitions

The following are the essential parameters and concepts that are used to assess and understand the data. They are explained as definitions in some cases and with examples and formulae in others. They are classified as "vocabulary" and "statistical quantities". You will come across some of these terms in the next sections of this chapter:

Term	Definition
Population	This is the universe of data. Typically, statisticians want to make a prediction about a group of objects (Indians, galaxies, countries, and more). All the members of the group are called the population.

Term	Definition
Sample	Most of the times, it is not feasible to work on the entire population. So, statisticians collect a representative sample from the population and do all their calculations on them. The subset of the population that is chosen for the analysis is called a **sample**. It is always cheaper to compile the sample compared to the population or census. There are several techniques to collect samples: • **Stratified sampling**: This is defined as the process of dividing the members of the population into homogeneous subgroups before sampling. Each subgroup should be mutually exclusive, and every element of the population should be assigned to a subgroup. • **Cluster sampling**: This method of sampling ensure n unique clusters where each cluster has elements with no repetition.
Sample size	This is an obvious dilemma that every statistician has been through. How big should be the size of the sample? The bigger the sample, the higher will be the accuracy. However, the cost of collection and analysis also rise accordingly. So, the challenge is to find an optimum sample size where the results are accurate, and the costs are lower.
Sampling Bias	Bias is a systematic error that impacts the outcome in some way. Sampling bias is a consistent error that arises due to the sample selection.
Variable	It is one of the measurements of the sample or population. If we are taking all the members of a class, then their age, academic background, gender, height, and so on, become the variables. Some variables are independent. This means they do not depend on any other variable. Some are dependent.
Randomness	An event is called random if its outcome is uncertain before it happens. An example of a random event is the value of the price of gold tomorrow afternoon at 1 P.M.
Mean	It is equal to the sum of all the values in the sample divided by the total number of observations in the sample.

Term	Definition
Median	Median is a midpoint value between the lowest and highest value of a data set. This is also called the second quartile (designated Q2) = cuts data set in half = 50th percentile. If there is no exact midpoint (that is, the observations in the sample are even), then the median is the average of the two points in the middle.
Mode	This is the most frequently occurring value of the variable. A data can be unimodal (single mode), or multimodal (frequent multiple values). If the data obeys normal distribution (about which you will learn later), the mode is obtained using the empirical formula: *mean – mode = 3 x (mean - median)*
Standard deviation	It is an average measure of how much each measurement in the sample deviates from the mean. Standard deviation is also called the standard deviation of the mean. $$\sigma = \sqrt{\frac{1}{n-1}\sum_{i=1}^{i=n}\left(x_i - \overline{x}\right)^2}$$

Probability

Before we start understanding the probability, let's first look at why we need to consider uncertainty in the first place. Any real-life action is always associated with the uncertainty of the result or the outcome. Let's take some examples; will I be able to catch the train on time today? Will the sales of our top-selling product continue to be in the top position this quarter? If I toss a coin, will I get a heads or tails? Will I be able to go to the airport in *t* minutes?

There can be many sources of uncertainty:

- Uncertainty due to lack of knowledge, as a result of insufficient data, incomplete analysis, and inaccurate measurements
- Otherwise, uncertainty can also be due to complexity, as a result of incomplete processing conditions

In the real world, we need to use probabilities and uncertainties to summarize our lack of knowledge and ability to predict an outcome.

Let's elaborate on the last previous example.

Can I go to the airport in 25 minutes? There could be many problems, such as incomplete observations on the road conditions, noisy sensors (traffic reports), or uncertainty in action, say a flat tire or complexity in modeling the traffic. To predict the outcome, there should definitely be some assumptions made, and we need to deal with uncertainty in a principled way; this is called **probability**. In short, probability is a study of randomness and uncertainty.

In probability, an experiment is something that can be repeated and has uncertainty in the result. A single outcome of an experiment is referred to as a single event, and an event is a collection of outcomes. A **sample space** probability is a list of all the possible outcomes of an experiment.

The probability of the event *E* is represented as *P(E)* and is defined as the likelihood of this event occurring.

 The Probability of an Event P(E) = the number of ways an event can happen / the number of possible outcomes

For example, for a coin that is tossed, there are two possibilities: heads or tails.

The probability of heads is *P(H) = ½ = 0.5*

When a dice is thrown, there are six possibilities, which are 1, 2, 3, 4, 5, and 6.

The probability of 1 is *P(1) = 1/6 = 0.16667*

The probability of rolling any event, *E*, *P(E)*, must be between *0* and *1* (inclusive).

$$0 \leq P(E) \leq 1$$

The value of *0* for probability indicates that an event is impossible, and the value of *1* indicates the certainty of the event. If there are *n* events, then the summation of the probability of each event is *1*. This can be represented as:

If *S = {e1, e2, ...en}* then *P(e1) +P(e2)+...P(en) = 1*

There are many ways to determine the probability:

- **Classical method**: This is the method that we used to define probability in the previous section. This method requires equally likely outcomes. So, if an experiment has equally likely *n* events and there are *m* possibilities, the event E can then occur.

  P(E) = the number of ways the event E can occur / the number of possible outcomes = m/n.

  For example, a bag of chocolates contains five brown covered chocolates, six yellow covered chocolates, two red covered chocolates, eight orange covered chocolates, two blue covered chocolates, and seven green covered chocolates. Suppose that a candy is randomly selected. What is the probability of a candy being brown?

  P (B) = 5/30

- **Empirical method**: The empirical method of probability computation is also called relative frequency, as this formula requires the number of times an experiment is repeated. This method defines the probability of the event *E*, which is the number of times an event is observed over the total number of times the experiment is repeated. The basis on which the probability is computed in this case is either observations or experiences.

  P(E) = Frequency of E / the number of trials of the experiment.

  For example, we want to compute the probability of a grad student to pick medicine as their major. We pick, let's say, a sample of 200 students and 55 of them pick medicine as majors, then:

  P(someone picking medicine) = 55/200 = 0.275

- **Subjective method**: This method of probability uses some fair and computed, or educated assumptions. It usually describes an individual's perception of the likelihood of an event to occur. This means the individual's degree of belief in the event is considered, and thus can be biased. For example, there is a 40% probability that the physics professor would not turn up to take the class.

Types of events

Events can be mutually exclusive, independent, or dependent in nature.

Mutually exclusive or disjoint events

Mutually exclusive events are the events that cannot happen at the same time. In short, the probability of the two events occurring at the same time is *0. P(1)* and *P(5)*. When a dice is rolled, there are mutually exclusive events. A Venn diagram representation of mutually exclusive events is depicted here:

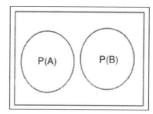

For mutually exclusive events A and B the Addition rule is:

$$P(A \text{ or } B) = P(A) + P(B)$$

For mutually exclusive events A and B the Multiplication rule is:

$$P(A \text{ and } B) = P(A) \times P(B)$$

Independent events

If the outcome of one event does not impact the outcome of another event, the two events are called independent events. For example, event A is that it rained on Sunday, and event B is the car having a flat tire. These two events are not related and the probability of one does not impact the other. An independent event can be mutually exclusive but not vice versa.

Multiplication rule in the case of independent events A and B is:

$$P(A \text{ and } B) = P(A) \times P(B)$$

Dependent events

Dependent events are the events where the occurrence of one event can influence the occurrence of another event. For example, a student who takes English as their first major can take political science as the second major. The Venn representation of dependent events is depicted here:

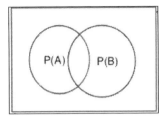

Addition rule for dependent event A and B is:

$$P(A \text{ or } B) = P(A) + P(B) - P(A \text{ and } B)$$

Multiplication rule for dependent event A and B is:

$$P(A \text{ and } B) = P(A) \times P(B)$$

Types of probability

In this section, we will take a look at the different types of probabilities, which are listed as follows:

- **Prior and posterior probability**: Prior probability is the probability that an event E occurs without any prior information or knowledge of any assumptions in the problem context.

  Let's take an example. If your friend was travelling by air and you were asked if they have a man or a woman as their neighbor, as the basis formula of probability works, there is a 0.5 (50%) probability that it can be a man and a 0.5 (50%) probability that it can be a woman. These values can change when more information is provided, and the probability that is measured then is called the posterior probability.

- **Conditional probability**: Conditional probability is defined as the probability that an event occurs, given another event already occurred. *P(B|A)* is interpreted as the probability of event B, given event A.

  For example, let's compute the probability that a person will be hit by a car while walking on the road. Let *H* be a discrete random variable describing the probability of a person being hit by a car, taking the hit as 1 and not as 0.

  Let *L* be a discrete random variable describing the probability of the cross traffic's traffic light state at a given moment, taking one from *{red, yellow, green}*:

  P(L=red) = 0.7,

  P(L=yellow) = 0.1,

P(L=green) = 0.2.

P(H=1 | L=R) = 0.99,

P(H | L=Y) = 0.9 and

P(H | L=G) = 0.2.

Using the conditional probability formulae, we get the following:

P(H=1 and L=R) = P(L=R)*P(H | L=R) = 0.693;

P(H=1 and L=Y) = 0.1*0.9 = 0.09

Similarly, if the probability of getting hit while red is on is 0.99, the probability of not getting hit is 0.01. So, *P(H=0 | L=R) = 0.01.* From these, we can compute the probability of *H=0* and *L=R.*

- **Joint probability**: Joint probability is the probability of two or more things happening together. In a two variable case, *f(x,y | θ)* is the joint probability distribution, where *f* is the probability of *x* and *y* together as a pair, given the distribution parameters—*θ.* For discrete random variables, the joint probability mass function is:

$$P(X \text{ and } Y) = P(X).P(Y \mid X) = P(Y).P(X \mid Y)$$

You already saw this while studying the conditional probability. Since these are probabilities, we have the following:

$$\sum_x \sum_y P(X = x \text{ and } Y = y) = 1$$

- **Marginal probability**: Marginal probability is represented by *f(x | θ)* where *f* is the probability density of *x* for all the possible values of *y*, given the distribution parameters—*θ.* The marginal probability in a random distribution is determined from the joint distribution of *x* and *y* by summing over all the values of *y.* In a continuous distribution, it is determined by integrating over all the values of *y.* This is called **integrating out** the variable *y.* For discrete random variables, the marginal probability mass function can be written as *P(X = x).* This is as follows:

$$P(X = x) = \sum_y P(X = x, Y = y) = \sum_y P(X = x \mid Y = y) P(Y = y)$$

From the above equation, $P(X = x, Y = y)$ is the joint distribution of X and Y, and $P(X = x \mid Y = y)$ is the conditional distribution of X, given Y. The variable Y is marginalized out. These bivariate marginal and joint probabilities for discrete random variables are often displayed as two-way tables (as illustrated next). We will show the computations in a worked out problem in the next section.

For example, suppose two dices are rolled, and the sequence of scores *(X1, X2)* is recorded. Let *Y=X1+X2* and *Z=X1−X2* denote the sum and difference of the scores respectively. Find the probability density function of *(Y, Z)*. Find the probability density function of *Y*. Find the probability density function of *Z*. Are *Y* and *Z* independent?

Assuming that *X1* and *X2* are independent, they can take 36 possibilities, as shown in the table here:

X1	X2	Y (X1+X2)	Z (X1-X2)
1	1	2	0
1	2	3	-1
1	3	4	-2
1	4	5	-3
1	5	6	-4
1	6	7	-5
2	1	3	1
2	2	4	0
2	3	5	-1
2	4	6	-2
2	5	7	-3
2	6	8	-4
3	1	4	2
3	2	5	1
3	3	6	0
3	4	7	-1
3	5	8	-2
3	6	9	-3
4	1	5	3
4	2	6	2
4	3	7	1
4	4	8	0
4	5	9	-1
4	6	10	-2
5	1	6	4
5	2	7	3
5	3	8	2
5	4	9	1
5	5	10	0
5	6	11	-1
6	1	7	5
6	2	8	4
6	3	9	3
6	4	10	2
6	5	11	1
6	6	12	0

Let's now construct the joint, marginal, and conditional table. In this, we will have values of Z as rows and Y as columns. Y varies from 2 to 12 and Z varies from -5 to 5. We can fill all the conditional distributions just by counting. For example, take $Z=-1$; we see that this happens when $Y=3, 5, 7, 9, 11$. We also note that the probability of each one of them (say, the conditional probability that $Z=-1$, given $Y=3$) is *1/36*. We can fill the table like this for all the values:

Z \ Y	2	3	4	5	6	7	8	9	10	11	12	Marginal Z
-5	0	0	0	0	0	1/36	0	0	0	0	0	1/36
-4					1/36		1/36					1/18
-3				1/36		1/36		1/36				1/12
-2			1/36		1/36		1/36		1/36			1/9
-1		1/36		1/36		1/36		1/36		1/36		5/36
0	1/36		1/36		1/36		1/36		1/36		1/36	1/6
1		1/36		1/36		1/36		1/36		1/36		5/36
2			1/36		1/36		1/36		1/36			1/9
3				1/36		1/36		1/36				1/12
4					1/36		1/36					1/18
5						1/36						1/36
	1/36	1/18	1/12	1/9	5/36	1/6	5/36	1/9	1/12	1/18	1/36	

So, the bottom row is the marginal distribution of Y. The right-most column is the marginal distribution of Z. The total table is the joint distribution. Clearly, they are dependent.

Distribution

Distributions are either discrete or continuous probability distributions, depending on whether they define probabilities associated with discrete variables or continuous variables:

Discrete	Continuous
Bernouli	Normal
Binomial	T distribution
Negative binomial	Gamma
Geometric	Chi Square
Poisson	Exponential
	Weibull
	F Distribution

We will cover a few of the previously mentioned distributions here.

In this section, our major emphasis is on modeling and describing a given property of the data. To understand how crucial this skill is, let's look at a few examples:

- A bank wants to look at the amount of cash withdrawn per transaction in an ATM machine over a period of time to determine the limits of transaction
- A retailer wants to understand the number of broken toys that he is getting in every shipment
- A manufacturer wants to understand how the diameter of a probe is varying between various manufacturing cycles
- A pharmaceutical company wants to understand how the blood pressures of millions of patients are impacted by its new drug

In all these cases, we need to come up with some precise quantitative description of how the observed quantity is behaving. This section is all about this. Anyway, intuitively, what do you think are the qualities that you would like to measure to gain an understanding?

- What are all the values that a given variable is taking?
- What is the probability of taking a given value and what values have the highest probability?
- What is the mean/median, and how much is the variance?
- Given a value, can we tell how many observations fall into it and how many fall away from it?
- Can we give a range of values where we can tell 90% of the data lies?

Actually, if we can answer these questions, and more importantly if we develop a technique to describe such quantities, we are more or less unstoppable as far as this property is considered!

There are two prime observations to be made here. First, a property when distributed the way it is has all the qualities it takes to be a random variable (knowing one value of the quantity does not help us know the next value). Then, if we know the probability mass function or the distribution function of this random variable, we can compute all the previous matter. This is why it is so important to understand mathematics. In general, we follow (for that matter, almost anybody interested in analyzing the data that follows) a systematic process in describing a quantity:

1. We will first understand the random variable.
2. Next, we will compute the probability mass (or distribution) function.

3. Then, we will predict the all-important parameters (mean and variance).
4. Then, we will check with experimental data to see how good our approximations are.

For example, the number of vans that have been requested for rental at a car rental agency during a 50-day period is identified in the following table. The observed frequencies have been converted into probabilities for this 50-day period in the last column of the table:

Possible demand X	Number of days	Probability [P(X)]
3	3	0.06
4	7	0.14
5	12	0.24
6	14	0.28
7	10	0.2
8	4	0.08

The expected value is 5.66 vans, as shown here:

Possible demand X	Probability [P(X)]	Weighted Value [XP(X)]
3	0.06	0.18
4	0.14	0.56
5	0.24	1.2
6	0.28	1.68
7	0.2	1.4
8	0.08	0.64
	1	E(X) = 5.66

Similarly, variance computation is given next:

Possible demand X	Probability [P(X)]	Weighted Value [XP(X)]	Squared demand (X2)	Weighted Square [X2P(X)]
3	0.06	0.18	9	0.54
4	0.14	0.56	16	2.24
5	0.24	1.2	25	6
6	0.28	1.68	36	10.08
7	0.2	1.4	49	9.8
8	0.08	0.64	64	5.12
	1	E(X) = 5.66		E(X2) = 33.78

The standard deviation is a square root of variance and is equal to 1.32 vans. Let's systematically analyze various distributions.

Bernoulli distribution

This is the simplest distribution that one can think of. Many a times, a property takes only discrete values; like a coin toss, a roll of the dice, the gender of people, and so on. Even if they are not exactly discrete, we can transform them by binning in some cases. For example, when we look at the net worth of individuals, we can redivide them as rich and poor (**discrete quantity**) based on the exact wealth they have (**continuous quantity**). Let's say that the probability of the property taking a given value is p (of course, the probability of it not taking is $(1-p)$). If we collect the large sample sufficiently, then how does the dataset look? Well, there will be some positives (where the variable took the value) and negatives (where the variable does not take the value). Assume that we denote positive with 1 and negative with 0.

Then, we have the following:

The mean = weighted average of probabilities = $1*p + 0*(1-p) = p$

Binomial distribution

This is an extension of the Bernoulli idea. Let's take a specific example. You are working in a population bureau and have the data of all the families in a state. Let's say you want to identify the probability of having two male children in families that have exactly two children. As you can see, a family can have two children in only four different ways: MM, MF, FM, and FF. As we consider having a male child as the event of interest, then the probability that there are only male children is *0.25 (1/4)*. The probability of there being one male child is *0.5 (0.25+0.25) (1/4+1/4)*, and no male child is *0.25 (1/4)*.

So, if you look at 100 families, what is the probability that 20 families have exactly two male children? We will come to the solution later. Let's extend the argument to find the probability of having all the males in families with three children: The total possibilities are FFF, FFM, FMF, FMM, MFM, MMF, MFF, and MMM (eight total possibilities). The probability for all three to be male is *1/8*. The probability for two of the three being male is *3/8*. The probability for one of the three to be male is *3/8*. The probability for none to be male is *1/8*. Note that the total probability of all the events is always equal to 1.

Poisson probability distribution

Now, let's try to extend the Binomial theorem to infinite trials, but with a catch. The examples that we have taken (coin toss and more) have an interesting property. The probability of the event occurring in a trial does not change even if we increase the number of trials. However, there are a great number of examples, whereas the number of trials (or its equivalent) increases, the corresponding probability of the event decreases. So, we need to reduce the time interval to zero, or the number of observations to infinity to ensure that we see only a single success or failure in any trial. In this limiting case, the probability that we see r successes in n observations can be computed as follows:

$$\lim_{n \to \infty} c_r^n \left(\frac{\lambda}{n} \right)^r \left(1 - \frac{\lambda}{n} \right)^{n-r}$$

$$\lim_{n \to \infty} \frac{n!}{r!(n-r)!} \frac{\lambda^r}{n^r} \left(1 - \frac{\lambda}{n} \right)^{n-r}$$

The probability distribution of a Poisson random variable X is as given below. This considers representing the number of successes occurring in a given time interval:

$$P(X = r) = \frac{\lambda^r e^{-\lambda}}{r!}$$

Here, r is the rth trial and λ = a mean number of successes in the given time interval or the region of space.

Exponential distribution

Let's now look at the Poisson example and ask ourselves a different question. What is the probability that the inspector does not see the first car until t hours? In this case, it may not be relevant, but when we work on the failure of a component, it makes sense to understand what time the probability of not seeing the failure is high. So, let's say the sighting of the car (or first failure) follows the Poisson process. Then, let's define L, a random variable that is the probability that the inspector will not see the first car until time t as the time before the first sighting of the car. From the Poisson distribution, the probability that she will not see the first car in 1 hour is as follows:

$$P(X = 0) = \frac{e^{-\lambda}\lambda^0}{0!} = e^{-\lambda}$$

The probability that that she will not see a car in the second hour also is the same, and the probability that she will not see the car in t hours is $e^{-\lambda t}$ ($e^{-\lambda *} e^{-\lambda *}...times$). The probability that she will see the car in the first t hours then is $1-e^{-\lambda t}$.

The applications of exponential distribution are as follows:

- Time to the first failure in a Poisson process
- Distance of the dispersion of seeds from the parent plant
- The expected lifetime of an organism, ignoring the aging process (where the end occurs due to accidents, infections, and more)

Normal distribution

Normal distribution is a very widely used class of continuous distribution. It is also often called the bell curve because the graph of its probability density resembles a bell. Most of the real-life data such as weights, heights, and more (particularly when there are large collections) can be well approximated by a normal distribution.

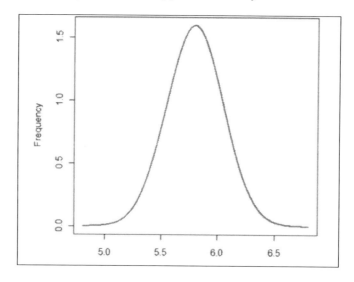

Once we know the values of the heights, the number of samples that have this value can be mathematically described as follows:

$$f(x) = \frac{1}{\sigma\sqrt{2\pi}} e^{-(x-\mu)^2/2\sigma^2}$$

Here, σ is the standard deviation and μ is the mean. To describe a normal distribution, we just need to know two concepts (average and SD).

Every normal curve adheres to the following *rule*:

- About 68% of the area under the curve falls within one standard deviation of the mean
- About 95% of the area under the curve falls within two standard deviations of the mean
- About 99.7% of the area under the curve falls within three standard deviations of the mean

Collectively, these points are known as the **empirical rule** or the **68-95-99.7 rule**.

Relationship between the distributions

While we know that more or less everything converges to a normal distribution, it is best to understand where each one fits. The following chart helps in this:

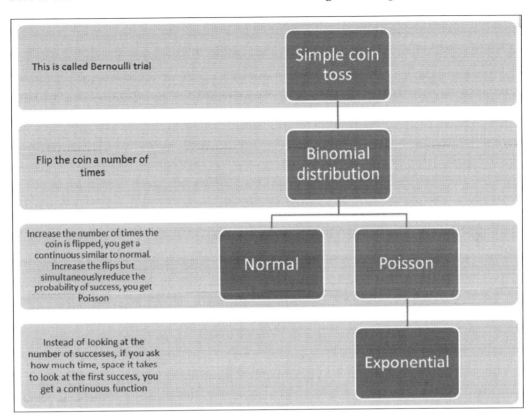

Bayes' theorem

Before we go into the Bayes' theorem, we mentioned at the beginning of this chapter what is at the Bayesian learning is the Bayes theorem.

Let's start with an example. Assume that there are two bowls of nuts; the first bowl contains 30 cashew nuts and 10 pistachios and the second bowl contains 20 of each. Let's choose one bowl randomly and pick a nut with eyes closed. The nut is cashew. Now, what is the probability that the bowl chosen is the first bowl? This is a conditional probability.

So, *p(Bowl 1 | cashew)* or the probability that it is bowl 1, given the nut is cashew, is not an easy and obvious one to crack.

If the question was to put the other way, *p(cashew | bowl1)* or the probability that the nut is cashew, given bowl 1 is easy, *p(cashew | Bowl 1) = ¾.*

As we know, *p(cashew | Bowl 1)* is not the same as *p(Bowl 1 | cashew)*, but we can use one value to get another value, and this is what Bayes' theorem is all about.

The first step of defining the Bayes' theorem conjunction is commutative; following are the steps:

p (A and B) =p (B and A),

Further, the probability of A and B is the probability of A and the probability of B, given A:

p (A and B) = p (A) p (B | A), similarly

p (B and A) = p (B) p (A | B)

so,

p (A) p (B | A) = p (B) p (A | B) and

$$p(A|B) = \frac{p(A)p(B|A)}{p(B)}$$

And that's Bayes' theorem!

It might not be very obvious, but it is a very powerful definition.

Now, let's apply this to solve the previous *nut* problem to find *p(bowl1 cashew)*, and we can derive it if we can get *p(cashew | bowl 1)*:

p (bowl1 cashew) = (p(bowl1) p(cashew | bowl1)) / p (cashew)

p (bowl1) = ½

p (cashew | bowl1) = ¾

p (cashew) = total cashews / total nuts (between bowl1 and bowl2) = 50/80 = 5/8

Putting it together, we have the following:

p (bowl1 cashew) = ((1/2) (3/4))/(5/8)= 3/5 = 0.6

The additional aspect that needs to be considered now is how to feature in the changes that come over time as the new data comes in. This way, the probability of a hypothesis can be measured in the context of the data at a given point in time. This is called the diachronic interpretation of the Bayes' theorem.

Following is the restating Bayes' theorem with the hypothesis (*H*) for the given data (*D*):

$$p(H \mid D) = \frac{p(H)\,p(D \mid H)}{p(D)}$$

p (H) is the probability of the hypothesis *H* before seeing the data *D*.

p (D) is the probability of data *D* under any hypothesis, which is usually constant.

p (H|D) is the probability of the hypothesis *H* after seeing the data *D*.

p (D|H) is the probability of data *D* given the hypothesis *H*.

p (H) is called prior probability; *p (H|D)* is posterior probability; *p (D|H)* is the likelihood; and *p (D)* is the evidence:

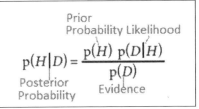

Naïve Bayes classifier

In this section, we will look at the Naïve Bayes classifiers and how they are used to solve the classification problems. The Naïve Bayes classifier technique is based on the Bayes' theorem and assumes the predictors to be independent, which means knowing the value of one attribute does influence the value of any other attribute. The independence assumption is what makes Naïve Bayes *naïve*.

Naïve Bayes classifiers are easy to build, do not involve any iterative process, and work very well with large datasets. Despite its simplicity, Naïve Bayes is known to have often outperformed other classification methods.

We need to compute the probability of an assumption given a class.

That is, $P(x_1, x_2, \ldots x_{n|y})$. Obviously, there are multiple pieces of evidence represented by $x_1, x_2, \ldots x_n$.

Hence, we start with an assumption that $x_1, x_2, \ldots x_n$ are conditionally independent, given y. Another simple way of defining this is that we need to predict an outcome given multiple evidence as against a single evidence. To simplify, we uncouple these multiple pieces of evidence:

P(Outcome | Multiple Evidence) = [P(Evidence1 | Outcome) x P(Evidence2 | outcome) x ... x P(EvidenceN | outcome)] x P(Outcome) / P(Multiple Evidence)

This is also written as follows:

P(Outcome | Evidence) = P(Likelihood of Evidence) x Prior probability of outcome / P(Evidence)

In order to apply Naïve Bayes to predict an outcome, the previously mentioned formula will need to be run for every outcome. Just run this formula for each possible outcome, and in the case of a classification problem, the outcome will be a class. We will look at the famous fruit problem to help you understand this easily.

Given any three important characteristics of a fruit, we will need to predict what fruit it is. To simplify the case, let's take three attributes—long, sweet, and yellow; and three classes of fruit—banana, orange, and others. Let there be 1,000 data points in the training set, and this is how the available information looks like:

Type	Long	Not long	Sweet	Not sweet	Yellow	Not yellow	Total
Banana	400	100	350	150	450	50	500
Orange	0	300	150	150	300	0	300
Others	100	100	150	50	50	150	200
Total	500	500	650	350	800	200	1000

Some derived values/prior probabilities from the previous table are as follows:

Probability of Class

p (Banana)= 0.5 (500/1000)

p (Orange)= 0.3

p (Others) = 0.2

Probability of Evidence

p *(Long)= 0.5*

p *(Sweet)= 0.65*

p *(Yellow) = 0.8*

Probability of Likelihood

p *(Long | Banana) = 0.8*

p *(Long/Orange) = 0 P(Yellow/Other Fruit) =50/200 = 0.25*

p *(Not Yellow | Other Fruit)= 0.75*

Now, given a fruit, let's classify it based on attributes. First, we run probability for each of the three outcomes, take the highest probability, and then classify it:

p *(Banana |/Long, Sweet and Yellow) = p (Long | Banana) x p (Sweet | Banana) x p (Yellow | Banana) x p (banana) /p (Long) xp (Sweet) x. p (Yellow)*

p *(Banana | | Long, Sweet and Yellow) =0.8 x 0.7 x 0.9 x 0.5 / p (evidence)*

p *(Banana | | Long, Sweet and Yellow) =0.252/ p (evidence)*

p *(Orange | | Long, Sweet and Yellow) = 0*

p *(Other Fruit/Long, Sweet and Yellow) = p (Long/Other fruit) x p (Sweet/Other fruit) x p (Yellow/Other fruit) x p (Other Fruit)*

= (100/200 x 150/200 x 50/150 x 200/1000) / p (evidence)

= 0.01875/ p (evidence)

With the largest margin of *0.252 >> 0.01875,* we can now classify this Sweet/Long/Yellow fruit as likely to be a *Banana.*

As Naïve Bayes assumes a gaussian distribution for each of the features, it is also called the Gaussian Naïve Bayes classifier.

Naïve Bayes is particularly good when there is missing data. In the next sections, let's look at different types of Naïve Bayes classifiers.

Multinomial Naïve Bayes classifier

As we have seen in the previous section, Naïve Bayes assumes independence of the model against the distribution for a feature. In the case of a multinomial Naïve Bayes, the $p(x_i|y)$ is a multinomial distribution; in short, a multinomial distribution is assumed for each of the features. The case that fits this variant is that of a document where we need to compute the word count. A simple algorithm of multinomial Naïve Bayes is given here:

```
TRAINMULTINOMIALNB(C, D)
 1   V ← EXTRACTVOCABULARY(D)
 2   N ← COUNTDOCS(D)
 3   for each c ∈ C
 4   do N_c ← COUNTDOCSINCLASS(D, c)
 5       prior[c] ← N_c/N
 6       text_c ← CONCATENATETEXTOFALLDOCSINCLASS(D, c)
 7       for each t ∈ V
 8       do T_ct ← COUNTTOKENSOFTERM(text_c, t)
 9       for each t ∈ V
10       do condprob[t][c] ← (T_ct+1)/(Σ_t'(T_ct'+1))
11   return V, prior, condprob

APPLYMULTINOMIALNB(C, V, prior, condprob, d)
 1   W ← EXTRACTTOKENSFROMDOC(V, d)
 2   for each c ∈ C
 3   do score[c] ← log prior[c]
 4       for each t ∈ W
 5       do score[c] += log condprob[t][c]
 6   return arg max_{c∈C} score[c]
```

The Bernoulli Naïve Bayes classifier

The Bernoulli Naïve Bayes classifier attaches a Boolean indicator to a word as one if it belongs to a document under examination and zero if it does not. The focus of this variation is that it considers the count of occurrence or non-occurrence of a word in a specific document under consideration. The non-occurrence of a word is an important value as it is used in the computation of the conditional probabilities of the occurrence of a word. The Bernoulli Naïve Bayes algorithm is detailed here:

```
TRAINBERNOULLINB(C, D)
1   V ← EXTRACTVOCABULARY(D)
2   N ← COUNTDOCS(D)
3   for each c ∈ C
4   do Nc ← COUNTDOCSINCLASS(D, c)
5       prior[c] ← Nc/N
6       for each t ∈ V
7       do Nct ← COUNTDOCSINCLASSCONTAININGTERM(D, c, t)
8           condprob[t][c] ← (Nct + 1)/(Nc + 2)
9   return V, prior, condprob

APPLYBERNOULLINB(C, V, prior, condprob, d)
1   Vd ← EXTRACTTERMSFROMDOC(V, d)
2   for each c ∈ C
3   do score[c] ← log prior[c]
4       for each t ∈ V
5       do if t ∈ Vd
6           then score[c] += log condprob[t][c]
7           else  score[c] += log(1 − condprob[t][c])
8   return arg max_{c∈C} score[c]
```

	Multinomial Naïve Bayes	**Bernoulli Naïve Bayes**
Model Variable	Here, a token is generated and checked for occurrence in a position	Here, a document is generated and checked for occurrence in a document
Document	$d = \left\langle t_1, \ldots, t_k, \ldots, t_{n_d} \right\rangle, t_k \in V$	$d = \left\langle e_1, \ldots, e_i, \ldots, e_M \right\rangle,$ $e_i \in \{0,1\}$
Estimation of the parameter	$\hat{P}(X = t \mid c)$	$\hat{P}(U_i = e \mid c)$
Rule	$\hat{P}(c) \prod_{1 \leq k \leq n_d} \hat{P}(X = t_k \mid c)$	$\hat{P}(c) \prod_{t_i \in V} \hat{P}(U_i = e_i \mid c)$
Occurrences	This considers multiple occurrences	This considers single occurrences
Size of the document	Large documents are handled	Good with smaller documents
Features	This supports handling more features	This is good with lesser features
Estimation of a term	$\hat{P}(X = the \mid c) \approx 0.05$	$\hat{P}(U_{the} = 1 \mid c) \approx 1.0$

Implementing Naïve Bayes algorithm

Refer to the source code provided for this chapter for implementing Naïve Bayes classifier (source code path .../chapter9/... under each of the folders for the technology).

Using Mahout

Refer to the folder .../mahout/chapter9/naivebayesexample/.

Using R

Refer to the folder .../r/chapter9/naivebayesexample/.

Using Spark

Refer to the folder .../spark/chapter9/naivebayesexample/.

Using scikit-learn

Refer to the folder .../python-scikit-learn/chapter9/naivebayesexample/.

Using Julia

Refer to the folder .../julia/chapter9/naivebayesexample/.

Summary

In this chapter, you have learned Bayesian Machine learning and how to implement Naïve Bayes classifiers association rule-based learning with Mahout, R, Python, Julia, and Spark. Additionally, we covered all the core concepts of statistics, starting from basic nomenclature to various distributions. We have covered the Bayes' theorem in depth with examples to understand how to apply it to the real-world problems.

In the next chapter, we will be covering the regression-based learning techniques and in specific, the implementation for linear and logistic regression.

10
Regression based learning

Regression analysis allows us to mathematically model the relationship between two variables using simple algebra. In this chapter, we will focus on covering another supervised learning technique: regression analysis or regression-based learning. In the previous chapter, we covered the basics of statistics that will be of use in this chapter. We will start with understanding how multiple variables can influence the outcome, and how statistical adjustment techniques can be used to arbitrate this influence, understand correlation and regression analysis using real world examples, and take a deep dive into concepts such as confounding and effect modification.

You will learn the basic and advanced concepts of this technique and get hands-on implementation guidance in simple, multiple linear regression, polynomial regression and logistic regression using Apache Mahout, R, Julia, Apache Spark, and Python.

At the end of this chapter, readers will have understood the uses and limitations of regression models, learned how to fit linear and logistic regression models to data, statistically inferencing the results and finally, assessing and diagnosing the performance of the models.

The following diagram depicts different learning models covered in this book, and the techniques highlighted in orange will be dealt in detail in this chapter:

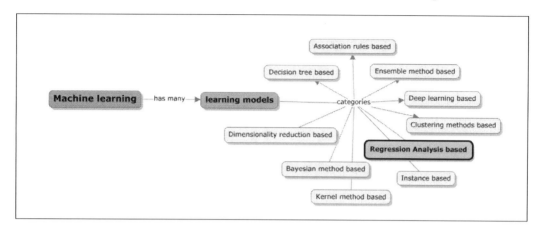

The topics listed here are covered in depth in this chapter:

- Introduction to correlation and regression analysis; revision of additional statistical concepts such as covariance and correlation coefficients. We will cover the properties of expectation, variance, and covariance in the context of regression models and ANOVA model and diagnostics

- You will learn simple, linear and multiple linear regressions: linear relationships, linear models, basic assumptions (normality, homoscedasticity, linearity, and independence), and least squares estimation. Overall, you will learn model diagnostics and selection.

- You will be presented with an overview of generalized linear models (GLMs) and a listing of the regression algorithms under GLM. Also, the phenomena of confounding and effect modification will be presented, and hence realization and adjustments for the same.

- An introduction to logistic regression, understanding odds and risk ratios, model building logistic regression models, and assessing the same will be covered.

- Sample implementation using Apache Mahout, R, Apache Spark, Julia, and Python (scikit-learn) libraries and modules will also be covered.

Regression analysis

Under supervised learning techniques, the learning models that are categorized under statistical methods are instance-based learning methods, Bayesian learning methods, and regression analysis. In this chapter, we will focus on regression analysis and other related regression models. Regression analysis is known to be one of the most important statistical techniques. As mentioned, it is a statistical methodology that is used to measure the relationship and check the validity and strength of the relationship between two or more variables.

Traditionally, researchers, analysts, and traders have been using regression analysis to build trading strategies to understand the risk contained in a portfolio. Regression methods are used to address both classification and prediction problems.

We have covered some key statistical concepts in the earlier chapter; in this chapter, we will cover some more concepts that are quite relevant in the context of regression analysis. To name a few concepts, we have the measurement of variability, linearity, covariance, coefficients, standard errors, and more.

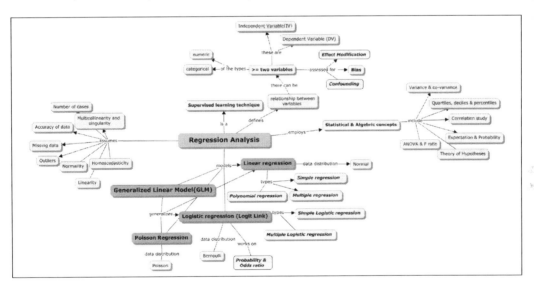

Revisiting statistics

In the earlier chapter, where we learned the Bayesian learning methods, we covered some core statistical measures such as mean, median, mode, and standard deviation. Let's now extend this to some more measures such as variance, covariance, correlation, and the first and second moments of the distribution of a random variable.

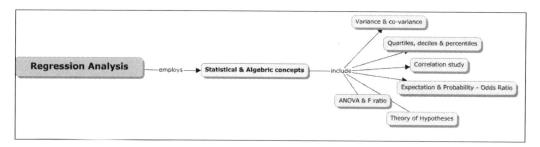

Variance is the square of standard deviation. If you recollect what standard deviation is, it is an average measure of how much each measurement in the sample deviates from the mean. It is also called the standard deviation of the mean. We can theoretically compute standard deviations for mode and median.

The range is defined as a span of values over which the dataset is spread. Range usually is represented as minimum and maximum values.

Quartiles, deciles, and percentiles subdivide a distribution of measurements that are similar to the median. The median is known to divide the distribution into half while quartile, decile, and percentile divide the distribution into 1/25, 1/10 and 1/100 respectively.

First quartile (designated Q1) OR lower quartile is the 25th percentile.

Third quartile (designated Q3) OR upper quartile is the 75th percentile.

interquartile range = third quartile – first quartile

Symmetric and **skewed data**: Median, mean and mode for symmetric, positively, and negatively skewed data is represented here:

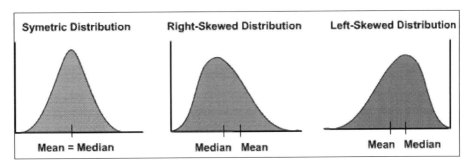

Symmetric distribution has equal mean and median values. For a positively skewed distribution, the median is greater than the mean and for a negatively skewed distribution, the mean value is greater than the median's value.

The outlier is an observation that is separated from the main cluster of the data. It can impact measures such as mean in a very significant way. Let's take an example to understand this better. We want to understand the average wealth of a group of five people. Say, the individual assets are valued at USD 1M, USD 1.2M, USD 0.9M, USD 1.1M, and USD 12M.

1+1.2+0.9+1.1+12=16.2

16.2/5=3.24

The last observation had an unrealistic impact on the measurement. Let's now see how the median is impacted. Let's sort the assets in ascending order: 0.9M, 1.0M, 1.1M, 1.2M, and 12M. The median is 1.1M. There are two important concepts we must understand. Outliers influence mean more significantly than the median.

So, you should check the data carefully before choosing the correct statistical quantity.

Mean represents the average value of the variable and median represents the value of the average variable.

Covariance is when there are two or more variables of interest (such as stocks of companies, physical properties of materials, etc.); it becomes important to understand whether there is any relation between them. Precisely, what we want to understand is if one of them is varying how does the other variable vary.

In statistics, two terms explain this behavior:

The first one is known as covariance. For a data set comprising n points of two variables x and y, the following equation depicts the computation of covariance:

$$\rho_{xy} = \frac{\sum_1^n (x_i - \bar{x})(y_i - \bar{y})}{n}$$

However, covariance can be a very large number. It is best to express it as a normalized number between -1 and 1 to understand the relation between the quantities. This is achieved by normalizing covariance with standard deviations of both the variables (sx and sy).

This is called **correlation coefficient** between x and y.

$$Cor(x,y) = \rho_{xy}/\sigma_x\sigma_y$$

Correlation measures the strength of linear dependence between X and Y and lies between -1 and 1. The following graph gives you a visual understanding of how the correlation impacts the linear dependence:

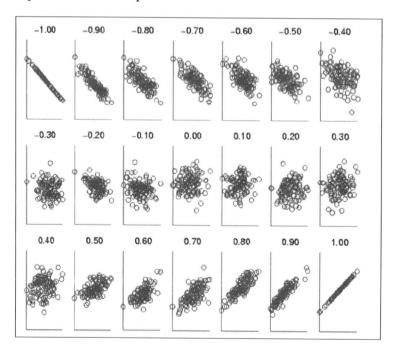

Before we get into the specifics of various regression models, let's first look at the steps for implementing a regression model and analyzing the results.

The mean and variances are the *first and second moments* of the probability distribution functions of random variables. They are computed as follows:

$$\text{Mean} = \mu = \int_a^b xP(x)dx$$

$$\text{Variance} = \sigma^2 = \int_a^b x^2 P(x)dx$$

After computing the probability distribution for a given random variable, we will compute the mean variance through simple integration.

Let's compute all these measures using a real-world example.

Following is the data of the stock prices of three companies (company A, company B, and company C) during a period of 14 days. First, compute the returns using the next formula:

Returns = (current day's price-yesterday's price)/yesterday's price

From this return, compute mean, median, and pairwise correlation. Do not use the built-in libraries. Use the base formulae even if you use Excel.

Company A	Company B	Company C
498.3	243.7	250.15
515.25	245.75	250.25
506.4	242.7	250.25
504.8	244.65	253.55
536.95	250.95	236.8
512.55	227.4	219.1
525.65	240.3	206.5
538.95	243.8	216.45
510.45	235.25	217.9
503	238.35	215.3
500.75	231.4	218.15
496.45	228.15	217.55
492.3	219.7	215.15
496.6	218	205.4

First, let's compute the returns using the formula given previously.

Company A	Company B	Company C	A (returns)	B (returns)	C (returns)
498.3	243.7	250.15			
515.25	245.75	250.25	0.0340157	0.008412	0.0004
506.4	242.7	250.25	-0.017176	-0.012411	0
504.8	244.65	253.55	-0.00316	0.0080346	0.013187
536.95	250.95	236.8	0.0636886	0.0257511	-0.06606
512.55	227.4	219.1	-0.045442	-0.0938434	-0.07475
525.65	240.3	206.5	0.0255585	0.0567282	-0.05751
538.95	243.8	216.45	0.025302	0.0145651	0.048184
510.45	235.25	217.9	-0.052881	-0.0350697	0.006699
503	238.35	215.3	-0.014595	0.0131775	-0.01193
500.75	231.4	218.15	-0.004473	-0.0291588	0.013237
496.45	228.15	217.55	-0.008587	-0.0140449	-0.00275
492.3	219.7	215.15	-0.008359	-0.037037	-0.01103
496.6	218	205.4	0.0087345	-0.0077378	-0.04532

If we had to compute the mean, the values would be as follows:

	A (returns)	B (returns)	C (returns)
	0.0340157	0.008412	0.0004
	-0.017176	-0.012411	0
	-0.00316	0.0080346	0.013187
	0.0636886	0.0257511	-0.06606
	-0.045442	-0.0938434	-0.07475
	0.0255585	0.0567282	-0.05751
	0.025302	0.0145651	0.048184
	-0.052881	-0.0350697	0.006699
	-0.014595	0.0131775	-0.01193
	-0.004473	-0.0291588	0.013237
	-0.008587	-0.0140449	-0.00275
	-0.008359	-0.037037	-0.01103
	0.0087345	-0.0077378	-0.04532
Sum	0.0026265	-0.1026342	-0.18764
Mean	0.000202	-0.0078949	-0.01443

To find the median, we will first sort the return values in ascending order and then mark the mid value.

	A (returns)	B (returns)	C (returns)
	-0.05288	-0.09384	-0.07475
	-0.04544	-0.03704	-0.06606
	-0.01718	-0.03507	-0.05751
	-0.01459	-0.02916	-0.04532
	-0.00859	-0.01404	-0.01193
	-0.00836	-0.01241	-0.01103
Median	-0.00447	-0.00774	-0.00275
	-0.00316	0.008035	0
	0.008735	0.008412	0.0004
	0.025302	0.013177	0.006699
	0.025558	0.014565	0.013187
	0.034016	0.025751	0.013237
	0.063689	0.056728	0.048184

Finally, let's compute the covariance and then correlations using the formulae given in the previous covariance section.

A (returns)	B (returns)	C (returns)	Cov(A,B)	Cov(B,C)
-0.0528806	-0.093843	-0.07475	0.004562	0.005184
-0.0454419	-0.103097	0.00133	0.001505	
-0.0171761	-0.03507	-0.05751	0.000472	0.001171
-0.014595	-0.029159	-0.04532	0.000315	0.000657
-0.0085871	-0.014045	-0.01193	5.41E-05	-1.50E-05
-0.0083594	-0.012411	-0.01103	3.87E-05	-1.50E-05
A (returns)	B (returns)	C (returns)	Cov(A,B)	Cov(B,C)
-0.0044732	-0.007738	-0.00275	-7.30E-07	-1.84E-06
-0.0031596	0.0080346	0	-5.40E-05	0.00023
0.0087345	0.008412	0.0004	0.000139	0.000242
0.025302	0.0131775	0.006699	0.000529	0.000445
0.0255585	0.0145651	0.013187	0.00057	0.00062
0.0340157	0.0257511	0.013237	0.001138	0.000931
0.0636886	0.0567282	0.048184	0.004103	0.004047
		Covariance	0.001015	0.001154
		Correlation	0.939734	0.942151

Properties of expectation, variance, and covariance

Let's combine the understanding of the previous and current chapters and conclude them.

This distribution of a variable is the probability of taking a particular value. The expectation is the population mean (which is the probability of the weighted average).

We can define a variance and standard deviation of the mean.

Finally, if we are looking at two different variables, we can define covariance and correlations. Now, let's understand how the expectations and variance of two groups can be computed. This becomes particularly useful in the next sections where we will analyze two variables together for linear regression is given here:

$E(x+y) = E(x) + E(y)$

$E(x+a) = E(x) + E(a) = a + E(x)$

$E(kx) = kE(x)$

Here is a very interesting rule:

$$E\left(\sum_{i=1}^{n} a_i x_i\right) = \sum_{i=1}^{n} a_i E(x_i)$$

Essentially, this rule says that if we have a portfolio of properties in a given fraction, then the total expectation is the weighted sum of the individual expectations. This is a crucial concept in the portfolio of analytics. If there is a portfolio of 30% company A, 50%, company B, and 20% company C stocks, the expected return of our portfolio is:

E (Portfolio) = 0.3 E(Company A) + 0.5 E(Company A) + 0.2 E (Company A)

Properties of variance

Given X, a random variable:

$Var(X+Y) = Var(X)+Var(Y)+2Cov(X,Y)$

$V(x+a) = V(x)$ (the variance does not change when a constant is added)

$V(ax) = a2\ V(x)$

Let's prove this as it is not obvious:

Say, $Y= aX$

$E(Y) = an\ E(X)$ (from the previous set of relations)

$Y-E(Y) = a(X-E(X))$

Squaring both sides and taking expectations:

$E(Y-E(Y))^2 = a^2\ E(X-E(x))^2$

However, the left-hand side is the variance of Y, and the right-hand side is the variance of X:

$Var\ (Y) = a^2 Var(X)$

Another couple of interesting properties of variance can be derived from the above. It follows directly that

$Var\ (-y) = Var\ (y)$

Let's now look at the variance of the portfolio:

$$v \sum a_i X_i = \sum a_i^2\ v\ (x_i) + 2\ \sum \sum a_i a_j cov\ (x_i, x_j)$$

So, if you have a portfolio of three stocks, the variance of your portfolio (or the standard deviation that is its square root) varies as shown previously. The standard deviation is often called the risk of the portfolio. Ideally, it needs to be as low as possible. From the previous formula, this can be done in two ways:

1. By selecting the elements whose variance is very low
2. By selecting the elements whose covariance is very negative

This is a crucial approach to a successful investment.

Properties of covariance

Following are the properties of covariance:

$cov(X, Y) = E[XY] - E[X]E[Y]$

$cov(x, a) = 0$

$cov(x, x) = var(x)$

$cov(y, x) = cov(x, y)$

$cov(ax, by) = abcov(x, y)$

$$cov(X+a, Y+b) = cov (X, Y)$$

$$cov(aX+bY, cW+dV) = accov(X,W) + adcov(X,V) + bccov(Y,W) + bdcov(Y,V)$$

$$Cor(X,Y) = E[XY]/\sigma X \sigma Y$$

Let's now see this using a real-world example.

Example

Two of your best friends, Ana and Daniel, are planning to invest in stock markets. As you are the most experienced investor in your friends circle, they approached you for advice. You know Daniel can handle a 10% risk whereas Ana wants the least possible risk. You obviously want to maximize the returns for both. They both want to invest in three items: gold bonds, a top IT company, and a top bank.

	Gold	IT	Bank
Returns	15	25	17
SD	5	15	10

SD—Standard Deviation

Correlations can be computed as follows:

	Gold	IT	Bank
Gold	1	-1	-0.5
IT	-1	1	0.5
Bank	-0.5	0.5	1

Now, let's derive the advice systematically.

Let's first create a list of all the possible weights (assuming you need to compute up to a single decimal point) for three assets. There can be approximately 66 values possible. This means that our friends must pick from one of these choices to invest. Now, calculate the returns for each possible portfolio (a unique combination of weights) using the following formula (again use any language you like):

$$Return\ from\ portfolio = W_g\ X\ R_g + W_i\ X\ R_i + w_b\ X\ R_b W_g$$

$$W_i, W_b = weights\ and$$

$$R_i, R_g, R_b = returns$$

This is because the expectation of a portfolio is the summation of the expectations of individual portfolio multiplied by individual weights.

The values for the first five portfolios are:

Portfolio1	0	1	0	25
Portfolio2	0	0.9	0.1	24.2
Portfolio3	0	0.8	0.2	23.4
Portfolio4	0	0.7	0.3	22.6
Portfolio5	0	0.6	0.4	21.8

Compute all the other values.

Calculate the risk of each portfolio using the following formula:

$$\text{Return} = \text{Sqrt} ((wg*sdg)^2 + (Wi*sdi)^2 + (Wb*sdb)^2 + (2*Wg*sdg*Wi*sdi*rgi) + (2*Wi*sdi*Wb*sdb*rib) + (2*Wb*sdb*wg*sdg*rbg))$$

sdg, sdb, sdi = Risks and rij = correlations of i and j

This is exactly the same formula for the variance of a portfolio as given in one of the previous sections.

wg	wi	wb	SD
0	1	0	15
0	0.9	0.1	14.03
0	0.8	0.2	13.11
0	0.7	0.3	12.28
0	0.6	0.4	11.53

Now lets compute all the other values.

Now, all that is needed is to recommend the balanced portfolios for both Ana and Daniel as their risk appetites are known to you. As Ana prefers zero risk, we will pick the point that corresponds to 17.2% returns and 0.87 risks. You can look up in the table and confirm that this is obtained with the portfolio of 0.7, 0.2, and 0.1 (Gold, IT, and Bank). As Daniel can take 10% risk, we will see the portfolio that corresponds to 10% risk, which has the highest return.

Again, this can be read as 0.2, 0.7, and 0.1.

ANOVA and F Statistics

In cases like bivariate and multivariate distributions, a good quantity to understand is the way the variance is distributed within the populations or groups and between the populations or groups. This is the process of grouping data into multiple subsets. As you can clearly see, in such situations it really helps to know how variance is distributed among them. Such an analysis is called the **ANOVA (Analysis of Variance)**. The calculations involved are fairly straightforward.

Let's take three samples that have their own mean and distribution as depicted here:

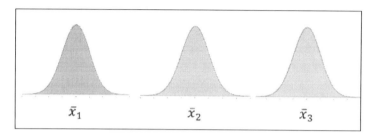

And in terms of an example, see the following:

Sample 1= {3, 2, 1}

Sample 2= {5, 3, 4}

Sample 3= {5, 6, 7}

Mean for Sample 1 = 2

Mean for Sample 2 = 4

Mean for Sample 3 = 6

Overall grand mean = (3+2+1+5+3+4+5+6+7) / 9 = 4

The grand mean (which will be the population mean if the groups cover the entire population) is equal to the mean of means.

Is it possible that the three means come from the same population? If one mean value is very different or far from the others, would that mean they are not from the same population? Or are they equally far apart?

All the previous samples are about relative distance measures from the grand mean.

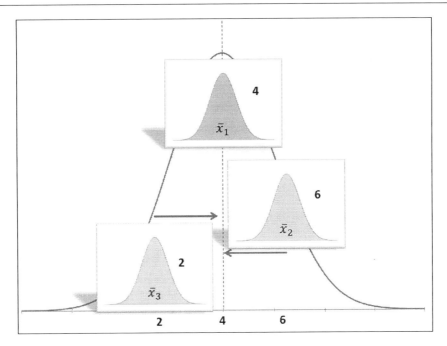

Let's now compute the sum of the squares of the entire sample set:

$(3 - 4)^2 + (2 - 4)^2 + \ldots = 30$

We could have calculated the variance by dividing the previously mentioned quantity with the degrees of freedom $(n*m\text{-}1)$:

n — number of elements in each sample

m — number of samples

The property that we are trying to establish does not change. Hence, let's just stick with the sum of squares instead of the variance. Now, let's compute two quantities: the sum of squares of the group and between the groups.

- **The sum of squares of the group**: Let's take the first group (3, 2, and 1) where the mean is 2. The variation (we are not calling it variance. But, it is definitely a measure of variance) within the group is equal to $(3\text{-}2)2+\ldots=2$. Similarly, variation within group 2 and group 3 are equal to 2 and 2. So, the total variation contributed within the groups is 6. The total number of the degrees of freedom within each group is $n\text{-}1$. The total degrees of freedom is $(n\text{-}1)*m$. This is 6 in this case.

- **The sum of squares between the groups**: This is measured as the distances between the mean of the group, and the grand mean, which is multiplied by the number of elements in the group mean of group 1 is 2, and grand mean is 4. So, the variation of this group from the grand mean is *(2-4)2 * 3 = 12*. The variation for the second group is 0 and for the third is 12. So, the variation between the groups is 24. The degree of freedom, in this case, is *m-1 = 2*.

So, let's document this:

	Variation	DOF
Total	30	8(mn-1)
Within	6	6(m(n-1)
Between	24	2(m-1)

So, we see that of the total variation of 30, 6 is contributed by variation within and 24 is contributed by variation between the groups. So most likely, it makes sense to group them separately. Now, let's do some kind of inferential statistics here. Let's assume that the previous values are the ranks obtained by three coaching centers. We want to know whether putting people in a coaching center actually has an impact on their final rank.

Let's start with a hypothetical argument.

Null Hypothesis is that coaching centers do not have an impact on the rank. Alternative coaching centers do have an impact on the rank.

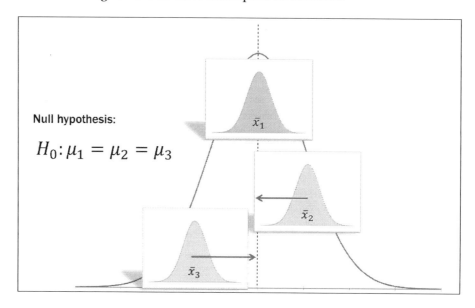

Null hypothesis:

$$H_0: \mu_1 = \mu_2 = \mu_3$$

If we observe, this measure is not about the values being equal, but it would be a check if the samples come from the same larger population. This measure is called the variability among or between the sample means.

So in short, ANOVA is a variability ratio represented as follows:

ANOVA = Variance Between / Variance Within = Distance between the overall mean / internal spread

Total Variance = Variance Between + Variance Within

This process of separating total variance into two components is called partitioning:

- If the variance between the means is > variance within the means, it will mean that the variability ratio is > 1. Hence, we can conclude that the samples do not belong to the same population.

- If the variance between the means and within the means is similar, then the ratio almost becomes 1, and this would indicate an overlap.

- If the variance between the means < the variance with the means, it will mean that the samples are close to the overall mean or the distributions *melt* together.

So, as we can see while dealing with multiple variables that there can be many factors that influence the outcome. Each of these variables will need to be assessed for the independent effect on the relationship between variables. In the next section, two concepts, **confounding** and **effect modification**, will explain the different types of influence factors on the outcome.

Confounding

We will start understanding what confounding is using an example. Let's assume we are doing a study where we want to determine if the risk of developing heart disease has anything to do with smoking. When a study was done on sample data that had a mix of smokers and non-smokers and those who were detected to have a heart disease over a period of time, a measure of association such as a *risk ratio* was done, and it was found to be 2.0. This can be interpreted as the risk of a smoker developing a heart disease being twice as much as that of a non-smoker. Now, when we look closely at the data, let's assume that we find the age distribution among the smokers and non-smokers is not the same, and it turns out that the age of smokers in the sample is much higher than the age of non-smokers. If we had to correlate this piece of information, is the outcome of developing heart disease to do with the old age, smoking or both?

An ideal way of measuring the quantitative effect of smoking on developing heart disease is to take a sample of people, observe them smoke over a period of time, collect the data on heart disease development, use the same set of people, and go back in time to run the same assessment when they are not smoking. This would help measure the counterfactual outcomes. The same group of people represents both smokers and non-smokers. Since this is not a possibility, we need to assume there is *exchangeability*. Non-smokers describe smokers if they ever smoke and vice-versa. This, in other words, means the two groups are comparable in all respects/aspects. In the cases where the data samples are not comparable, the condition is termed as confounding, and the property that is responsible for it (in this case, age) is called the **confounder**. If we have to explain this with an example, the fact that all non-smokers are younger, the non-smokers will under-estimate the outcome of older smokers had they not smoked.

This condition can be represented as shown here:

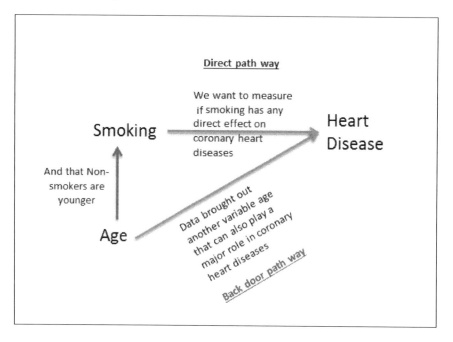

What we observe is that there is a backdoor pathway (through the age property). Confounding can thus be defined in a much simpler term, that is, *the existence of a backdoor pathway*.

 Confounding is a situation in which the effect or association between exposure and outcome is distorted by the presence of another variable.

Effect modification

Effect modification is the condition when exposures have different values for different groups. This can be observed when the measures of association estimation, like odds ratio, rate ratio, and risk ratio values, are very close to a weighted average of group-specific estimates from the association.

The effect modifier is the variable that differentially (this can mean positively or negatively) modifies the observed effect on the outcome.

Let's look at an example. Breast cancer can occur both in men and women; the ratio occurs in both men and women, but the rate at which it occurs in women is 800 times more than men, and the gender factor is a differentiating one for obvious reasons.

If the effect modifier is not properly identified, this could result in an incorrect crude estimate, and this results in missing the opportunity to understand the relationship between the risk factor and the outcome.

The following steps need to be followed to study the effect modification for analyzing the data:

1. Gather information on potential effect modifiers.
2. Study the effect of the effect modifier, measure the difference, and hold on from matching the values.
3. Stratify the data by potential effect modifiers and calculate estimates of the effect of the risk on the outcome. Determine if effect modification is present. If so, the estimates can be presented/used.

To review, confounders mask a true effect and effect modifiers mean that there is a different effect for different groups.

Regression methods

As we learned, regression allows us to model the relationship between two or more variables, especially when a continuous dependent variable is predicted, based on several independent variables. The independent variables used in regression can be either continuous or dichotomous. In cases where the dependent variable is dichotomous, logistic regression is applied. In cases where the split between the two levels of dependent variables is equal, then both linear and logistic regression would fetch the same results.

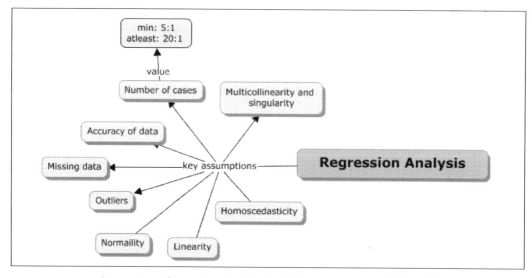

Assumptions of regression (most apply to linear regression model family)

- **Sample cases size**: In order to apply regression models, the cases-to-Independent Variables (IVs) ratio should ideally be 20:1 (for every IV in the model, there need to be 20 cases), the least being 5:1(5 cases for every IV in the model).

- **Data accuracy**: Regression assumes the basic validity of data, and it is expected to run basic data validations before running regression methods. For example, if a variable can have values between 1-5, any value not in the range will need to be corrected.

- **Outliers**: As we learned, outliers are those data points that usually have extreme values and don't naturally appear to be a part of the population. Regression assumes that the outlier values are handled.

- **Missing data**: It is important to look for missing data and address the same. If a specific variable has many missing values, it might be good to eliminate the variable unless there are too many variables with many missing values. Once the regression process is run, the variable that has no values can be a candidate for exclusion. And to avoid the risk of losing data through elimination, missing value techniques will need to be applied

- **Normal distribution**: It is necessary for the data to be checked to ensure that your data is normally distributed. Plotting data on a histogram is a way to check if the data is normally distributed. The following histogram is an example of normal distribution:

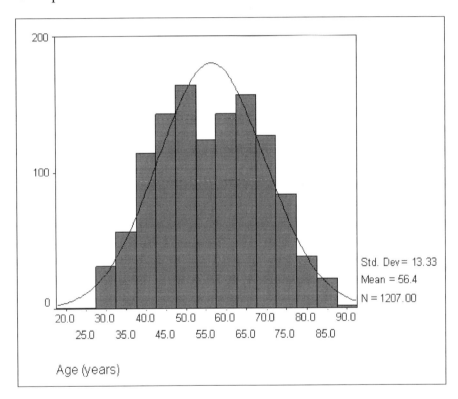

- **Linear behavior**: Linear behavior is, in simple terms, seeing a straight line relationship between the dependent and independent variables. Any non-linear relationship between the IV and DV is ignored. A bivariate scatterplot is used to test for linearity.

- **Homoscedasticity**: Homoscedasticity refers to the constant changes to an independent variable for a change in the dependent variable. The following scatter plot is an example of data being homoscedastic, and we can see the concentration of plottings in the center:

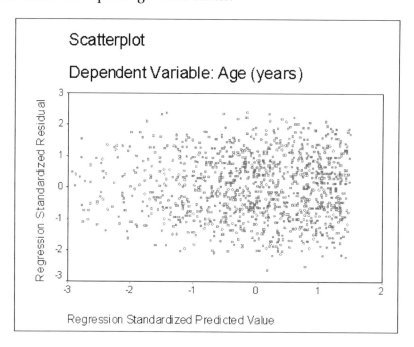

Similar to the assumption of linearity, violation of the assumption of homoscedasticity does not invalidate regression but weakens it.

- **Multicollinearity and singularity**: Multicollinearity is a case where independent variables are highly correlated. In the case of singularity, the independent variables are perfectly correlated and, usually, one IV is a combination of one or more other IVs. Both multicollinearity and singularity can be easily identified using the correlation between IVs.

From the following section onwards, we will cover each of the regression methods in depth as listed in the concept map here:

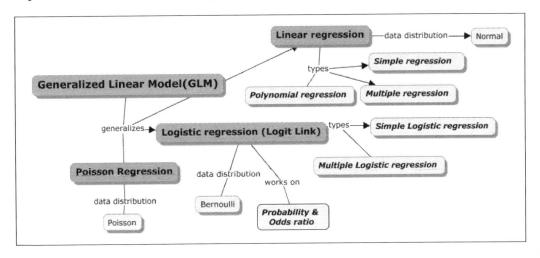

Simple regression or simple linear regression

In this case, we will be working with just two variables; one dependent variable and another independent variable. Simple linear regression is all about comparing two models; one where there is no independent variable and the best fit line is formed using the dependent variable, and the other that uses the best-fit regression line. Now let's look at an example to understand the best fit line and regression line definitions.

We will start with a real-world example. Let's assume there is a real-estate dealer and for every real-estate transaction that he does, he gets a commission. Very obviously, the commission amount dependents on the value of the transaction; the higher the value of the transaction, the higher the commission. So in this case, the commission becomes a dependent variable, and the transaction amount becomes an independent variable. In order to predict what could possibly be the next commission amount, let's consider the sample data of the last six transactions as follows:

Trns #	Commision ($)
1	5000
2	17000
3	11000
4	8000
5	14000
6	5000

Let's assume that we do not have data for the overall transaction amount. If we were to predict the next commission given in the previous data, we start by plotting it on a graph as shown here:

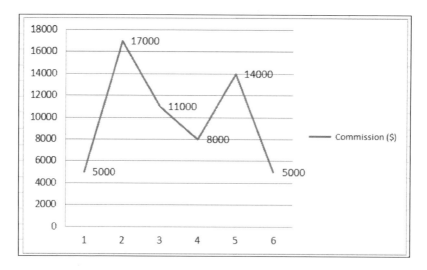

One of the options we have to identify the next commission amount that is given in the data is to compute the mean, which is the best prediction for the sample.

Trns #	Commision ($)
1	5000
2	17000
3	11000
4	8000
5	14000
6	5000
Mean	10000

Let's plot this point on the graph and this would become the *best* fit. Plotting the mean value on the previous graph:

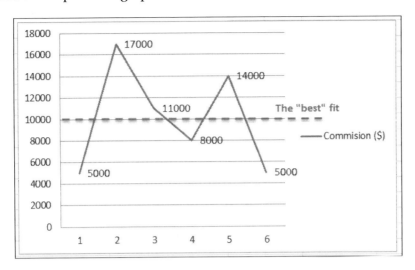

Computing the distance for each point from the mean gives the values that are shown in the next graph. This distance measure is called error or residual. The sum of the error for all the points is always found to be zero, and this is the measure of the goodness of the fit.

Trns #	Commision ($)	error
1	5000	-5000
2	17000	7000
3	11000	1000
4	8000	-2000
5	14000	4000
6	5000	-5000
Total Error		0

Plotting the distance on the graph.

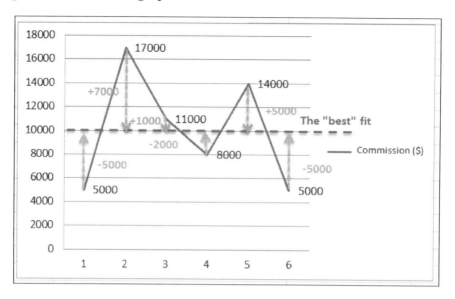

We have learned in our earlier chapters about the **SSE (Sum Squared Error)** value. The error is squared because it makes the value positive and also emphasizes larger deviations. The following table shows the SSE values computed for the sample data:

Trns #	Commision ($)	error	error $\wedge$ 2
1	5000	-5000	25000000
2	17000	7000	49000000
3	11000	1000	1000000
4	8000	-2000	4000000
5	14000	4000	16000000
6	5000	-5000	25000000
		SSE	120000000

The overall goal of a simple linear regression is to build a model that minimizes SSE to a maximum extent. Until now, we have seen the best fit using a single variable, which is the dependent variable. Now, let's assume we get the data for another independent variable in our example. This, in fact, gets us a new regression line that is different from the best fit line that we arrived at previously. It is expected that the new independent variable should significantly reduce the SSE value. In other words, this new regression line should be a better fit for the given data.

If there is no difference in the earlier best-fit line and the regression line, this would mean that the identified independent variable has no influence on the outcome. Overall, simple linear regression is designed to find the best fitting line using the data that would have the least amount of SSE value.

Let's now add the independent variable data into our analysis—the real-estate transaction value, as shown in the table here:

Transaction ($)	Commision ($)
34000	5000
108000	17000
64000	11000
88000	8000
99000	14000
51000	5000

We will plot a scatter plot between the dependent and the independent variable.

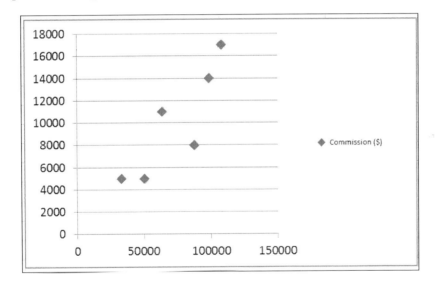

There could be multiple lines/equations possible in this context as shown in the next graph. In case the data seems to be falling in line, we can proceed. If the data points are scattered all over the place, this is an indication that there is no linearity in data, and we could choose to stop deriving the regression line. We could choose to compute the correlation coefficient here as follows:

r = 0.866

This indicates that the relationship between the two variables is strong, and we can proceed to build the regression model.

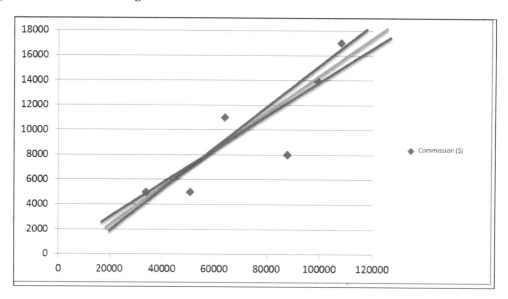

Let's now compute the mean for the x and y-axis; here are the values:

	Transaction ($)	Commision ($)
	34000	5000
	108000	17000
	64000	11000
	88000	8000
	99000	14000
	51000	5000
Mean	74000	10000

These mean values are to then be plotted as a centroid onto the scattered plot, as shown here:

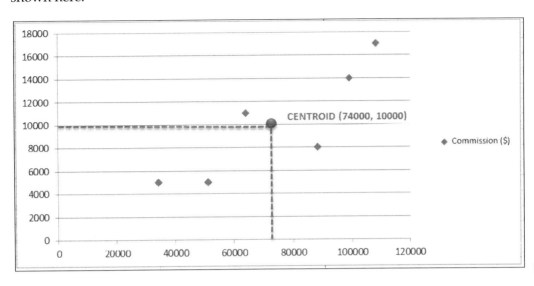

The best-fit regression line has to go through the centroid that comprises the mean of the x and y variables. The calculations are as follows:

$$\hat{y}_i = b_0 + b_1 x_i$$

$$b_1 = \frac{\sum (x_i - \bar{x})(y_i - \bar{y})}{\sum (x_i - \bar{x})^2}$$

$\bar{x} = mean\ of\ the\ independent\ variable \quad x_i = value\ of\ independent\ variable$

$\bar{y} = mean\ of\ the\ dependent\ variable \quad\quad y_i = value\ of\ dependent\ variable$

	Transaction ($)	Commision ($)	Txn Deviation	Comm Deviation	Dev Product	Square Txn Dev
	34000	5000	-40000	-5000	200000000	1600000000
	108000	17000	34000	7000	238000000	1156000000
	64000	11000	-10000	1000	-10000000	100000000
	88000	8000	14000	-2000	-28000000	196000000
	99000	14000	25000	4000	100000000	625000000
	51000	5000	-23000	-5000	115000000	529000000
Mean	74000	10000		Sum	615000000	4206000000

The final regression line equation looks like this:

$$\hat{y}_i = b_0 + b_1 x_i \qquad b_0 = -0.8188 \qquad b_1 = 0.1462$$

$$\text{intercept} \qquad\qquad \text{slope}$$

$$\hat{y}_i = -0.8188 + 0.1462x$$

OR

$$\hat{y}_i = 0.1462x - 0.8188$$

Plotting the previous equation on the scatter plot looks like this:

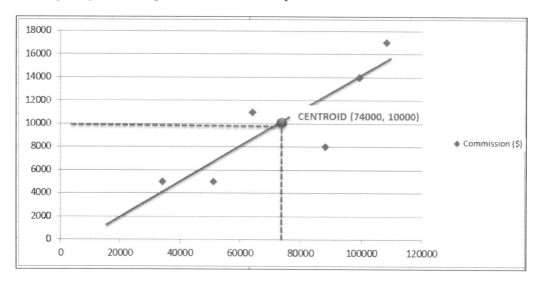

Multiple regression

Multiple regression is an extension of simple linear regression with one important difference, that there can be two or more independent variables used for predicting or explaining the variance in one dependent variable. Adding more independent variables does not necessarily make the regression better. There could potentially be two problems that could arise, one of which is over-fitting. We have covered this in the earlier chapters. Too many independent variables can add to the variance but in reality, they add nothing to the model thus causing over-fitting. Also, adding more independent variables adds more relationships. It is not only that the independent variables are potentially related to the dependent variables, but also there could be a dependency between the independent variables themselves. This condition is called multicollinearity. The ideal expectation is that the independent variables are correlated with the dependent variables, but not with each other.

As a result of over-fitting and multicollinearity issues, there is a need for preparatory work before a multiple regression analysis work is to be started. The preparatory work can include computing correlations, mapping scatter plots, and running simple linear regression among others.

Let's say, we have one dependent variable and four independent variables, and there is a multicollinearity risk. This means there are four relationships between the four independent variables and one dependent variable, and among the independent variables, there could be six more. So, there are 10 relationships to consider as shown here. DV stands for dependent variable and IV stands for independent variable.

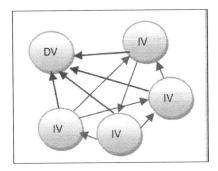

Some independent variables are better than others for predicting the dependent variable, and some might not contribute anything to the prediction. There is a need to decide which one of the dependent variables to consider.

In multiple regression, each coefficient is interpreted as the estimated change in y corresponding to a one-unit change in the variable, while the rest of the variables are assumed constant.

The following are the multiple regression equations.

$$y = \boxed{\beta_0 + \beta_1 x_1 + \beta_2 x_2 + \cdots \beta_p x_p} + \boxed{\epsilon}$$

linear parameters   error

$$E(y) = \beta_0 + \beta_1 x_1 + \beta_2 x_2 + \cdots \beta_p x_p$$

error term assumed to be zero

$$\hat{y} = b_0 + b_1 x_1 + b_2 x_2 + \cdots b_p x_p$$

$b_0, b_1, b_2, \ldots b_p$ are the estimates of $\beta_0, \beta_1, \beta_2, \ldots \beta_p$

$\hat{y}$ = predicted value of the dependent variable

Let's say we want to fit an independent variable as a function of a lot of variables (x, y, and x^2). We can follow a simple procedure to get the coefficients of all the variables. This is applicable for linear, quadratic, and cubic functions.

The following is the step-by-step process:

1. Order all the points of each variable in a separate column.
2. Combine all the columns of the independent variables to be represented as a matrix.
3. Add a column to the 1's at the beginning of the matrix.
4. Name this matrix as X Matrix.
5. Make a separate column matrix of all independent variables and call it Y Matrix.
6. Compute the coefficients using the formula here (this is the least square regression):

   $B = (X^T X)^{-1} X^T Y$

This is a matrix operation, and the resulting vector is the coefficient.

In multiple regression, a lot of preparatory work needs to be done before running the regression model. It is necessary to step back and perform some analysis on the variables in consideration. Some basic scatter plots can be plotted to check for any correlations and to analyze the relationships between the dependent variables. Techniques like scatter plots, correlation analysis, and individual or group regressions can be used. In case there are any qualitative or categorical variables, we will need to use dummy variables to build the regression model.

Polynomial (non-linear) regression

While the linear regression model $y = X\beta + \varepsilon$ is a general model that will fit any linear relationship in the unknown parameter β, polynomial models are applicable in cases where the analyst knows that curvilinear effects are present in the true response function. Polynomial models are also used as approximating functions to the unknown and possibly very complex nonlinear relationship. The polynomial model is the Taylor series expansion of the unknown function.

If the two variables are linearly related, the scatterplot looks like the following:

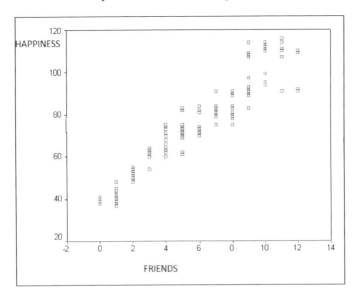

From the previous bivariate scatterplot, it is clear that there is a linear relationship between friends and happiness. The graph says *more friends, more happiness*. What if we talk about a curvilinear relationship between the variables, the number of friends and happiness? This means as the number of friends grows, the happiness grows but only to a certain point. The following graph shows this behavior in data:

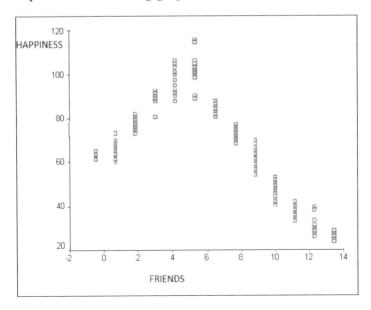

If the data is not linear, then the process is to make it linear by transforming IVs or the DV so that there is a linear relationship between them. This transformation will not always work as there might be a genuine non-linearity in data and behavior. In this case, we will need to include the square of the independent variables in the regression. This is also known as a polynomial/quadratic regression. The **least squares** method is used to fit a polynomial regression model as it minimizes the variance in the estimation of the coefficients.

Generalized Linear Models (GLM)

Let's look at the reasons why a linear regression model does not work.

Simple linear regression is a quantitative variable predicting another, multiple regression. It is an extended simple linear regression, but with more independent variables and finally, a nonlinear or polynomial regression is the case where there are two quantitative variables, but the data is curvilinear.

Now, running a typical linear regression, in the same way, has some problems. Binary data does not have a normal distribution. This is where the need for other regression models comes in. Secondly, the predicted values of the dependent variable can be beyond 0 and 1, which is against the concept of probability. Finally, probabilities are often non-linear and can take majorly low or high values at the extremes.

GLM is a generalization of linear regression that supports cases where the independent variables can have distribution error models other than normal distribution. GLM generalizes linear regression as it allows the linear model to be related to the independent variable through a link function, and it also allows the degree of the variance of each measure is a function of its predicted value.

In short, GLM generalizes linear, logistic, and Poisson regression models.

Logistic regression (logit link)

Logistic regression is an extension of linear regression where the dependent variable is a categorical variable that is responsible for the classification of the observations.

For example, if Y denotes whether a particular customer is likely to purchase a product (1) or unlikely to purchase (0), we have a categorical variable with two categories or classes (0 and 1). Logistic regression can solve a classification problem where the class is unknown. This is done using the predictor values classifying a new observation, where the class is unknown, into one of the classes, based on the variable.

The examples are as follows:

- Classifying customers as returning (1) or non-returning (0)
- Predicting if a loan would be approved or rejected, given the credit score

One of the important uses can be to find similarities between predictor values.

Before we start taking a deep dive into logistic regression, let's revisit the concept of probability and the odds that were covered in the earlier chapter.

Probability = outcomes of interest / all possible outcomes.

For example, when a fair coin is tossed, *P(heads)* = ½ = *0.5*. When a dice is rolled, *P(1 or 2)* = *2/6* = *1/3* = *0.33*. In a deck of cards, *P(diamond card)* = *13/52* = *¼* = *0.25*.

Odds = P(something happening)/P(something not happening) = p/1-p

For example, when a coin is tossed, *odds(heads* = *0.5/0.5= 1)*. When a dice is rolled, *odds(1 or 2)* = *0.333/0.666* = *½* = *0.5*. In a deck of cards, *odds(diamond card)* = *0.25/0.75* = *1/3* = *0.333*.

The odds ratio is the ratio of two odds.

For example, when a coin is tossed, in case of a fair flip:

P(heads) = *½= 0.5* and *odds(heads)* = *0.5/0.5* = *1* = *1:1*

In case of a loaded coin flip:

P(heads) = *0.7 and odds(heads)* = *0.7/0.3* = *2.333*

Odds ratio= odds1/odds0 = *2.333/1* = *2.333*

This means the odds of getting a heads when a loaded coin is flipped is 2.333 times greater than a fair coin.

Overall, logistic regression seeks to:

- **Model** the probability of the event occurring depending on the values of the independent variables, which can be categorical or numerical
- **Estimate** the probability of an event occurring versus not occurring
- **Predict** the effect of a set of variables on a binary response variable
- **Classify** the observations to belong to a particular category based on the probability estimation

Odds ratio in logistic regression

The odds ratio for a variable in logistic regression denotes how the odds for one variable changes with the increase of a unit in that variable, keeping the rest of the variables constant.

Let's take an example to understand this—whether the body weight is dependent on sleep apnea or not. Let's assume that the body weight variable has an odds ratio of 1.07. This means one pound increased in weight could potentially increase the odds of having slept apnea by 1.07 times. This might not be significant. In the case of a 10-pound increase in weight, the odds increase to 1.98, which doubles the odds of the person having slept apnea. It is important that we separate the probability and the odds measures. For example, though the increase in weight by 20 pounds increases the odds of the person having slept by 4 times, the probability that the person's weight has increased by 20 pounds could potentially be very low.

In logistic regression, there are two important steps:

1. Finding the probability of belonging to a particular class. So, if $Y = 0$ or 1, the probability of belonging to *class 1* is *P(Y=1)*.

2. We will need to use the cut-off values of the probabilities to ensure that each case gets into one of the classes. In case of binary cut-off, a *P(Y=1) > 0.5* will be categorized as *1* and *P(Y=0) < 0.5* will be categorized as *0*.

Model

y_i is normally distributed and takes the value of either 0 or 1 for $i = 0,1,...,n$.

y_i is equal to {0, 1} where $P(y_i = 1) = p$ and $P(y_i = 0) = 1-p$

$Y = a + bx$ for $P(y_i = 1)$

$p_i = a + bx_i$

Note that p_i will not take values between $(0, 1)$. This is fixed by using a non-linear function of predictors such as:

$$p_i = \frac{1}{1+e^{-(a+bx_i)}} \quad \textit{(This is called the logistic response function)}$$

Clearly, this takes a value between 0 and 1 as x varies from $-\infty$ to ∞. From this, $a+bx_i$ can be obtained as follows:

$$\log \frac{p_i}{1-p_i} = a+bx_i$$

$$\frac{p_i}{1-p_i} = e^{\hat{a}+\hat{b}x_i}$$

$$\widehat{p_i} = \frac{e^{\hat{a}+\hat{b}x_i}}{1+e^{\hat{a}+\hat{b}x_i}}$$

The following curve shows how the function varies:

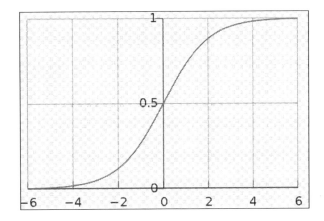

Poisson regression

Poisson regression, in the context of GLM, is a count of data with the independent variable having Poisson distribution and the link function applied is a logarithm of the response that can be modeled using a linear combination of unknown parameters.

Implementing linear and logistic regression

Refer to the source code provided for this chapter for implementing linear regression. (source code path .../chapter10/... under each of the folders for the technology)

Using Mahout

Refer to the folder `.../mahout/chapter10/linearregressionexample/`.

Refer to the folder `.../mahout/chapter10/logisticregressionexample/`.

Using R

Refer to the folder `.../r/chapter10/linearregressionexample/`.

Refer to the folder `.../r/chapter10/logisticregressionexample/`.

Using Spark

Refer to the folder `.../spark/chapter10/linearregressionexample/`.

Refer to the folder `.../spark/chapter10/logisticregressionexample/`.

Using scikit-learn

Refer to the folder `.../python-scikit-learn/chapter10/linearregressionexample/`

Refer to the folder `.../python-scikit-learn/chapter10/logisticregressionexample/`

Using Julia

Refer to the folder `.../julia/chapter10/linearregressionexample/`.

Refer to the folder `.../julia/chapter10/logisticregressionexample/`.

Summary

In this chapter, you learned regression analysis-based machine learning and, in particular, how to implement linear and logistic regression models using Mahout, R, Python, Julia, and Spark. Additionally, we covered other related concepts of statistics such as variance, covariance, and ANOVA among others. We covered regression models in depth with examples to understand how to apply them to real-world problems. In the next chapter, we will cover deep learning methods.

11
Deep learning

Until now, we covered a few supervised, semi-supervised, unsupervised, and reinforcement learning techniques and algorithms. In this chapter, we will cover neural networks and its relationship with the deep learning practices. The traditional learning approach was about writing programs that tell the computer what to do, but neural networks are about learning and finding solutions using observational data that forms a primary source of input. This technique's success depends on how the neural networks are trained (that is, the quality of the observational data). Deep learning refers to methods of learning the previously referenced neural networks.

The advancement in technology has taken these techniques to new heights where these techniques demonstrate superior performance, and are used to solve some key non-trivial requirements in computer vision, speech recognition, and **Natural Language Processing** (**NLP**). Large companies such as Facebook and Google, among many others, have adopted deep learning practices on a substantial basis.

The primary aim of this chapter is to enforce mastering the neural networks and related deep learning techniques conceptually. With the aid of a complex pattern recognition problem, this chapter covers the procedure to develop a typical neural network, which you will be able to use to solve a problem of a similar complexity. The following representation shows all the learning methods covered in this book, highlighting the primary subject of learning in this chapter—*Deep learning*.

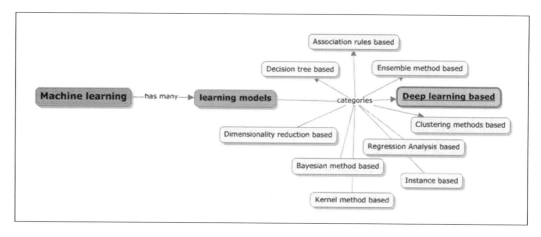

The chapter covers the following topics in depth:

- A quick revisit of the purpose of Machine learning, types of learning, and the context of deep learning with details on a particular problem that it solves.

- An overview of neural networks:
    - Human brain as the primary inspiration for neural networks
    - The types of neural network architectures and some basic models of neurons
    - A simple learning example (digit recognition)
    - An overview of perceptrons, the first generation of neural networks and what they are capable of doing and what they are not capable of doing

- An overview of linear and logistic output neurons. An introduction to back the propagation algorithm and applying the derivatives of back propagation algorithm for solving some real-world problems

- The concepts of cognitive science, the softmax output function, and handling multi-output scenarios

- Applying convolution nets and the problem of object or digit recognition
- **Recurrent neural networks (RNN)** and Gradient descent method
- Signal processing as the principle of component analysis and autoencoders; the types of autoencoders which are deep and shallow autoencoders
- A hands-on implementation of exercises using Apache Mahout, R, Julia, Python (scikit-learn), and Apache Spark

Background

Let's first recap the premise of Machine learning and reinforce the purpose and context of learning methods. As we learned, Machine learning is about training machines by building models using observational data, against directly writing specific instructions that define the model for the data to address a particular classification or a prediction problem. The word *model* is nothing but a *system* in this context.

The program or system is built using data and hence, looks as though it's very different from a hand-written one. If the data changes, the program also adapts to it for the next level of training on the new data. So all it needs is the ability to process large-scale as opposed to getting a skilled programmer to write for all the conditions that could still prove to be heavily erroneous.

We have an example of a Machine learning system called spam detector. The primary purpose of this system is to identify which mail is spam and which is not. In this case, the spam detector is not coded to handle every type of mail; instead, it learns from the data. Hence, it is always true that the precision of these models depends on how good the observational data is. In other words, the features extracted from the raw data should typically cover all the states of data for the model to be accurate. Feature extractors are built to extract standard features from the given sample of data that the classifier or a predictor uses.

Some more examples include recognizing patterns such as speech recognition, object recognition, face detection, and more.

Deep learning is a type of Machine learning that attempts to learn prominent features from the given data, and thus tries to reduce the task of building a feature extractor for every category of data (for example, image, voice, and so on.). For a face detection requirement, a deep learning algorithm records or learns features such as the length of the nose, the distance between the eyes, the color of the eyeballs, and so on. This data is used to address a classification or a prediction problem and is evidently very different from the traditional **shallow learning algorithm**.

The human brain

The human brain is known to be one of the most implausible organs in the human body. The brain is essentially what makes us, humans, intelligent. It is responsible for building our perceptions based on what we experience regarding our senses of touch, smell, sight, vision, and sound. These experiences are collected and stored as memories and emotions. Inherently, the brain is what makes us intelligent without which, we probably are just primitive organisms in the world.

The brain of a newborn infant is capable of solving problems that any complex and powerful machine cannot solve. In fact, just within a few days of birth, the baby starts recognizing the face and voice of his/her parents and starts showing the expressions of longing to see them when they are not around. Over a period, they begin associating sounds with objects and can even recognize an object given a sight. Now, how do they do this? If they come across a dog, how do they recognize it to be a dog; also, do they associate a barking sound with it and mimic the same sound?

It is simple. Every time the infant comes across a dog, his/her parents qualify it to be a dog, and this reinforces the child's model. In case they qualify the child to be wrong, the child's model would incorporate this information. So, a dog has long ears, long nose, four legs, a long tail, and can be of different colors such as black, white or brown, making a barking sound. These characteristics are recognized through sight and sound that an infant's brain records. The observational data thus collected drives the recognition of any new object henceforth.

Now, let's say the infant sees a wolf for the first time; he/she would identify a wolf to be a dog by looking at the similarity of its characteristics s. Now, if the parent feeds in the definite differences on the first sighting, for example, a difference in the sound that it makes, then it becomes a new experience and is stored in memory, which is applied to the next sighting. With the assimilation of more and more such examples, the child's model becomes more and more accurate; this process is very subconscious.

For several years, we have been working toward building machines that can be intelligent with brains as those of humans. We are talking about robots that can behave as humans do and can perform a particular job with similar efficiency to humans beings, such as driving a car, cleaning a house, and so on. Now, what does it take to build machines as robots? We probably need to build some super-complex computational systems that solve the problems our brain can solve in no time. This field that works on building artificially intelligent systems is called deep learning.

Following are some formal definitions of deep learning:

According to Wikipedia, Deep learning is a set of algorithms for machine learning that attempts to model high-level abstractions in data by using model architectures composed of multiple non-linear transformations.

According to `http://deeplearning.net/`, Deep learning is the new area of Machine learning research that has been introduced with the objective of moving Machine learning closer to one of its original goals—Artificial Intelligence.

This subject has evolved over several years; the following table lists research areas across the years:

Research Area	Year
Neural networks	1960
Multilayer Perceptrons	1985
Restricted Boltzmann Machine	1986
Support Vector Machine	1995
Hinton presents the **Deep Belief Network (DBN)** New interests in deep learning and RBM State of the art MNIST	2005
Deep Recurrent Neural Network	2009
Convolutional DBN	2010
Max-Pooling CDBN	2011

Among many others, some key contributors to this field are Geoffrey Hinton, Yann LeCun, Honglak Lee, Andrew Y. Ng, and Yoshua Bengio.

The following concept model covers different areas of Deep learning and the scope of topics covered in this chapter:

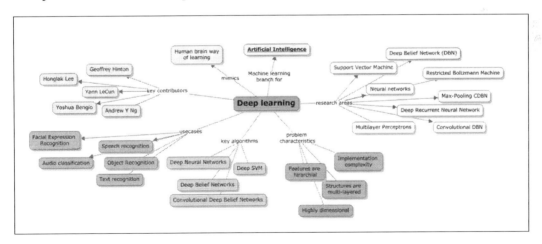

Let's look at a simple problem on hand; the requirement is to recognize the digits from the handwritten script given here:

For a human brain, this is very simple as we can recognize the digits as 287635. The simplicity with which our brain interprets the digits is perceptive that it undermines the complexity involved in this process. Our brain is trained to intercept different visuals progressively due to the presence of visual cortices, with each cortex containing more than 140 million neurons that have billions of connections between them. In short, our brain is no less than a supercomputer that has evolved over several millions of years and is known to adapt well to the visual world.

If a computer program has to crack the recognition of the digits, what should be the rules to identify and differentiate a digit from another?

Neural networks are one such field being researched for several years and is known to address the need for multilayered learning. The overall idea is to feed a large number of handwritten digits; an example of this data (training) is shown in the following image, and that can learn from these examples. This means the rules are automatically inferred from the provided training data. So, the larger the training dataset, the more accurate would be the prediction. If we are posed with a problem to differentiate the digit 1 from the digit 7 or the digit 6 from the digit 0, some minor differences will need to be learned. For a zero, the distance between the starting and ending point is minimal or nothing.

The difference is basically because these learning methods have been targeted to mimic a human brain. Let's see what makes this a difficult problem to solve.

In summary, with deep learning being a subset of Machine learning, we know that this involves the technique of feeding examples and a model that can evaluate the pattern to evolve it in case it makes a mistake. Thus, over a period of time, this model would solve the problem with the best possible accuracy.

If this needs to be represented mathematically, let's define our model to be a function $f(x,\theta)$.

Here, x is the input that is provided as a vector of values and θ is a reference vector that the model uses to predict or classify x. So, it is θ that we need to expose to a maximum set of examples in order to improve the accuracy.

Let's take an example; if we were to predict whether a visitor to a restaurant would come back based on two factors—one is the amount of bill (x_1) and the other is his/her age(x_2). When we collect data for a specific duration of time and analyze it for an output value that can be 1(in case the visitor came back) or -1(if the visitor has not come back). The data, when plotted, can take any form—from a linear relationship or any other complex form, as shown here:

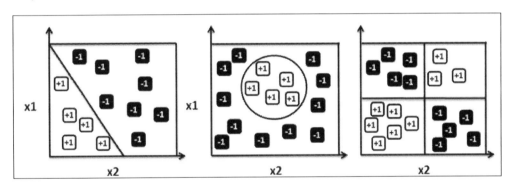

Something like a linear relationship looks straight forward and more complex relationships complicate the dynamics of the model. Can parameter θ have an optimal value at all? We might have to apply optimization techniques and in the next sections to follow, we will cover these techniques such as perceptrons and gradient descent methods among others. If we want to develop a program to do this, we need to know what our brain does to recognize these digits, and even if we knew, these programs might be very complex in nature.

Neural networks

Neural computations have been a primary interest of the study to understand how parallel computations work in neurons (the concept of flexible connections) and solve practical problems like a human brain does. Let's now look at the core fundamental unit of the human brain, the *neuron*:

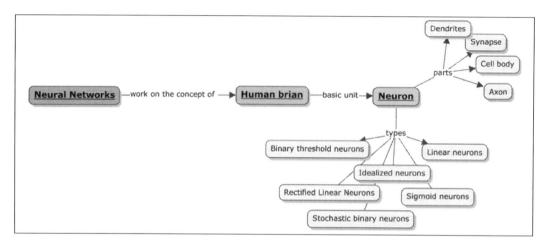

Neuron

The human brain is all about neurons and connections. A neuron is the smallest part of the brain, and if we take a small rice grain sized piece of the brain, it is known to contain at least 10000 neurons. Every neuron on an average has around 6000 connections with other neurons. If we look at the general structure of a neuron, it looks as follows.

Every feeling that we humans go through, be it thought or emotion, is because of these millions of cells in our brain called neurons. As a result of these neurons communicating with each other by passing messages, humans feel, act, and form perceptions. The diagram here depicts the biological neural structure and its parts:

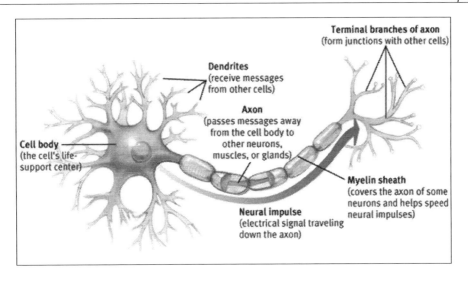

Every neuron has a central cell body; as any cell, in general, it has an axon and a dendritic tree that are responsible for sending and receiving messages respectively with other neurons. The place where axons connect to the dendritic tree is called a synapse. The synapses themselves have an interesting structure. They contain transmitter molecules that trigger transmission, which can either be positive or negative in nature.

The inputs to the neurons are aggregated, and when they exceed the threshold, an electrical spike is transmitted to the next neuron.

Synapses

The following diagram depicts the model of a synapse depicting the flow of messages from axon to dendrite. The job of the synapse is not just the transmission of messages, but in fact, adapt themselves to the flow of signals and have the ability to learn from past activities.

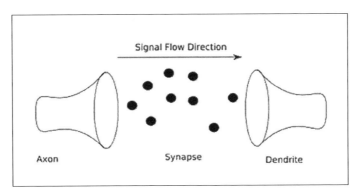

As an analogy in the field of Machine learning, the strength of the incoming connection is determined on the basis of how often it is used, and thus its impact on the neuron output is determined. This is how new concepts are learned by humans subconsciously.

There can additionally be external factors such as medication or body chemistry that might impact this learning process.

Now we will finally summarize how the learning happens inside the brain with the help of the following list:

- Neurons communicate with other neurons or sometimes receptors. The cortical neurons use spikes for communication.

- The strengths of connections between neurons can change. They can take positive or negative values by either establishing and removing connections between neurons or by strengthening the connection based on the influence that a neuron can have over the other. A process called **long-term potentiation (LTP)** occurs that results in this long-term impact.

- There are about 10^{11} neurons having weights that make the computations that the human brain can do more efficiently than a workstation.

- Finally, the brain is modular; different parts of the cortex are responsible for doing different things. Some tasks infuse more blood flow in some regions over the other and thus, ensuring different results.

Before schematizing the neuron model into the **artificial neural network (ANN)**, let us first look at different types, categories, or aspects of neurons, and in specific the Artificial neuron or Perceptron, the deep learning equivalent of a biological neuron. This approach is known to have produced extremely efficient results in some of the use cases we listed in the previous section. ANNs are also called feed-forward neural networks, **Multi-Layer Perceptrons (MLP)**, and, recently, deep networks or learning. One of the important characteristics has been the need for feature engineering, whereas deep learning represents applications that require minimum feature engineering, where learning happens through multiple learned layers of neurons.

Artificial neurons or perceptrons

It is obvious that artificial neurons draw inspiration from biological neurons, as represented previously. The features of an artificial neuron are listed here:

- There is a set of inputs received from other neurons that activate the neuron in context
- There is an output transmitter that transfers signals or an activation of the other neurons
- Finally, the core processing unit is responsible for producing output activations from the input activations

Idealizing for a neuron is a process that is applied to building models. In short, it is a simplification process. Once simplified, it is possible to apply mathematics and relate analogies. To this case, we can easily add complexities and make the model robust under identified conditions. Necessary care needs to be taken in ensuring that none of the significantly contributing aspects are removed as a part of the simplification process.

Linear neurons

Linear neurons are the simplest form of neurons; they can be represented as follows:

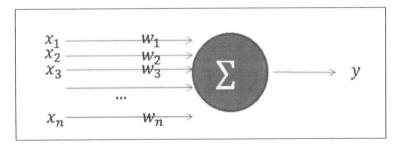

The output y is a summation of the product of the input x_i and its weight w_i. This is mathematically represented as shown here:

$$y = b + \sum_{i=1}^{n}\left(w_i x_i\right)$$

Here, b is the bias.

A graph representation of the previous equation is given as follows:

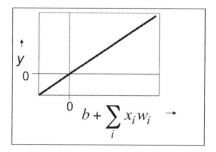

Rectified linear neurons / linear threshold neurons

Rectified linear neurons are similar to linear neurons, as explained in the preceding section, with a minor difference where the output parameter value is set to zero in cases where it is less than (<) zero (0), and in case the output value is greater than (>) zero (0), it continues to remain as the linear weighted sum of the inputs:

$$z = b + \sum_i x_i w_i$$

$$y = \begin{cases} z & \text{if } z > 0 \\ 0 & \text{otherwise} \end{cases}$$

Binary threshold neurons

The binary threshold neurons were introduced by McCulloch and Pitts in 1943. This class of neurons first have the weighted sum of the inputs computed, similar to the linear neurons. If this value exceeds a defined threshold, a fixed size spike to activity is sent out. This spike is called as the *truth value of a proposition*. Another important point is the output. The output at any given point in time is binary (0 or 1).

The equation that demonstrates this behavior is given here:

$$z = \sum_{i=1}^{n} \left(w_i x_i \right)$$

And

$y = 1$ if $z \geq \theta$,

$y = 0$ otherwise

here $\theta = -b$ *(bias)*

(OR)

$$z = b + \sum_{i=1}^{n} \left(w_i x_i \right)$$

And

$y = 1$ if $z \geq 0$,

$y = 0$ otherwise

Moreover, a graphical representation of the previous equation is given here:

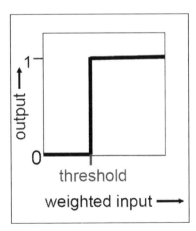

Sigmoid neurons

Sigmoid neurons are highly adopted in artificial neural networks. These neurons are known to provide the output that is smooth, real-valued, and therefore a bounded function of all the inputs. Unlike the types of the neurons that we have seen until now, these neurons use the logistic function.

The logistic function is known to have an easy-to-calculate derivative that makes learning easy. This derivative value is used in computing the weights. Following is the equation for the sigmoid neuron output:

$$z = b + \sum_{i=1}^{n}(w_i x_i)$$

$$y = \frac{1}{1 + e^{-z}}$$

The diagrammatic/graphical representation is as follows:

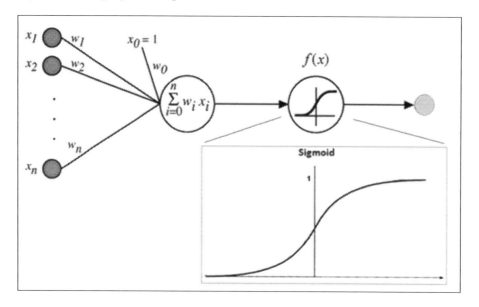

Stochastic binary neurons

Stochastic binary neurons use the same equation as logistic units, with one important difference that the output is measured for a probabilistic value, which measures the probability of producing a spike in a short window of time. So, the equation looks like this:

$$z = b + \sum_{i=1}^{n}\left(w_i x_i\right)$$

$$p\left(s=1\right) = \frac{1}{1+e^{-z}}$$

Moreover, the graphical representation of this equation is:

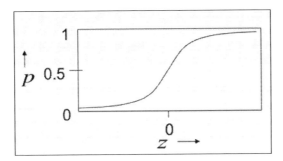

Overall, what we can observe is that each neuron takes in a weighted sum of a bunch of inputs on which a non-linear activation function is applied. Rectified linear function is typically applied for solving regression problems and for classification problems, logistic functions are applied. A generic representation of this can be given as follows:

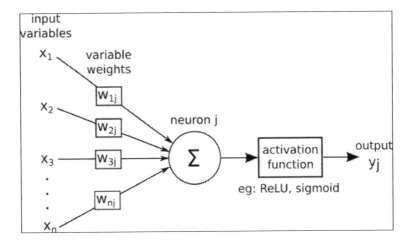

Now, these inputs can be fed into a series of layers of neurons. Let's look at what happens next and how this happens. The input layer pushes input values; the hidden layers of neurons then take the values as input. It is possible to have multiple layers within these hidden layers, where the output from one layer feeds as the input to the subsequent layer. Each of these layers can be responsible for the specialized learning. Moreover, finally, the last in the hidden layer feeds into the final output layer. This typical structure of an ANN is illustrated next. Every circle in the next diagram represents a neuron. The concept of the **Credit Assignment Path (CAP)** refers to the path from input to output. In the feed-forward networks, the length of the path is the total number of hidden layers along with the output layer. The following diagram shows a feed-forward neural network with a single hidden layer and connections between layers:

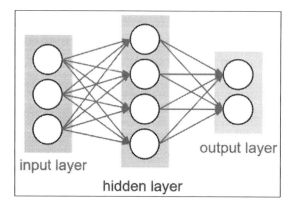

The case of two hidden layers are shown in here:

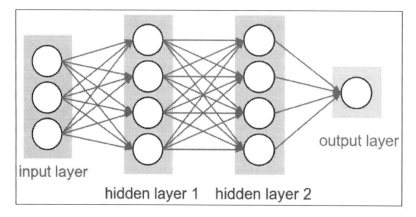

Neural Network size

Computing the number of neurons or parameters is shown here:

- For the single layer network:

  Total number of neurons = 4 + 2 = 6 (inputs are not counted)

  Total weights = [3 x 4] + [4 x 2] = 20

  Total bias = 4 + 2 = 6, for 26 learnable parameters.

- For the two layer network:

  Total number of neurons = 4 + 4 + 1 = 9 (inputs are not counted)

  Total weights = [3 x 4] + [4 x 4] + [4 x 1] = 12 + 16 + 4 = 32

  Total bias = 4 + 4 + 1 = 9 for 41 learnable parameters

So, what is the optimal size of neural networks? It is important to identify the possible number of hidden layers along with the size of each layer. These decisions determine the capacity of the network. A higher value helps to support a higher capacity.

Let's take an example where we will try three different sizes of the hidden layer by obtaining the following classifiers:

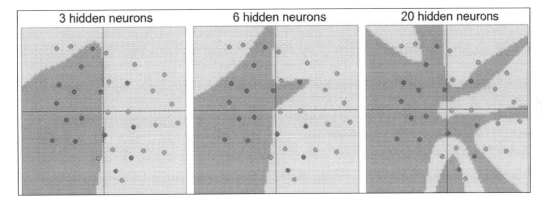

Clearly, with more neurons, functions with higher complexity can be expressed, which is good, but we need to watch out for the over-fitting case. So, a smaller-sized network works well for simpler data. With the increasing data complexity, the need for a bigger size arises. The trade-off is always between handling the complexity of the model versus. over-fitting. Deep learning addresses this problem as it applies complex models to extremely complex problems and handles over-fitting by taking additional measures.

An example

A face recognition case using the multi-layered perceptron approach is shown next:

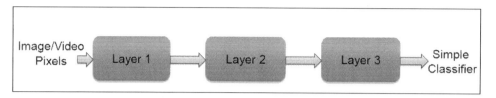

Multiple layers take this image as input and finally, a classifier definition is created and stored.

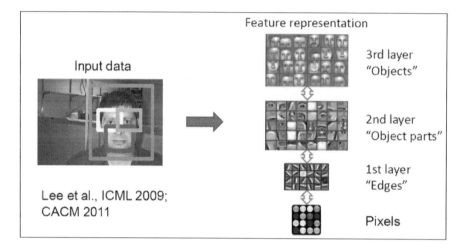

Given a photograph, each layer focuses on learning a specific part of the photograph and finally stores the output pixels.

Some key notes on the weights and error measures are as follows:

- The training data is the source of learning the weights of neurons
- The error measure or the cost function is different from the regression and classification problems. For classification, log functions are applied, and for regression, least square measures are used.
- These methods help to keep these error measures in check by updating the weights using convex optimization techniques such as decent gradient methods

Neural network types

In this section, we will cover some key types of neural networks. The following concept map lists a few principal types of neural networks:

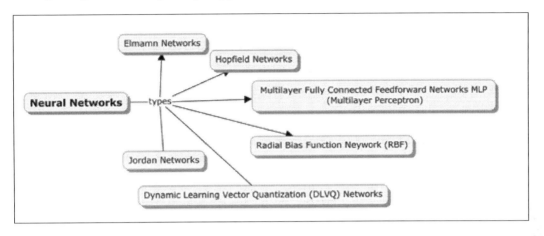

Multilayer fully connected feedforward networks or Multilayer Perceptrons (MLP)

As covered in the introductory sections about neural networks, an MLP has multiple layers where the output of one layer feeds as an input to a subsequent layer. A multilayer perceptron is represented as shown in the following diagram:

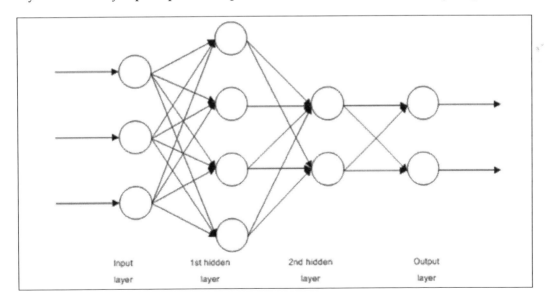

Jordan networks

Jordan networks are partially recurrent networks. These networks are the current feedforward networks with a difference of having additional context neurons inside the input layer. These context neurons are self-imposed and created using the direct feedback from input neurons. In Jordon networks, the number of context neurons is always equal to the input neurons. The following diagram depicts the difference in the input layer:

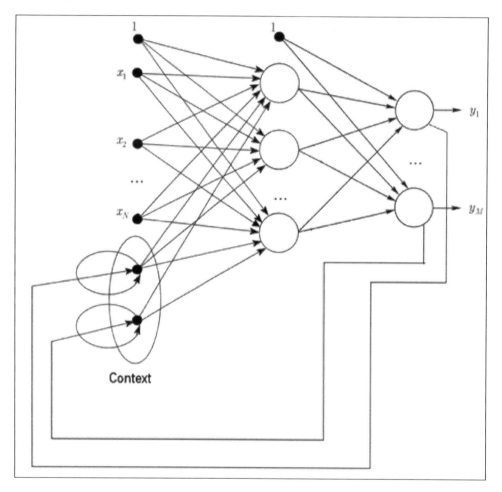

Elman networks

Elman networks, just as Jordon networks, are partially recurrent feedforward networks. These networks also have context neurons, but in this case, the main difference is that the context neurons receive the feed from the output neurons, and not from the hidden layers. There is no direct correlation between the number of context neurons and input neurons; rather, the number of context neurons is the same as the number of hidden neurons. This, in turn, makes this model more flexible, just as the number of hidden neurons do on a case-by-case basis:

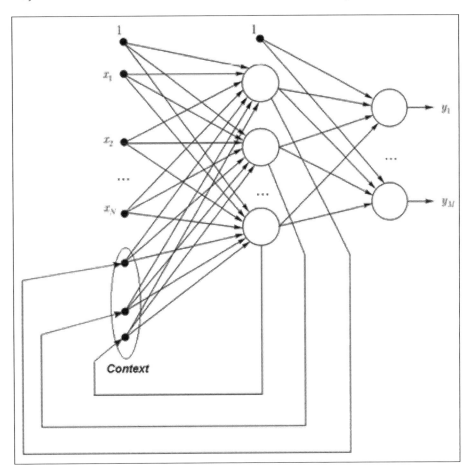

Radial Bias Function (RBF) networks

Radial Bias Function networks are also feed-forward neural networks. These networks have a special hidden layer of special neurons called radially symmetric neurons. These neurons are for converting the distance value between the input vector and the center using a Gaussian measure. The advantage of this additional layer is that it gives an additional capability to determine the number of layers required without a manual intervention. The choice of the linear function determines the optimal output layer. Therefore, the learning happens relatively faster in these networks even in comparison to back propagation.

The only downside of this method is its ability to handle large input vectors. The diagram below depicts the hidden layer of radially symmetric neurons.

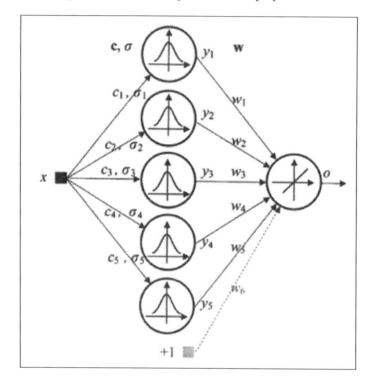

Hopfield networks

Hopfield networks work around a concept called *energy of network*. This is nothing but an optimal local minima of the network that defines an equilibrium state for the functionality. Hopfield networks target the state of achieving this equilibrium state. An equilibrium state is when the output of one layer becomes equal to the output of the previous layer. The following diagram depicts how the input and output states are checked and managed in the Hopfield network:

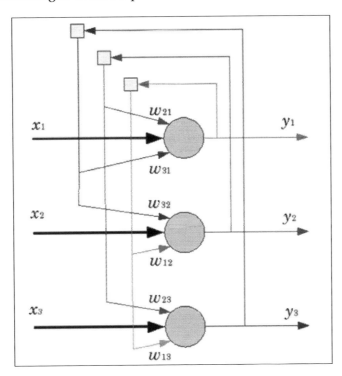

Dynamic Learning Vector Quantization (DLVQ) networks

The **Dynamic Learning Vector Quantization (DLVQ)** network model is another variation of neural networks that starts with a smaller number hidden layers and dynamically generates these hidden layers. It is important to have similarities in patterns that belong to the same class; hence, this algorithm best suits classification problems, such as recognition of patterns, digits, and so on.

Gradient descent method

In this section, we will look at one of the most popular ways of optimizing the neural network, minimizing the cost function, minimizing errors, and improving the accuracy of the neural network: the Gradient descent method. The graph here shows the actual versus. The predicted value along with the cases of inaccuracy in the predictions:

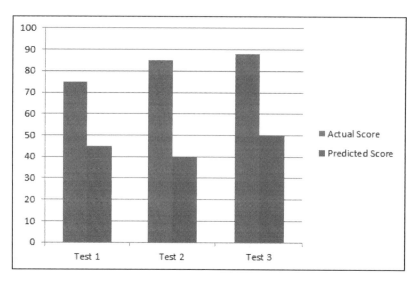

Backpropagation algorithm

Taking forward the topic of training the networks, the Gradient descent algorithm helps neural networks to learn the weights and biases. Moreover, to compute the gradient of the cost function, we use an algorithm called backpropagation. Backpropagation was first discussed in the 1970s and became more prominent regarding its application only in the 1980s. It was proven that neural network learning was much faster when backpropagation algorithm was employed.

In the earlier sections of this chapter, we saw how a matrix-based algorithm works; a similar notation is used for the backpropagations algorithm. For a given weight w and bias b, the cost function C has two partial derivatives which are $\partial C/\partial w$ and $\partial C/\partial b$.

Some key assumptions regarding the cost function for backpropagation are stated here. Let's assume that the cost function is defined by the equation here:

$$C = \frac{1}{2n} \sum_{x} \|y(x) - a^{L}(x)\|^{2}$$

Where, n = number of training examples

x = sum across the individual training sets

$y = y(x)$ is the expected output

L = total number of layers in the neural network

$a^L = a^L(x)$ is the output activation vector

Assumption 1: The overall cost function can be an average of the individual cost functions. For x individual training sets, the cost function can now be stated as follows:

$$C = \frac{1}{n} \sum_x C_x$$

Moreover, the cost function for an individual training set can be as follows:

$$C_x = \frac{1}{2} \|y - a^L\|^2$$

With this assumption, since we can compute the partial derivatives for each training set x as $\partial_x C / \partial w$ and $\partial_x C / \partial b$, the overall partial derivative functions $\partial C / \partial w$ and $\partial C / \partial b$ can be an average of the partial derivatives for each training set.

Assumption 2: This hypothesis is about the cost function C that C can be the function of outputs from the neural networks as shown here:

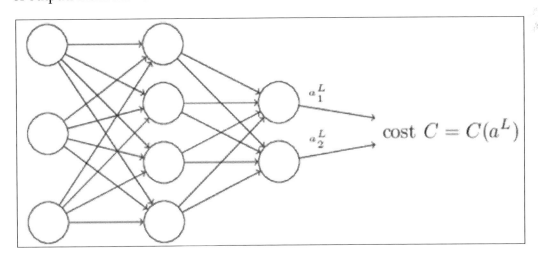

Extending the previous equation of the cost function, the quadratic cost function for each training example set x can now be written as follows. We can see how this acts as a function of the output activations as well.

$$C = \frac{1}{2}\|y - a^L\|^2 = \frac{1}{2}\sum_j (y_j - a_j^L)^2$$

Back propagation is about the impact the weights and bias have on the overall cost function value.

First, we compute the error in the jth neuron in the lth layer, δ_j^l, and then use this value to calculate the partial derivatives that relate to this error δ_j^l:

$$\partial C / \partial w_{jk}^l \text{ and } \partial C / \partial b_j^l$$

The error function δ_j^l of the jth neuron in the lth layer can be defined as:

$$\delta_j^l \equiv \frac{\partial C}{\partial z_j^l}$$

Thus, the error for the layer L δ^L can be computed as well. This, in turn, helps to compute the gradient of the cost function.

The following equations are used by the back propagation algorithm in sequence, as shown here:

Equation 1: The computing error in the layer L, δ^L, given the neuron at the position j.

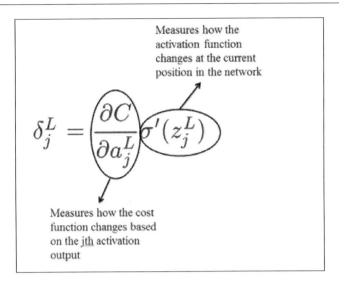

Equation 2: The computing error in the layer L, δ^L, given the error in the next layer δ^{L+1}.

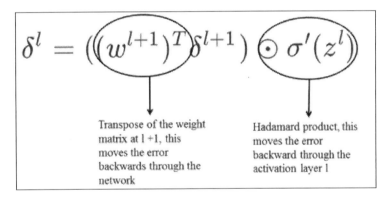

The Hadamard product is a matrix multiplication technique that is used for element-wise matrix multiplication as shown here:

$$\begin{bmatrix} 1 \\ 2 \end{bmatrix} \odot \begin{bmatrix} 3 \\ 4 \end{bmatrix} = \begin{bmatrix} 1 * 3 \\ 2 * 4 \end{bmatrix} = \begin{bmatrix} 3 \\ 8 \end{bmatrix}$$

The notation $\odot$ is used to represent this method.

Equation 3: This equation measures the impact on the cost and gives a change in the bias:

$$\frac{\partial C}{\partial b_j^l} = \delta_j^l$$

Moreover, we will get the following from equations 1 and 2:

$$\frac{\partial C}{\partial b} = \delta$$

This is because the error value is the same as the rate of change of the partial derivative.

Equation 4: This equation is used to compute the rate of change of the cost as a relationship to the weight.

$$\frac{\partial C}{\partial w_{jk}^l} = a_k^{l-1} \delta_j^l$$

At every stage of these algorithms, there is some kind of learning that impacts the overall output from the network.

The final backpropagation algorithm as compiled is explained here:

1. The input layer x, and for $x = 1$ Set the activation as a^1.
2. For each of the other layers $L = 2, 3, 4 \dots L$, compute the activations as:

$$z^l = w^l a^{l-1} + b^l \text{ and } a^l = \sigma(z^l)$$

3. Compute the error δ^L using equations 1 and 2.

4. Backpropagate the error for $l = L\text{-}1, L\text{-}2, \ldots 2, 1$ using the equation 3.

5. Finally, compute the gradient of the cost function using equation 4.

If we observe the algorithm, the error vectors δ^l are calculated backwards, starting from the output layer. This is the fact that the cost is a function of outputs from the network. To understand the impact of earlier weights on the cost, a chain rule needs to be applied that works backwards through all the layers.

Softmax regression technique

Softmax regression is also known as multinomial logistic regression. This section does not cover the concept of logistic regression in depth as it is covered in the chapter related to a regression in this book. Instead, we will specifically look at understanding how this technique is employed in digit recognition-related problems in deep learning use cases.

This technique is a special case of the logistic regression that works for multiple classes. As we learned, the result of logistic regression is a binary value {0,1}. Softmax regression facilitates handling $y(i)\text{<--}\{1,\ldots,n\}$, where n is the number of classes against the binary classification. In the MNIST digit recognition case, the value n is 10, representing 10 different classes. For example, in the MNIST digit recognition task, we would have $K=10$ different classes.

As a result of its ability to process multiple classes, this technique is used actively in neural network-based, problem-solving areas.

Deep learning taxonomy

The feature learning taxonomy for deep learning cases is depicted here:

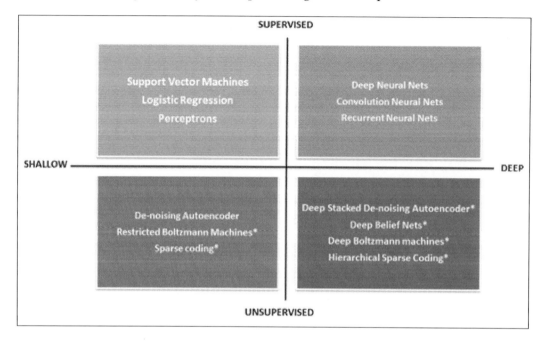

Some of the frameworks that are used to implement neural network applications are listed here:

- Theano is a Python library
- Torch a Lua programming language
- Deeplearning4J is an open, source Java-based framework that works with Spark and Hadoop
- Caffe is a C++ based framework

Convolutional neural networks (CNN/ ConvNets)

CNN, also known as convolution nets (ConvNets), are a variation of the regular neural networks.

Let us recap the function of the regular neural network. Regular neural networks have a single vector-based input that is transformed through a series of hidden layers where the neurons in each layer are connected with the neurons in its neighboring layers. The last layer in this series provides the output. This layer is called the output layer.

When the input to the neural network is an image and does not just fit into a single vector structure, the complexity grows. CNN have this slight variation where the input is assumed as a three-dimensional vector having depth (D), height (H) and width (W). This assumption changes the way the neural network is organized and the way it functions. The following diagram compares the standard three layers neural network with the CNN.

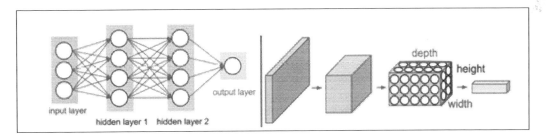

As we see, the convolutional net shown previously arranges neurons in a three-dimensional way; every layer in the network transforms this into a 3D output of neuron activations.

Convolution network architecture comprises a fixed set of layers designated for specialized functions. The most critical layers are as follows:

- **Convolutional layer (CONV)**
- **Pooling layer (POOL)**
- **Full-connected (FC) layer**

In some cases, the activation function is written as another layer (RELU); a distinct normalization layer for FC layer conversion may exist.

Convolutional layer (CONV)

The convolutional layer forms the core of convolution nets. This layer is responsible for holding the neurons in a three-dimensional format and is therefore responsible for a three-dimensional output. The following is an example of an input volume with the dimensions 32 x 32 x 3. As shown, each neuron is connected to a particular input region. Along the depth, there can be many neurons; we can see five neurons in the example.

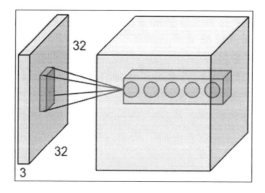

The diagram here shows how the net convolution function works in the neuron function representation:

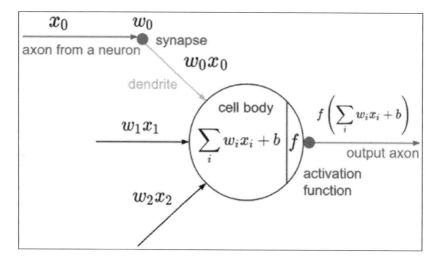

That said, the core function of the neuron remains unchanged and is responsible for computing the product of weights and the inputs followed by an observation of non-linear behavior. The only difference is the restrictions on the connectivity to the local regions.

Pooling layer (POOL)

There can be multiple convolution layers and, between these convolution layers, there can be a pooling layer. The pooling layer is responsible for reducing the chances of over-fitting by reducing the spatial size of the input volume. The reduction of the spatial size implies reducing the number of parameters or the amount of computations in the network. The MAX functions contribute to reducing the spatial size. The pooling layers use the MAX functions and apply it on every slice in the three-dimensional representation, sliced depth-wise. Usually, the pooling layers apply filters of size 2 X 2 applied along both width and height. This can discard around 75% of the activations.

Overall, the pooling layer has the following characteristics:

- Always considers a volume size of W1×H1×D1 as an input
- Applies stride S and spatial extent F and generates the W2×H2×D2 output where:

W2=(W1−F)/S+1

H2=(H1−F)/S+1

D2=D1

Fully connected layer (FC)

The fully connected layer is very similar to the regular or traditional neural networks, responsible for establishing extensive connections to the previous layer activations. The connection activations are computed using matrix multiplication techniques. More details on this can be found upon referring to the earlier sections of this chapter.

Recurrent Neural Networks (RNNs)

RNNs are a special case of neural networks that are known to be very efficient in remembering information, because the hidden state is stored in a distributed manner, and so it can hold more information about the experiences. These networks also apply non-linear functions to update the hidden state. The following diagram depicts how the hidden states link in RNNs:

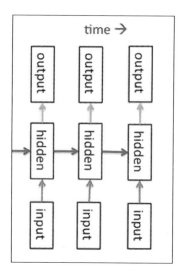

In most of the real world examples, the inputs and outputs are not independent of each other. For example, if we had to predict the next word, it would be important for us to know the words that came before it. As the word suggests, "Recurrent" Neural Networks execute the same task over and over again, where the input of one execution is the output of the previous execution. Usually, RNNs are known to go back only a few steps in the past and not always through all the iterations. The following diagram depicts how RNNs work; it shows how RNNs unfold across iterations:

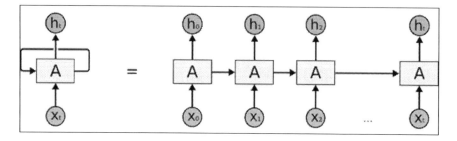

In the previous example, the requirement was to predict the next word, and if there were five words in the input, then RNN unfolds upto five layers.

Restricted Boltzmann Machines (RBMs)

RBMs came into existence to solve the difficulty in training RNNs. The rise of restricted recurrent models to handle these training difficulties simplified the problem context, and additionally, learning algorithms are applied to solve the problem. The Hopfield Neural Network is an example of a restricted model that addresses the previously described problem.

As a first step, Boltzmann machines came into existence. These models were a special case of Hopfield Neural Networks with a stochastic element. In this case, the neurons were of two categories: the ones that resulted in visible states and the others in hidden states. This was also similar to the Hidden Markov's model. A RBM is again a special case of Boltzmann machine, where the difference is primarily to do with the absence of connections between the neurons in the same layer. So, for the given states of the neurons of one group, the states of the neurons in the other group are independent. The following diagram depicts a typical RBN structure and the previous definition:

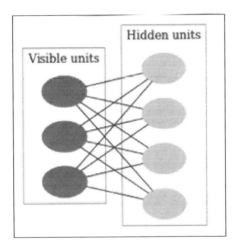

Taking this definition further for a deeper interpretation, some visible states of neurons are observable, and there are hidden states of neurons that are not visible or cannot directly be seen. There are a few probabilistic conclusions made on the hidden states based on the available visible states, and this is how the training model is formed.

In an RBM, the connectivity is restricted, and this, in turn, eases the inferencing and learning. It typically takes only one step to reach an equilibrium state with the visible states clamped. The following formula shows how the probability of the hidden state is computed, given that the information about the visible states is provided:

$$p(h_j = 1) = \cfrac{1}{1 + e^{-\left(b_j + \sum_{i \in vis} v_i w_{ij}\right)}}$$

Deep Boltzmann Machines (DBMs)

DBMs are a special case of conventional Boltzmann machines with a lot of missing connections, and, unlike the sequential stochastic updates, parallel updates are allowed for ensuring efficiency in the model.

DBMs restrict the connections between hidden variables and primarily use unlabeled data for training the models. Labeled data is used for fine-tuning the model. The following diagram depicts the general structure of a three-layered DBM:

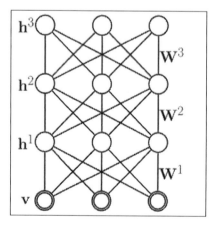

Autoencoders

Before we understand autoencoders, let's first learn about **autoassociators (AAs)**. The goal of AAs is to receive an input to the maximum possible precision.

The purpose of an AA is to receive the output as an image of the input as precisely as possible. There are two categories of AAs: one is generating AAs, and the second is synthesizing AAs. RBMs covered in the previous section are categorized as generating AAs, and autoencoders synthesize AAs.

An autoencoder is a type of neural network that has a single open layer. Applying backpropagation and unsupervised learning techniques, autoencoders start with an assumption that the target value is equal to the input value, $y = x$. The following diagram depicts an autoencoder that learns the function $h_{W,b}(x) \approx x$:

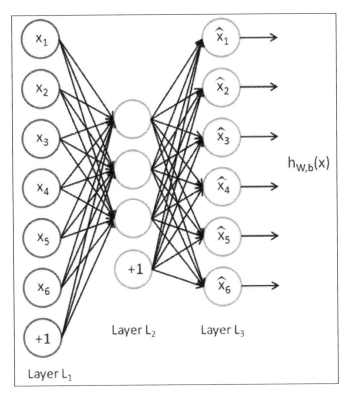

The layer in the middle is open, and as depicted in the previous diagram, for optimal output, it is essential for this layer to have lesser number of neurons than that of the input layer. The goal of this model is to learn an approximation to the identity function in such a way that the values of **Layer L$_3$** are equal to values in **Layer L$_1$**.

The data is compressed when it passes through the input to output layers. When an image of certain pixels, say 100 pixels (10 X 10 pixels), is input to the model for a hidden layer with 50 neurons, the expectation is that the network tries to compress the image by keeping the pixel configuration intact. This kind of compression is possible only if there are hidden interconnections and other characteristic correlations that can reduce the input data.

Another variation of an autoencoder is **denoising autoencoder (DA)**. The difference in this variation of autoencoder is its additional capability to recover and restore the state impacted by the corrupt input data.

Implementing ANNs and Deep learning methods

Refer to the source code provided for this chapter for implementing artificial neural networks and other deep learning methods covered in this chapters (source code path .../chapter11/... under each of the folders for the technologies).

Using Mahout

Refer to the folder .../mahout/chapter11/annexample/.

Refer to the folder .../mahout/chapter11/dlexample/.

Using R

Refer to the folder .../r/chapter11/annexample/.

Refer to the folder .../r/chapter11/dlexample/.

Using Spark

Refer to the folder .../spark/chapter11/annexample/.

Refer to the folder .../spark/chapter11/dlexample/.

Using Python (Scikit-learn)

Refer to the folder .../python-scikit-learn/chapter11/annexample/.

Refer to the folder .../python-scikit-learn/chapter11/dlexample/.

Using Julia

Refer to the folder .../julia/chapter11/annexample/.

Refer to the folder .../julia/chapter11/dlexample/.

Summary

In this chapter, we covered the model of a biological neuron and how an artificial neuron is related to its function. You learned the core concepts of neural networks, and how fully connected layers work. We have also explored some key activation functions that are used in conjunction with matrix multiplication.

12
Reinforcement learning

We have covered supervised and unsupervised learning methods in-depth in *Chapter 5*, *Decision Tree based learning*, with various algorithms. In this chapter, we will be covering a new learning technique that is different from both supervised and unsupervised learning called **Reinforcement Learning** (**RL**). Reinforcement Learning is a particular type of Machine learning where the learning is driven by the feedback from the environment, and the learning technique is iterative and adaptive. RL is believed to be closer to human learning. The primary goal of RL is decision making and at the heart of it lies **Markov's Decision Process** (**MDP**). In this chapter, we will cover some basic Reinforcement Learning methods like **Temporal Difference** (**TD**), certainty equivalence, policy gradient, dynamic programming, and more. The following figure depicts different data architecture paradigms that will be covered in this chapter:

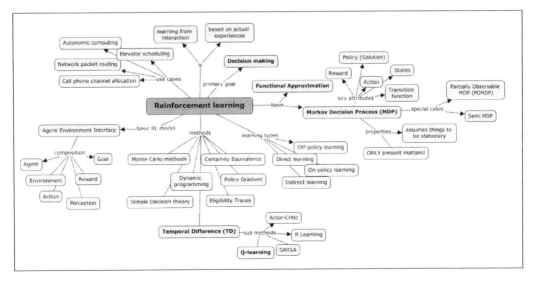

The following topics are covered in depth in this chapter:

- Recap of supervised, semi-supervised, and unsupervised learning, and the context of Reinforcement Learning.

- Understanding MDP is key to Reinforcement Learning. Regarding this, the following topics are covered in this chapter:
    - What does MDP mean, key attributes, states, reward, actions, and transitions (discounts)
    - The underlying process of MDP and how it helps in the decision process
    - Policies and value functions (also called utilities, as in a group of rewards) and how we assign value to an infinite sequence of rewards
    - **Bellman Equation** — the value iteration and policy iteration

- Regarding Reinforcement Learning, we will cover the following:
    - Planning and learning in MDP
    - Connection planning and functional approximation in RL
    - Different RL methods and approaches to RL, such as simple decision theory, the **temporal difference** (**TD**), dynamic programming, policy gradient, certainty equivalence, and eligibility traces
    - Key algorithms such as Q-learning, Sarsa, and others
    - Reinforcement learning applications

Reinforcement Learning (RL)

Let's do a recap of supervised, semi-supervised, and unsupervised learning, and set the context for Reinforcement Learning. In *Chapter 1, Introduction to Machine Learning,* we covered the basic definitions of supervised, semi-supervised, and unsupervised learning. Inductive learning is a reasoning process that uses the results of one experiment to run the next set of experiments and iteratively evolve a model from specific information.

The following figure depicts various subfields of Machine learning. These subfields are one of the ways the Machine learning algorithms are classified:

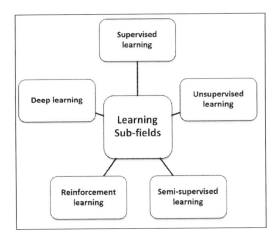

Supervised learning is all about operating to a known expectation, and in this case, what needs to be analyzed from the data being defined. The input datasets in this context are also referred to as **labeled** datasets. Algorithms classified under this category focus on establishing a relationship between the input and output attributes and uses this relationship speculatively to generate an output for new input data points. In the preceding section, the example defined for the classification problem is also an example of supervised learning. Labeled data helps build reliable models and are usually expensive and limited. The following diagram depicts the workflow for supervised learning:

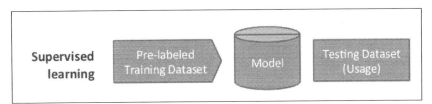

So, this is a function approximation, where given the *x*, *y* pairs, our goal is to find the function *f* that maps the new *x* to a proper *y*:

$y = f(x)$

In some of the learning problems, we do not have any specific target in mind to solve for; this kind of learning is specifically called unsupervised analysis or learning. The goal, in this case, is to decipher structures in data as against build mapping between input and output attributes of data, and in fact, the output attributes are not defined. These learning algorithms operate on an **unlabelled** dataset for this reason.

So, given a bunch of x's, the goal here is to define a function f that can give a concise description for a set of x's. Hence, this is called clustering:

$f(x)$

Semi-supervised learning is about using both labeled and unlabeled data to learn better models. It is important that there are appropriate assumptions for the unlabeled data as any incorrect assumptions can invalidate the model. Semi-supervised learning takes its motivation from the human way of learning.

The context of Reinforcement Learning

Reinforcement Learning is about learning that is focused on maximizing the rewards from the result. For example, while teaching toddlers new habits, rewarding toddlers every time they follow instructions works very well. In fact, they figure out what behavior helps them earn rewards. This is exactly what Reinforcement Learning is it is also called as credit assessment learning.

The most important thing in Reinforcement Learning is that, the model is additionally responsible for making decisions for which a periodic reward is received. The results, in this case, unlike supervised learning, are not immediate and may require a sequence of steps to be executed before the final result is seen. Ideally, the algorithm will generate a sequence of decisions that will help achieve the highest reward or utility.

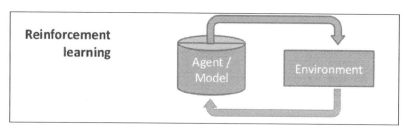

The goal of this learning technique is to measure the trade-offs effectively by exploring and exploiting the data. For example, when a person has to travel from a point A to point B, there will be many ways that include traveling by air, water, road, or on foot, and there is a significant value in considering this data measuring the trade-offs for each of these options. Another important aspect is, what would a delay in the rewards mean? Moreover, how it would affect learning? For example, in games like chess, any delay in reward identification may change or impact the result.

So, the representation is very similar to supervised learning, the difference being that the input is not x, y pairs but x, z pairs. The goal is to find a function f that identifies a y, given x and z. In the following sections, we will explore more of what the z is. The equation for definition of the goal function is as given here:

$y = f(x)$ given z.

A formal definition of Reinforcement Learning is as follows:

> *"Reinforcement Learning is defined as a way of programming agents by reward and punishment without needing to specify how the task is to be achieved."*
>
> *Kaelbling, Littman, & Moore, 96*

So, overall, RL is neither a type of neural network nor is an alternative to neural networks, but an orthogonal approach for Machine learning with emphasis being on learning feedback that is used for evaluating the learner's performance with no standard behavioral targets against which the performance is measured, for example, learning to ride a bicycle.

Let's now look at the formal or basic RL model and understand different elements in action. As a first step, let's understand some basic terms.

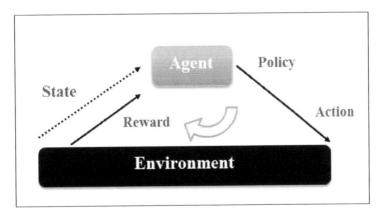

- **Agent**: An agent is an entity that is a learner as well as a decision maker, typically an intelligent program in this case.

- **Environment**: An environment is an entity that is responsible for producing a new situation given an action performed by the agent. It gives rewards or feedback for the action. So, in short, the environment is everything other than an agent.

- **State**: A state is a situation that an action lands an entity in.

- **Action**: An action is a step executed by an agent that results in a change in state.

- **Policy**: A policy is a definition of how an agent behaves at a given point in time. It elaborates the mapping between the states and actions and is usually a simple business rule or a function.

- **Reward**: A reward lays down short-term benefit of an action that helps in reaching the goal.

- **Value:** There is another important element in Reinforcement Learning, and that is a value function. While reward function is all about the short-term or immediate benefit of an action, a value function is about the good in long run. This value is an accumulation of rewards an agent is expected to get from the time the world started.

Examples of Reinforcement Learning

The easiest way to understand Reinforcement Learning is to look at some of the practical and real-world applications of it. In this section, we will list down and understand some of them.

- **Chess game**: In the game of chess, a player makes a move; this move is driven by an informed selection of an action that comes with a set of counter moves from the opponent player. The next action of the player is determined by what moves the opponent takes.

- **Elevator Scheduling**: Let's take an example of a building with many floors and many elevators. The key optimization requirement here is to choose which elevator should be sent to which floor and is categorized as a control problem. The input here is a set of buttons pressed (inside and outside the lift) across the floors, locations of the elevators, and a set of floors. The reward, in this case, is the least waiting time of the people wanting to use the lift. Here, the system learns how to control the elevators again; through learning in a simulation of the building, the system learns to control the elevators through the estimates of the value of actions from the past.

- **Network packet routing**: This is a case of defining a routing policy for dynamically changing networks. Q-learning techniques (covered a little later in the chapter) are used to identify which adjacent node the packet should be routed to. In this case, each node has a queue, and one packet is dispatched at a time.

- **Mobile robot behavior**: A mobile robot needs to decide between it reaching the recharge point or the next trash point depending on how quickly it has been able to find a recharge point in the past.

Evaluative Feedback

One of the key features that differentiates Reinforcement Learning from the other learning types is that it uses the information to evaluate the impact of a particular action than instructing blindly what action needs to be taken. Evaluative feedback on one hand indicates how good the action taken is while instructive feedback indicates what the correct action is irrespective of whether the action is taken or not. Although these two mechanisms are different in their way, there are some cases where techniques are employed in conjunction. In this section, we will explore some evaluative feedback methods that will lay the foundation for the rest of the chapter.

n-Armed Bandit problem

A formal definition of this problem with the original gambler analogy is given as follows:

According to Wikipedia, n-armed bandit problem is an issue where the "gambler" decides which machine to play, the order of play and the duration of play, he then plays and collects the reward that is unique for a machine with a goal to maximize the overall rewards.

Let's consider a case where there are thousands of actions that can be taken. Each action fetches a reward, and our goal is to ensure that we take actions in such a way that the total of the rewards is maximized over a period. The selection of a particular action is called a *play*.

An example case that explains the analogy of n-Armed Bandit the problem is that of a doctor who needs to choose from a series of options to treat a serious ailment where the survival of the patient becomes the reward for the choice of action (in this case, the treatment). In this problem, each action is associated with an expected reward for a selected action; this is called *value*. If the value of each action was known to us, solving n-armed bandit problem is easy as we will choose those actions that have a maximum value. It is only possible that we have the estimates of the values and are not certain about the actual values.

Now let us see the difference between exploration and exploitation.

Assuming we maintain the estimates of the values, if we choose an action with the greatest value (this action is called a greedy action), this situation is called exploitation, as we are best using the current knowledge on hand. Moreover, all the cases where any non-greedy action is chosen, it would be more of exploring, and it would help improve the estimates of the non-greedy action. While exploitation helps maximize the expected reward, exploration helps increase the total reward in the longer run. The short-term rewards are lower in the case of exploration while there might be better long-term total reward. For every action, exploration or exploitation approach can be chosen, and what works is a fine balance between these two techniques.

So, with this, we will now look at some techniques to best estimate the values for actions and to choose the best-suited actions.

Action-value methods

If value of an action a is $Q^*(a)$, then the assessed value of the tth play is $Q_t(a)$ I, the mean of the rewards given that action is chosen, the following equation represents this:

$Q_t(a) = (r1+r2+ \dots r_{ka})/ka$, where r is the reward and ka is the number of times the action a is chosen. This is one way of estimating action value and not necessarily the best way. Let's live with this and now look at the methods to choose actions.

The easiest action selection rule is to select an action or one of the actions, a, that has the highest estimated action value. So, for a given play t, choosing a greedy action a^* can be shown as follows:

$$Q_t(a^*) = \max_a Q_t(a)$$

This method by definition exploits the current knowledge with a little focus on whether the action is a better option. As an alternative to this method, we can choose to be greedy most of the time, and once in a while, select an action independent of the value estimation. With a probability of ε, this method is called the ε-**greedy method**.

Reinforcement comparison methods

We have been seeing in most of the selection methods that an action that has the largest reward has a higher likelihood of being selected than an action with a lesser reward. The important question is how to qualify whether a reward is big or small. We will always need to have a reference number that qualifies if a reward has a high value or a low value. This reference value is called **reference reward**. A reference reward, to start with, can be an average of previously received rewards. Learning methods that use this idea are called comparison reinforcement methods. These methods are more efficient than actor-value methods and form a basis for an actor-critic method that we will discuss in the sections to come.

The Reinforcement Learning problem – the world grid example

We will try to understand the Reinforcement Learning problem using a famous example: the grid world. This particular grid world is a 3X4 grid, as shown in the following screenshot, and is an approximation of the complexity of the world:

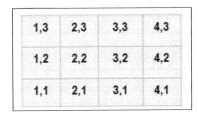

This example assumes the world is kind of a game where you start with a state called start state (from the location *1,1*). Let's assume four actions can be taken that include moving left, right, up, and down. The goal is to ensure using these actions that we move towards the goal that is represented in the location *4,3*. We need to avoid the red box that is shown in the location *4,2* like it is shown in the next image.

- **Start state**: position *(1,1)* --> The world starts here.
- **Success state**: position *(4,3)* --> The world ends here in a success state.
- **Failure state**: position *(4,2)* --> The world ends here in a failure state.
- When the world ends, we need to start over again.

- **Wall**: There is a roadblock or a wall shown in the position *(2,2)*. This position cannot be navigated:

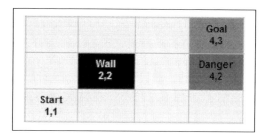

- To reach the goal *(4,3)* from the start point *(1,1)*, steps can be taken in the following directions:

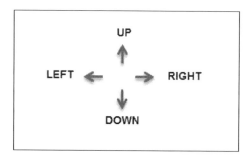

- Every step in a direction moves you from one position to another (position here is nothing but the state). For example, a movement in the *UP* direction from the position *(1,1)* will take you to the position *(1,2)* and so on.

- All directions cannot be taken from a given position. Let us consider the example shown in the following screenshot. From the position *(3,2)*, only *UP*, *DOWN*, and *RIGHT* can be taken. *LEFT* movement will hit the wall and hence cannot be taken. That said, only *UP* and *DOWN* movements make sense, as *RIGHT* will make a move to the danger position that results in failure in reaching the goal.

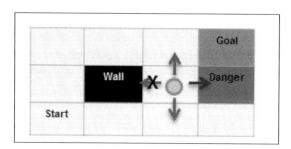

- Similarly, any of the positions in the boundaries of the grid will have limitations, for example, the position *(1,3)* allows *RIGHT* and *DOWN* movements and any other movements do not alter the position.

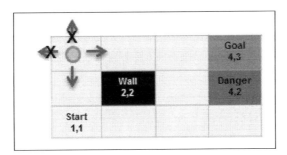

- Let's now look at the shortest path the from *Start (1,1)* to the *Goal (4,3)*. There are two solutions:

  ○ **Solution 1**: *RIGHT --> RIGHT --> UP --> UP --> RIGHT* (5 steps)

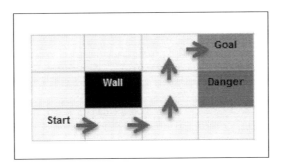

  ○ **Solution 2**: *UP --> UP --> RIGHT --> RIGHT --> RIGHT* (5 steps)

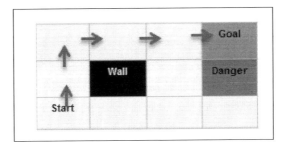

- In the real world, not all actions get executed as expected. There is a reliability factor that affects the performance, or rather, there is uncertainty. If we add a small caveat to the example and say that every time there is an action to move from one position to another, the probability that the movement is correct is 0.8. This means there is an 80% possibility that a movement executes as expected. In this case, if we want to measure the probability of Solution 1, (R-->R-->U-->U-->R) is succeeding:

Probability of actions happening as expected + Probability of actions not happening as expected

$$= 0.8 \times 0.8 \times 0.8 \times 0.8 \times 0.8 + 0.1 \times 0.1 \times 0.1 \times 0.1 \times 0.8$$

$$= 0.32768 + 0.00008 = 0.32776$$

- As we see, the element of uncertainty does change the result. In the next section, we will discuss the decision process framework that captures these uncertainties.

Markov Decision Process (MDP)

Markov's Decision Process is an essential framework or process to make decisions, and we will be bringing it up in most of the sections that follow on Reinforcement Learning.

Markov property is core to the Markov Decision Process, and it states that what matters is the present or current state and that the situation is stationary, which means that the rules do not change.

MDP tries to capture the world that we discussed in the preceding section that has the following features:

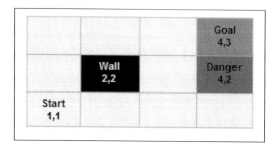

- **States**: In the preceding example, every grid position denotes a state
- **Model** (Transition function): A Transition function includes three attributes: given state, action, and the destination state. It describes the probability of an end state *s*, given the current state *s* and action *a*:

$$T (s, a, s') \sim P(s'/s, a)$$

- **Actions**: A(s), A In the preceding example, *A (1, 2) = UP* in the *UP, UP RIGHT, RIGHT, RIGHT* solution
- **Rewards**: *R(s), R(s,a), R(s,a,s1)* Rewards tell us the usefulness of entering into a state

  R(s): Reward for entering a state *s*

  R(s, a): Reward for the opening of a state *s* for an action *a*

  R(s, a,s1): Reward for the opening of a state *s1* for an action *a* given that you were in state *s*

- State, Action, Model and Rewards make the problem statement of MDP
- **Policy**: It is a solution for a problem; it says what action should be taken given a state:

  $\pi(s) \dashrightarrow a$

Basic RL model – agent-environment interface

As we have discovered, an RL problem is a straightforward way of learning from interaction to achieve a goal. Agent is the learner or decision-maker, and it interacts with the environment, and that is everything outside in this environment gives rise to rewards. The thing it interacts with, comprising everything outside the agent, is called the environment. The complete specification of an environment is defined as a task—a single instance of Reinforcement Learning problem.

The following model depicts the agent-environment interface:

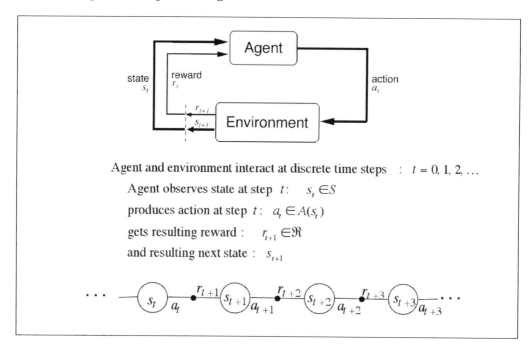

An environment model here means a context where an agent uses anything to predict the behavior of the environment for a given action. This environment model produces a prediction of the next state and the reward, given the action and the current state. There will be multiple next state rewards possible in case the model is stochastic. Again, these models can be distributed or sample-based. The distributed models identify all the potential probabilities, while a sample model produces the probability given that sample.

Finally, the goals of Reinforcement Learning can be defined as follows:

- In an environment where every action taken results in a new situation, RL is about how to take actions. The following can be the actions:
    - ° Define a policy that maps the action and the resultant situation
    - ° Identify the policy that results in highest rewards being given

Steps in Reinforcement Learning are as follows:

1. The agent observes the input state.
2. By applying the policy that is a decision-making function, an action is identified.

3. The action is executed that results in a state change.

4. As a consequence of this action, the agent receives a significant reward from the environment.

5. The details of the reward, given the change in the state, are recorded.

Delayed rewards

One of the aspects that differentiate Reinforcement Learning from supervised learning is *rewards*. In this section, we will explore what delayed rewards mean. As we know, every action that results in a particular state change results in a reward. The realization of this reward in some cases is not immediate. Let's look at an example a chess game. Let's assume it took 65 steps to end a chess game and only at the end of 65 steps or moves we get to know if we have won the game or lost it. Which of the 65 steps or moves were the cause of the success or failure is what is complex here. So, the reward is not known until the end of the game or the sequence of actions. Technically, we are looking at identifying which sequence of actions resulted in gaining the reward that was seen. This process is called **Temporal Credit Assignment**.

Now, in this journey of achieving the ultimate reward that is a success (+1) or failure (-1), every step or move or action would fetch a reward. Let's assume every step in solution 1 of the grid world problem fetches a reward of -0.4. The collective rewards that take to success or failure will determine long-term reward.

The policy

An optimal policy is a policy or solution that maximizes the expected long-term reward and can be represented by the following formula:

$$\pi *= argmax \ \pi \ (E \left[\sum_{t=0}^{\infty} r^t R(s_t)/\pi \right]$$

Now, let's measure the utility of a particular state(s) that depends on the policy (π):

$$R(s) \neq U^\pi(s) = E \left[\sum_{t=0}^{\infty} r^t R(s_t)/\pi , s_0 = s \right]$$

A reward to enter a state(s) (this is an immediate benefit) is not equal to the utility of that state (this is a long-term benefit of entering the state).

Now, we can define the optimal policy using the utility of the state value:

$$\pi *= argmax\pi \; E \left[\sum_{s1}^{\square} T(s, a, s1)U(s1) \right.$$

Now, if we have to define the utility of being in a state(s), it is equal to the reward for getting into that state, discounting the reward that we get from that point on:

$$U(s) = R(s) + \gamma \; max\pi \; E \left[\sum_{s1}^{\square} T(s, a, s1)U(s1) \right]$$

This is called **Bellman Equation**.

V^* is a value function for a policy, and the following is the Bellman optimality equation that expresses the fact that the value of a state with an optimal policy is the same as the best expected return from the best action for that state:

$$
\begin{aligned}
V^*(s) &= \max_{a \in \mathcal{A}(s)} Q^{\pi^*}(s, a) \\
&= \max_a E_{\pi^*} \left\{ R_t \mid s_t = s, a_t = a \right\} \\
&= \max_a E_{\pi^*} \left\{ \sum_{k=0}^{\infty} \gamma^k r_{t+k+1} \mid s_t = s, a_t = a \right\} \\
&= \max_a E_{\pi^*} \left\{ r_{t+1} + \gamma \sum_{k=0}^{\infty} \gamma^k r_{t+k+2} \mid s_t = s, a_t = a \right\} \\
&= \max_a E \left\{ r_{t+1} + \gamma V^*(s_{t+1}) \mid s_t = s, a_t = a \right\} \\
&= \max_{a \in \mathcal{A}(s)} \sum_{s'} \mathcal{P}^a_{ss'} \left[\mathcal{R}^a_{ss'} + \gamma V^*(s') \right].
\end{aligned}
$$

Reinforcement Learning – key features

Reinforcement Learning is not a set of techniques but is a set of problems that focuses on what the task is as, against how the task should be addressed.

Reinforcement Learning is considered as a tool for machines to learn using the rewards and punishments that are more trial-and-error driven.

Reinforcement Learning employs evaluative feedback. Evaluative feedback measures how effective the action taken is as against measuring the action if it is best or worst. (Note that supervised learning is more of an instructive learning and determines the correctness of an action irrespective of the action being executed.)

The tasks in Reinforcement Learning are more of related tasks. Associative tasks are dependent on the situation where actions that suit best to the given situation are identified and executed. Non-associative tasks are those that are independent of the particular situation, and the learner finds the best action when the task is stationary.

Reinforcement learning solution methods

In this section, we will discuss in detail some of the methods to solve Reinforcement Learning problems. Specifically, dynamic programming (DP), Monte Carlo method, and temporal-difference (TD) learning. These methods address the problem of delayed rewards as well.

Dynamic Programming (DP)

DP is a set of algorithms that are used to compute optimal policies given a model of environment like Markov Decision Process. Dynamic programming models are both computationally expensive and assume perfect models; hence, they have low adoption or utility. Conceptually, DP is a basis for many algorithms or methods used in the following sections:

1. **Evaluating the policy**: A policy can be assessed by computing the value function of the policy in an iterative manner. Computing value function for a policy helps find better policies.

2. **Improving the policy**: Policy improvement is a process of computing the revised policy using its value function information.

3. **Value iteration and Policy Iteration**: Policy evaluation and improvement together derive value and policy iteration. These are two of the most popular DP methods that are used to compute the optimal policies and value functions given complete knowledge of the MDPs.

The following algorithm depicts the iteration policy process:

1. Initialization
   $V(s) \in \Re$ and $\pi(s) \in \mathcal{A}(s)$ arbitrarily for all $s \in \mathcal{S}$

2. Policy Evaluation
   Repeat
       $\Delta \leftarrow 0$
       For each $s \in \mathcal{S}$:
         $v \leftarrow V(s)$
         $V(s) \leftarrow \sum_{s'} \mathcal{P}_{ss'}^{\pi(s)} \left[\mathcal{R}_{ss'}^{\pi(s)} + \gamma V(s') \right]$
         $\Delta \leftarrow \max(\Delta, |v - V(s)|)$
     until $\Delta < \theta$ (a small positive number)

3. Policy Improvement
       policy-stable $\leftarrow$ *true*
       For each $s \in \mathcal{S}$:
         $b \leftarrow \pi(s)$
         $\pi(s) \leftarrow \arg\max_a \sum_{s'} \mathcal{P}_{ss'}^a \left[\mathcal{R}_{ss'}^a + \gamma V(s') \right]$
         If $b \neq \pi(s)$, then *policy-stable* $\leftarrow$ *false*
       If *policy-stable*, then stop; else go to 2

Value iteration combines a solid policy improvement and process evaluation. The following are the steps involved:

Initialize V arbitrarily, e.g., $V(s) = 0$, for all $s \in \mathcal{S}^+$

Repeat
    $\Delta \leftarrow 0$
    For each $s \in \mathcal{S}$:
      $v \leftarrow V(s)$
      $V(s) \leftarrow \max_a \sum_{s'} \mathcal{P}_{ss'}^a \left[\mathcal{R}_{ss'}^a + \gamma V(s') \right]$
      $\Delta \leftarrow \max(\Delta, |v - V(s)|)$
until $\Delta < \theta$ (a small positive number)

Output a deterministic policy, π, such that
    $\pi(s) = \arg\max_a \sum_{s'} \mathcal{P}_{ss'}^a \left[\mathcal{R}_{ss'}^a + \gamma V(s') \right]$

Generalized Policy Iteration (GPI)

GPI is a way of categorizing Dynamic Programming (DP) methods. GPI involves interaction between two processes—one around the approximate policy, and the other around the approximate value.

In the first case, the process picks the policy as it is and performs policy evaluation to identify the true or exact value function associated with the policy. The other process picks the value function as the input and uses that to change the policy such that it improves the policy, which is its total reward. If you observe, each process changes the basis for the other process, and they work in conjunction to find a joint solution that results in an optimal policy and value function.

Monte Carlo methods

Monte Carlo methods in Reinforcement Learning learn policies and values from experience as samples. Monte Carlo methods have additional advantages over Dynamic Programming methods because of the following:

- Learning optimal behavior happens directly from the interactions with the environment without any model that simulates model dynamics.

- These methods can be used on simulated data or sample models; this feature becomes paramount in real-world applications.

- With Monte Carlo methods, we can easily focus on smaller sets of states, and we can explore a region of interest without necessarily going into complete state set.

- Monte Carlo methods are least impacted for any violation of Markov's property because the estimation for the value is not updated using any of the successor states. This also means that they do not bootstrap.

Monte Carlo methods are designed by the **Generalized Policy Iteration (GPI)** method. These methods provide an alternative way of evaluating the policies. For each state, instead of independently computing the value, an average value of the returns for starting at that state is taken, and this can be a good approximation of the value of that state. The focus is to apply action-value functions to improve the policies as this does not require environment's transition changes. Monte Carlo methods mix policy evaluation and improvement methods and can be implemented on a step-by-step basis.

How much of exploration is good enough? This is a crucial question to answer in Monte Carlo methods. It is not sufficient to select actions that are best based on their value; it is also important to know how much of this is contributing to ending reward.

Two methods can be used in this case—**on-policy** or **off-policy** methods. In an on-policy method, the agent is responsible for finding the optimal policy using exploration technique; and in off-policy methods, agent exploration is not central, but along with it learns a deterministic optimal policy that need not be related to the policy followed. In short, off-policy learning methods are all about learning behavior through behavior.

Temporal difference (TD) learning

TD learning is one of the unique techniques of Reinforcement Learning. Temporal difference learning is a combination of Monte Carlo methods and dynamic programming methods. The most discussed technique in Reinforcement Learning is the relationship between temporal difference (TD), dynamic programming (DP), and Monte Carlo methods:

1. Evaluate a policy that includes estimating the value function V^π for a given policy π.

2. Select an optimal policy. For policy selection, all the DP, TD, and Monte Carlo methods use a variation of generalized policy iteration (GPI). Hence, the difference in these three methods is nothing but these variations in GPI.

TD methods follow bootstrapping technique to derive an estimate; they fall back on the successor states and similar estimates.

Let's now look at some advantages of TD over DP and Monte Carlo methods. We will cover this in brief and without delving into too much of complexities. Following are the key benefits:

* TD methods do not require the model of the environment and probability distributions of the next states and rewards

* TD methods can easily and elegantly run in an online and incremental manner

Sarsa - on-Policy TD

Let's look at using TD methods for the control problems. We will continue to use GPI techniques, but now in conjunction with TD methods for the evaluation and prediction. While we need to have a balance between exploration and exploitation options, we have the option to choose on-policy or off-policy learning methods in here. We will stick to the on-policy method:

1. Learn the action-value function in relation to the state-value function. We will define $Q^\pi(s, a)$ for the policy π:

2. Learn the value of transition from one state-action pair to another state-action pair. This is computed iteratively as follows:

$$Q(s_t, a_t) \leftarrow Q(s_t, a_t) + \alpha \left[r_{t+1} + \gamma Q(s_{t+1}, a_{t+1}) - Q(s_t, a_t) \right].$$

This is defined as a Sarsa prediction method and is on-policy as the agent uses the identified policy to do this.

The Sarsa algorithm is stated as follows:

```
Initialize Q(s, a) arbitrarily
Repeat (for each episode):
    Initialize s
    Choose a from s using policy derived from Q (e.g., ε-greedy)
    Repeat (for each step of episode):
        Take action a, observe r, s′
        Choose a′ from s′ using policy derived from Q (e.g., ε-greedy)
        Q(s, a) ← Q(s, a) + α[r + γQ(s′, a′) − Q(s, a)]
        s ← s′; a ← a′;
    until s is terminal
```

Q-Learning – off-Policy TD

The Q-Learning technique that employs the off-policy learning method is one of the groundbreaking strategies of TD. This control algorithm called Q-learning (Watkins, 1989) in a simple form is defined as follows:

$$Q(s_t, a_t) \leftarrow Q(s_t, a_t) + \alpha \left[r_{t+1} + \gamma \max_a Q(s_{t+1}, a) - Q(s_t, a_t) \right].$$

We can see the optimal action-value function Q^* is directly approximated using the learned action-value function Q irrespective of the policy that it follows. This makes it an off-policy method.

There is still a small effect on the policy seen as the policy value functions are used and updated. Moreover, updates to all the pairs diligently mark convergence.

Based on this understanding, the Q-learning algorithm can be depicted as follows:

```
Initialize Q(s, a) arbitrarily
Repeat (for each episode):
    Initialize s
    Repeat (for each step of episode):
        Choose a from s using policy derived from Q (e.g., ε-greedy)
        Take action a, observe r, s'
        Q(s, a) ← Q(s, a) + α[r + γ max_a' Q(s', a') − Q(s, a)]
        s ← s';
    until s is terminal
```

Actor-critic methods (on-policy)

Actor-critic methods are temporal difference learning methods that ensure policy and value independence using a separate memory structure. In this case, the policy structure is called as an *actor*, and the value structure is called as a *critic*. The name critic comes from the fact that it criticizes the value of the policy. Since this critic always criticizes the value of the policy, it is also called the TD error. The following screenshot shows the actor-critic method flow:

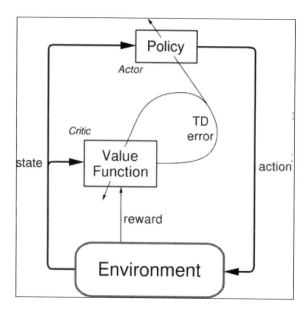

R Learning (Off-policy)

R-learning is an advanced Reinforcement Learning technique that is used in cases where there are no discounts with definitive and finite returns. The algorithm is as follows:

Initialize ρ and $Q(s, a)$, for all s, a, arbitrarily

Repeat forever:

$\quad s \leftarrow$ current state

$\quad$ Choose action a in s using behavior policy (e.g., ε-greedy)

$\quad$ Take action a, observe r, s'

$\quad Q(s, a) \leftarrow Q(s, a) + \alpha \left[r - \rho + \max_{a'} Q(s', a') - Q(s, a) \right]$

$\quad$ If $Q(s, a) = \max_{a} Q(s, a)$, then:

$\qquad \rho \leftarrow \rho + \beta \left[r - \rho + \max_{a'} Q(s', a') - \max_{a} Q(s, a) \right]$

Implementing Reinforcement Learning algorithms

Refer to the source code provided for this chapter to implement Reinforcement learning algorithms. (Source code path .../chapter12/... under each of the folder for the technology.)

Using Mahout

Refer to the folder .../mahout/chapter12/rlexample/.

Using R

Refer to the folder .../r/chapter12/rlexample/.

Using Spark

Refer to the folder .../spark/chapter12/rlexample/.

Using Python (Scikit-learn)

Refer to the folder .../python-scikit-learn/chapter12/rlexample/.

Using Julia

Refer to the folder .../julia/chapter12/rlexample/.

Summary

In this chapter, we explored a new learning technique called Reinforcement Learning. We saw how this was different from traditional supervised and unsupervised learning techniques. The goal of Reinforcement Learning is decision making and at the heart of it is MDP. We explored the elements of MDP and learned about it using an example. We then covered some fundamental Reinforcement Learning techniques that are on-policy and off-policy, and some of them are indirect and direct methods of learning. We covered dynamic programming (DP) methods, Monte Carlo methods, and some key temporal difference (TD) methods like Q-learning, Sarsa, R-learning, and actor-critic methods. Finally, we had hands-on implementations for some of these algorithms using our standard technology stack identified for this book. In the next chapter, we will cover ensemble learning methods.

13
Ensemble learning

This chapter is the concluding chapter of all the learning methods we have learned from *Chapter 5, Decision Tree based learning*. It is only apt to have this chapter as a closing chapter for the learning methods, as this learning method explains how effectively these methods can be used in a combination to maximize the outcome from the learners. Ensemble methods have an effective, powerful technique to achieve high accuracy across supervised and unsupervised solutions. Different models are efficient and perform very well in the selected business cases. It is important to find a way to combine the competing models into a committee, and there has been much research in this area with a fair degree of success. Also, as different views generate a large amount of data, the key aspect is to consolidate different concepts for intelligent decision making. Recommendation systems and stream-based text mining applications use ensemble methods extensively.

There have been many independent studies done in supervised and unsupervised learning groups. The common theme observed was that many mixed models, when brought together, strengthened the weak models and brought in an overall better performance. One of the important goals of this chapter details a systematic comparison of different ensemble techniques that combine both supervised and unsupervised techniques and a mechanism to merge the results.

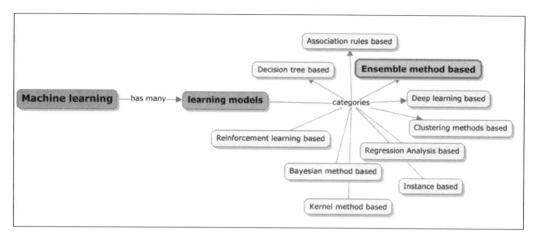

This chapter covers the following topics:

- An overview of ensemble methods based learning—the concept of *the wisdom of the crowd* and the key attributes.

- Core ensemble method taxonomy, real-world examples, and applications of ensemble learning

- Ensemble method categories and various representative methods:
    - **Supervised ensemble methods** provide an overview and a detailed coverage of concepts such as bagging, boosting, gradient boosting methods, and Random decision trees and Random forests
    - **Unsupervised ensemble methods** provide an overview of generative, direct and indirect methods that include clustering ensembles

- Hands-on implementation exercises using Apache Mahout, R, Julia, Python (scikit-learn), and Apache Spark

Ensemble learning methods

Ensemble, in general, means a group of things that are usually seen as a whole rather than in terms of the value as against the individual value. Ensembles follow a divide-and-conquer approach used to improve performance.

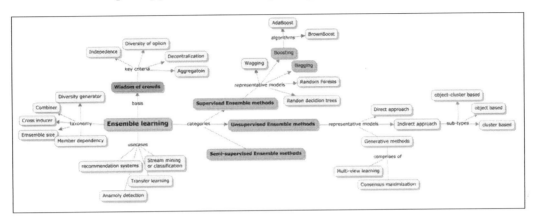

We will start understanding the specific algorithm with an introduction to the famous concept of the wisdom of the crowd.

The wisdom of the crowd

Imperfect judgments when aggregated in a right way result in a collective intelligence, thus resulting in a superior outcome. The wisdom of the crowd is all about this collective intelligence.

In general, the term crowd is usually associated with irrationality and the common perception that there is some influence, which sways the behavior of the crowd in the context of mobs and cults. However, the fact is that this need not always be negative and works well when working with collating intellect. The key concept of Wisdom of Crowds is that the decisions made by a group of people are always robust and accurate than those made by individuals. The ensemble learning methods of Machine learning have exploited this idea effectively to produce efficiency and accuracy in their results.

The term the wisdom of the crowd was coined by Galton in 1906. Once he attended a farmer's fair where there was a contest to guess the weight of an ox that is butchered and dressed. The closest guess won the prize from a total of 800 contestants. He chose to collect all the responses and analyze them. When he took the average of the guesses, he was shocked to notice that they were very close to the actual value. This collective guess was both better than the contestant who won the prize and also proved to be the best in comparison to the guesses by cattle experts. The democracy of thoughts was a clear winner. For such a useful output, it is important that each contestant had his/her strong source of information. The independent guess provided by the contestant should not be influenced by his/her neighbor's guess, and also, there is an error-free mechanism to consolidate the guesses across the group. So in short, this is not an easy process. Another important aspect is also to the fact these guesses were superior to any individual expert's guess.

Some basic everyday examples include:

- Google search results that usually have the most popular pages listed at the top

- In a game like "Who wants to be a billionaire", the audience poll is used for the answering questions that the contestant has no knowledge about. Usually, the answer that is most voted by the crowd is the right answer.

The results of the wisdom of the crowd approach is not guaranteed. Following is the basic criteria for an optimal result using this approach:

- **Aggregation**: There needs to be a foolproof way of consolidating individual responses into a collective response or judgment. Without this, the core purpose of collective views or responses across the board goes in vain.

- **Independence**: Within the crowd, there needs to be discipline around controlling the response from one entity over the rest in the crowd. Any influence would skew the response, thus impacting the accuracy.

- **Decentralization**: Individual responses have their source and thrive on the limited knowledge.

- **The diversity of opinion**: It is important that each person has a response that is isolated; the response's unusualness is still acceptable.

The word ensemble means grouping. To build ensemble classifiers, we first need to build a set of classifiers from the training data, aggregate the predictions made by these classifiers, and predict a class label of a new record using this data.

The following diagram depicts this process:

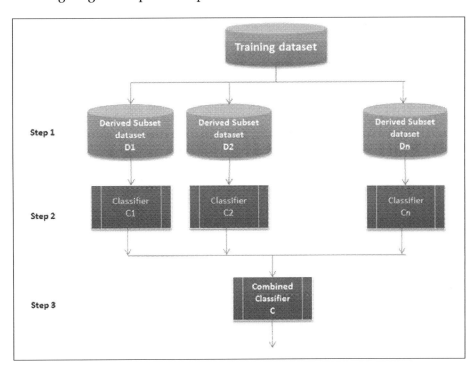

Technically, the core building blocks include a training set, an inducer, and an ensemble generator. Inducer handles defining classifiers for each of the sample training datasets. The ensemble generator creates classifiers and a combiner or aggregator that consolidates the responses across the combiners. With these building blocks and the relationships between them, we have the following properties that we will be using to categorize the ensemble methods. The next section covers these methods:

- **Usage of a combiner**: This property defines the relationship between the ensemble generator and the combiner

- **Dependency between classifiers**: This property defines the degree to which the classifiers are dependent on each other

- **Generating diversity**: This property defines the procedure used to ensure diversity across combiners

- **The size of the ensemble**: This property denotes the number of classifiers used in the ensembles

- **Cross inducers**: This property defines how the classifiers leverage the inducers. There are cases where the classifiers are built to work with a certain set of inducers

In summary, the building model ensembles first involves building experts and letting them provide a response/vote. The expected benefit is an improvement in prediction performance and produces a single global structure. Although, any interim results produced might end up being difficult to analyze.

Let's look at how the performance of an aggregated/combined classifier works better in a comprehensive manner.

Let's consider three classifiers that have an error rate of 0.35($\square$) or an accuracy of 0.65. For each of the classifiers, the probability that the classifier goes wrong with its prediction is 35%.

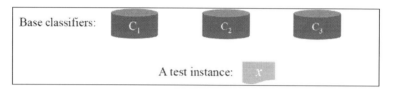

Given here is the truth table denoting the error rate of 0.35(35%) and the accuracy rate of 0.65(65%):

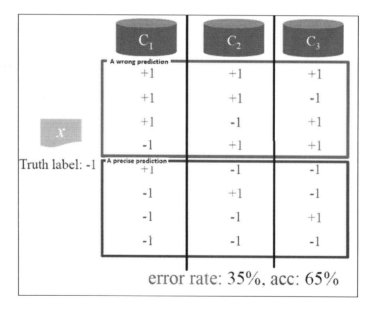

After the three classifiers are combined, the class label of a test instance is predicted by using the majority vote process across the combiners to compute the probability that the ensemble classifier makes an error. This is depicted in the formula given below.

$$\sum_{i=2}^{3}\binom{3}{i}\varepsilon^{i}(1-\varepsilon)^{3-i}=3\times0.35^{2}\times0.65+1\times0.35^{3}\times1=0.2817$$

Moreover, the accuracy is 71.83%. Very clearly, the error rate is lowered when aggregated across the classifiers. Now, if we extend this to 25 classifiers, the accuracy goes up to 94% as per the computation of the error rate (6%).

$$\sum_{i=13}^{25}\binom{25}{i}\varepsilon^{i}(1-\varepsilon)^{25-i}=0.06$$

Thus, the ensembles work as they give the bigger picture.

We have covered the criteria for the the wisdom of the crowd to work in the previous section. Let's now take the preceding case where we have 25 base classifiers, and see how the accuracy of the ensemble classifier changes for different error rates of the base classifier.

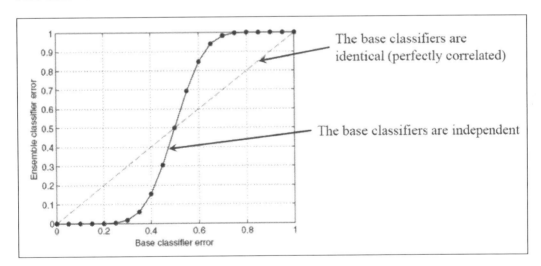

The base classifiers are identical (perfectly correlated)

The base classifiers are independent

The ensemble classifier's performance deteriorates and performs much worse than the base classifier in cases where the base classifier error rate is more than 0.5.

In the next section, we will cover some real-world use cases that apply ensemble methods.

Key use cases

Some of the key real-world applications of ensemble learning methods are detailed and discussed in this section.

Recommendation systems

The purpose of recommendation systems is to produce significant or meaningful recommendations to a community of users around the products that would possibly interest them. Some examples include suggestions related to decision-making process such as what books to read on Amazon, what movies to watch on Netflix, or what news to read on a news website. The business domain, or the context and the characteristics of the business attributes are the primary inputs to the design of recommendation systems. The rating (on a scale of 1-5) that users provide for each of the films is a significant input as it records the degree to which users interact with the system. In addition to this, the details of the user (such as demographics and other personal or profile attributes) are also used by the recommender systems to identify a potential match between items and potential users.

The following screenshot is an example of a recommendation system result on Netflix:

Anomaly detection

Anomaly detection or outlier detection is one of the most popular use cases or applications of ensemble learning methods. It is all about finding patterns in the data that look abnormal or unusual. Identifying anomalies is important as it may result in taking any decisive action. Some famous examples include (among many others):

- Fraud detection with credit cards
- Unusual disease detection in healthcare
- Anomaly detection in aircraft engines

Let's now expand on the example for anomaly detection in aircraft engines. Features of a plane engine which are considered to verify if it is anomalous or not are as follows:

- Heat generated(x_1)
- The intensity of vibration (x_2)
- With the dataset $= x_{(1)}, x_{(2)} \dots x_{(m)}$ marked, following are the anomalous and non-anomalous cases:

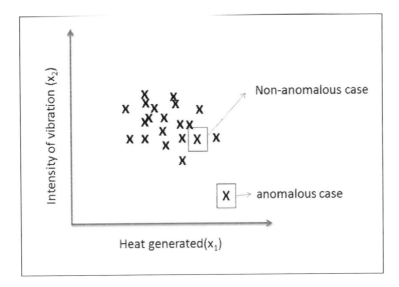

Transfer learning

Traditionally, all the Machine learning algorithms assume learning to happen from scratch for every new learning problem. The assumption is that no previous learning will be leveraged. In cases where the domains for the learning problems relate, there will be some learnings from the past that can be acquired and used. Some common examples include:

- The knowledge of French could help students learn Spanish
- The knowledge of mathematics could help students learn Physics
- The knowledge of driving a car could help drivers learn to drive a truck

In the Machine learning context, this refers to identifying and applying the knowledge accumulated from previous tasks to new tasks from a related domain. The key here is the ability to identify the commonality between the domains. Reinforcement learning and classification and regression problems apply transfer learning. The transfer learning process flow is as shown here:

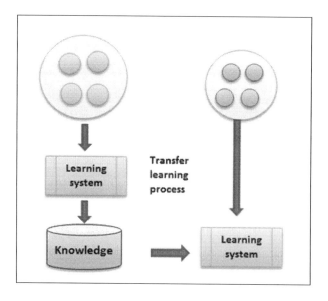

Stream mining or classification

Mining data that comes in as streams has now become a key requirement for a wide range of applications with the growing technological advancements and social media.

The primary difference between the traditional learning is that the training and test data sets evolved in a distributed way as they come in streams. The goal of prediction now becomes a bit complex as the probabilities keep changing for changing timestamps, thus making this an ideal context for applying ensemble learning methods. The next diagram shows how $P(y)$ changes with timestamp and changes to $P(x)$ and $P(y|x)$:

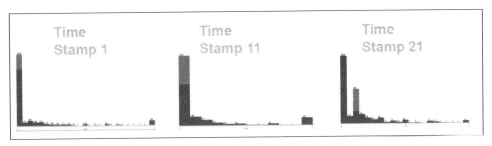

With ensemble learning methods, the variance produced by single models is reduced, and the prediction or result is more accurate or robust as the distribution is evolving.

Ensemble methods

As discussed in the previous sections, ensemble methods are now proven to be powerful methods for improving the accuracy and robustness of the supervised, semi-supervised, and unsupervised solutions. Also, we have seen how the dynamics of decision-making are becoming complex as different sources have started generating enormous amounts of data continuously. Effective consolidation is now critical for successful and intelligent decision making.

The supervised and unsupervised ensemble methods share the same principles that involve combining the diverse base models that strengthen weak models. In the sections to follow, let's look at supervised, semi-supervised, and unsupervised techniques independently and in detail.

The following model depicts various learning categories and different algorithms that cover both, combining the learning and consensus approaches to the ensemble learning:

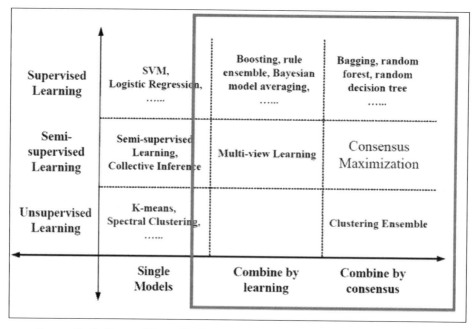

Source: On the Power of Ensemble: Supervised and Unsupervised Methods Reconciled
(http://it.engineering.illinois.edu/ews/)

Before we go deeper into each of the ensemble techniques, let's understand the difference between combining by learning versus combining by consensus:

	Benefits	Downside
Combining by learning	• Uses labeled data as a feedback mechanism • Has the potential to improve accuracy	• Works only with labeled data • There are chances of over-fitting
Combining by consensus	• Does not require labeled data • Has the potential to improve performance	• The valued feedback from the labeled data is missing • Works on the assumption that consensus is a good thing

Supervised ensemble methods

In the case of supervised learning methods, the input is always a labeled data. The *combining by learning* method includes boosting stack generalization and the rule ensembles techniques. The *combining by consensus* methods includes bagging, Random forests, and Random decision trees techniques. The following shows the process flow for combining by learning followed by another model for combining by consensus:

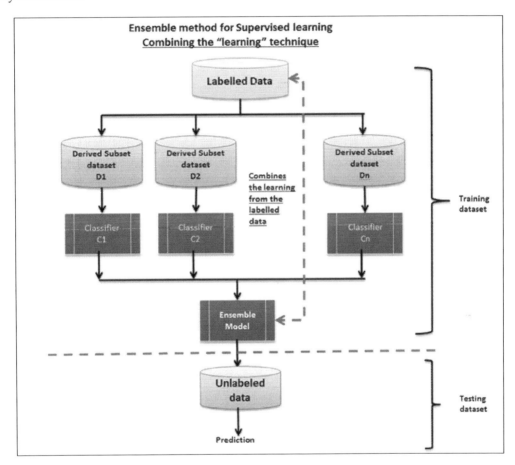

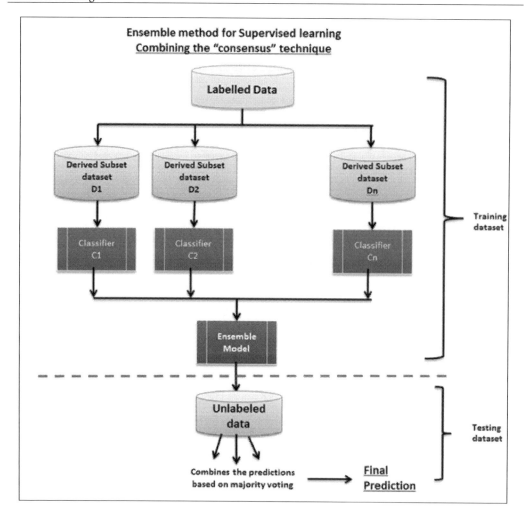

The supervised ensemble method problem statement is defined as follows:

- The input data set is $D=\{x_1, x_2, ..., x_n\}$ the respective labels are $L=\{l_1, l_2, ..., l_n\}$
- The ensemble method now generated a set of classifiers $C = \{f_1, f_2, ..., f_k\}$
- Finally, the combination of classifiers f^* minimizes generalization error as per the $f^*(x)= \omega_1 f_1(x)+ \omega_2 f_2(x)+ ....+ \omega_k f_k(x)$ formula

Boosting

Boosting is a pretty straightforward approach to calculating the output by applying a weighted average of all the outputs generated by multiple models. It is a framework for weak learners. The weights applied can be varied by using a powerful weighting formula to come up with a strong predictive model that addresses the pitfalls of these approaches and also works for a wider range of input data, using different narrowly tuned models.

Boosting has been successful in solving binary classification problems. This technique was introduced by Freund and Scaphire in the 1990s via the famous AdaBoost algorithm. Here listed are some key characteristics of this framework:

- It combines several base classifiers that demonstrate improved performance in comparison to the base classifier
- The weak learners are sequentially trained
- The data used for training each of the base classifiers is based on the performance of the previous classifier
- Every classifier votes and contributes to the outcome
- This framework works and uses the online algorithm strategy
- For every iteration, the weights are recomputed or redistributed where the incorrect classifiers will start to have their weights reduced
- Correct classifiers receive more weight while incorrect classifiers have reduced weight
- Boosting methods, though were originally designed for solving classification problems, are extended to handle regression as well

Boosting algorithm is stated next:

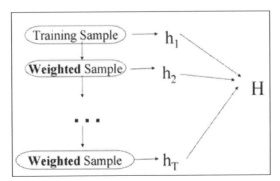

1. Train a set of weak hypotheses: $h_1, \ldots, h_T$.

2. Combine the hypothesis H as a weighted and majority vote of T weaker hypotheses.

$$H(x) = sign(\sum_{t=1}^{T} \alpha_t h_t(x))$$

3. Every iteration focuses on the misclassifications and recomputes the weights $D_t(i)$.

AdaBoost

AdaBoost is a linear classifier and constructs a stronger classifier $H(x)$ as a linear combination of weaker functions $h_t(x)$.

Given $(x_1, y_1), \ldots, (x_m, y_m)$ where $x_i \epsilon X$, $y_i \epsilon \{-1, +1\}$
Initialise weights $D_1(i) = 1/m$
Iterate $t=1, \ldots, T$:
- ☐ Train weak learner using distribution **Dt**
- ☐ Get weak classifier: $h_t : X \to R$
- ☐ Choose $\alpha_t \epsilon R$
- ☐ Update: $D_{t+1}(i) = \dfrac{D_t(i) \exp(-\alpha_t y_i h_t(x_i))}{Z_t}$

   ▪ where Zt is a normalization factor (chosen so that Dt+1 will be a distribution), and α_t:

   $$\alpha_t = \frac{1}{2} \ln\left(\frac{1-\varepsilon_t}{\varepsilon_t}\right) > 0$$

Output – the final classifier
$$H(x) = sign(\sum_{t=1}^{T} \alpha_t h_t(x))$$

The pictorial representation next demonstrates how the boosting framework works:

1. All the data points are labeled into two classes *+1* and *-1* with equal weights—*1*.

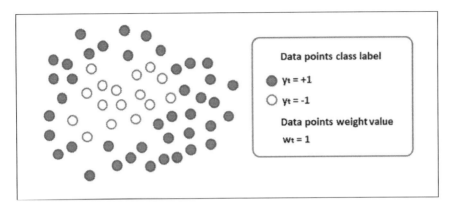

2. Apply a *p (error)* and classify the data points as shown here:

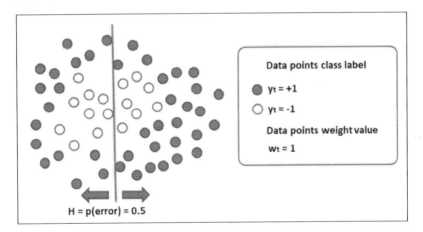

3. Recompute the weights.

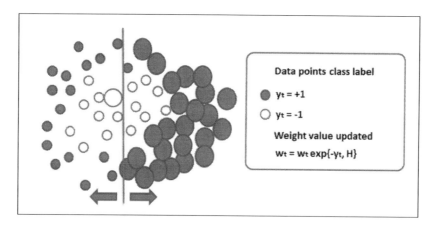

4. Have the weak classifiers participate again with a new problem set.

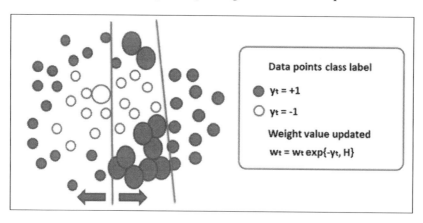

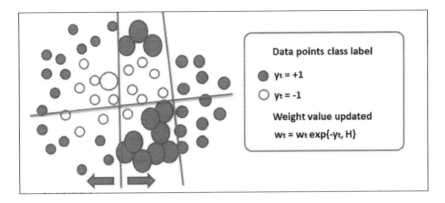

5. A strong non-linear classifier is built using the weak classifiers iteratively.

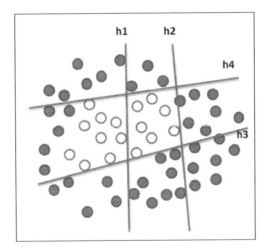

Bagging

Bagging is also called **Bootstrap Aggregation**. This technique of ensemble learning combines the *consensus* approach. There are three important steps in this technique:

1. Build the bootstrap sample that contains approximately 63.2% of the original records.
2. Classify training using each bootstrap sample.
3. Use the majority voting and identify the class label of the ensemble classifier.

This process decreases the prediction variance by generating additional data generation, based on the original dataset by combining the datasets of the same size repetitively. The accuracy of the model increases with a decrease in variance and not by increasing dataset size. Following is the bagging algorithm:

BAGGING

Training phase

1. Initialize the parameters
   - $\mathcal{D} = \emptyset$, the ensemble.
   - L, the number of classifiers to train.

2. For $k = 1, \ldots, L$
   - Take a bootstrap sample S_k from $\mathbf{Z}$.
   - Build a classifier D_k using S_k as the training set.
   - Add the classifier to the current ensemble, $\mathcal{D} = \mathcal{D} \cup D_k$.

3. Return $\mathcal{D}$.

Classification phase

4. Run $D_1, \ldots, D_L$ on the input $\mathbf{x}$.

5. The class with the maximum number of votes is chosen as the label for $\mathbf{x}$.

As per the previous algorithm steps, an example flow of the bagging algorithm and the process is depicted here:

1. **Training step**: For each iteration t, $t=1,\ldots T$, create N samples from the training sets (this process is called bootstrapping), select a base model (for example, decision tree, neural networks, and so on), and train it using the samples built.

2. **Testing step**: For every test cycle, predict by combining the results of all the T trained models. In the case of a classification problem, the majority of the voting approach is applied and for regression, it is the averaging approach.

Some of the error computations are done as follows:

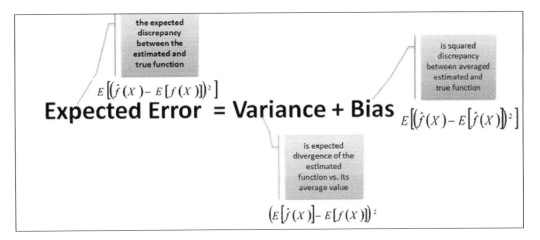

Bagging works both in the over-fitting and under-fitting cases under the following conditions:

- **For under-fitting**: High bias and low variance case
- **For over-fitting**: Small bias and large variance case

Here is an example of Bagging:

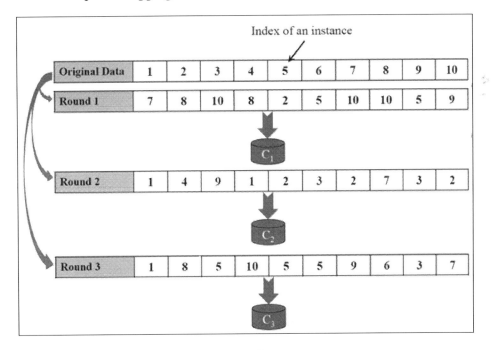

Wagging

Wagging is another variation of bagging. The entire dataset is used to train each model. Also, weights are assigned stochastically. So in short, wagging is bagging with additional weights that are assignment-based on the Poisson or exponential distribution. Following is the Wagging algorithm:

Require: I (an inducer), T (the number of iterations), S (the training set), d (weighting distribution).
Ensure: $M_t; t = 1, \ldots, T$
1: $t \leftarrow 1$
2: **repeat**
3:    $S_t \leftarrow S$ with random weights drawn from d.
4:    Build classifier M_t using I on S_t
5:    $t++$
6: **until** $t > T$

Random forests

Radom forests is another ensemble learning method that combines multiple Decision trees. The following diagram represents the Random forest ensemble:

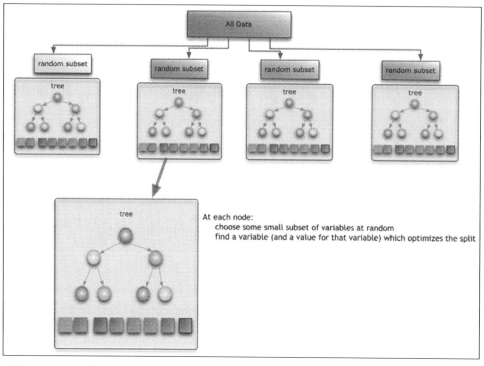

Source: https://citizennet.com/blog/2012/11/10/random-forests-ensembles-and-performance-metrics/

For a Random forest with T-trees, training of the decision tree classifiers is done as follows:

- Similar to the standard Bagging technique, a sample of *N* cases is defined with a random replacement to create a subset of the data that is about 62-66% of the comprehensive set.

- For each node, do as follows:
  - Select the *m* predictor variables in such a way that the identified variable gives the best split (binary split)
  - At the next node, choose other *m* variables that do the same

- The value of the *m* can vary
  - For Random splitter selection — *m=1*
  - For Breiman's bagger: *m= total number of predictor variables*
  - For Random forest, *m* is less than the number of predictor variables, and it can take three values: ½√m, √m, and 2√m

Now, for every new input to the Random forest for prediction, the new value is run down through all the trees and an average, weighted average, or a voting majority is used to get the predicted value.

> In *Chapter 5, Decision Tree based learning*, we have covered Random forests in detail.

Gradient boosting machines (GBM)

GBMs are one of the highly adopted Machine learning algorithms. They are used to address classification and regression problems. The basis for GBMs is Decision trees, and they apply boosting technique where multiple weak algorithms are combined algorithmically to produce a strong learner. They are stochastic and gradient boosted, which means that they iteratively solve residuals.

They are known to be highly customizable as they can use a variety of loss functions. We have seen that the Random forests ensemble technique uses simple averaging against GBMs, which uses a practical strategy of the ensemble formation. In this strategy, new models are iteratively added to the ensemble where every iteration trains the weak modeler to identify the next steps.

GBMs are flexible and are relatively more efficient than any other ensemble learning methods. The following table details the GBM algorithm:

Algorithm 1 Friedman's Gradient Boost algorithm

Inputs:

- input data $(x, y)_{i=1}^{N}$
- number of iterations M
- choice of the loss-function $\Psi(y, f)$
- choice of the base-learner model $h(x, \theta)$

Algorithm:

1: initialize $\widehat{f_0}$ with a constant
2: **for** $t = 1$ to M **do**
3:      compute the negative gradient $g_t(x)$
4:      fit a new base-learner function $h(x, \theta_t)$
5:      find the best gradient descent step-size ρ_t:

$$\rho_t = \arg\min_\rho \sum_{i=1}^{N} \Psi\left[y_i, \widehat{f}_{t-1}(x_i) + \rho h(x_i, \theta_t)\right]$$

6:      update the function estimate:
$$\widehat{f}_t \leftarrow \widehat{f}_{t-1} + \rho_t h(x, \theta_t)$$
7: **end for**

Gradient boosted regression trees (GBRT) are similar to GBMs that follow regression techniques.

Unsupervised ensemble methods

As a part of unsupervised ensemble learning methods, one of the consensus-based ensembles is the clustering ensemble. The next diagram depicts the working of the clustering-based ensemble:

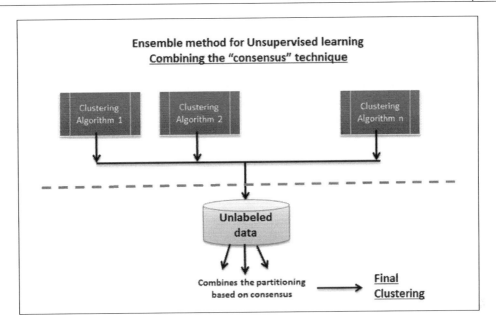

For a given unlabeled dataset $D=\{x_1, x_2, \ldots, x_n\}$, a clustering ensemble computes a set of clusters $C = \{C_1, C_2, \ldots, C_k\}$, each of which maps the data to a cluster. A consensus-based unified cluster is formed. The following diagram depicts this flow:

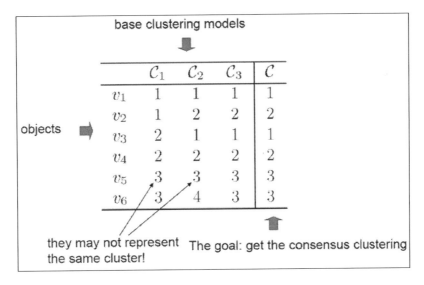

Implementing ensemble methods

Refer to the source code provided for this chapter to implement the ensemble learning methods (only supervised learning techniques). (source code path `.../chapter13/...` under each of the folders for the technology).

Using Mahout

Refer to the folder `.../mahout/chapter13/ensembleexample/`.

Using R

Refer to the folder `.../r/chapter13/ensembleexample/`.

Using Spark

Refer to the folder `.../spark/chapter13/ensembleexample/`.

Using Python (Scikit-learn)

Refer to the folder `.../python (scikit-learn)/chapter13/ensembleexample/`.

Using Julia

Refer to the folder `.../julia/chapter13/ensembleexample/`.

Summary

In this chapter, we have covered the ensemble learning methods of Machine learning. We covered the concept of *the wisdom of the crowd*, how and when it is applied in the context of Machine learning, and how the accuracy and performance of the learners are improved. Specifically, we looked at some supervised ensemble learning techniques with some real-world examples. Finally, this chapter has source code examples for the gradient boosting algorithm using R, Python (scikit-learn), Julia, and Spark Machine learning tools and recommendation engines using the Mahout libraries.

This chapter covers all the Machine learning methods and in the last chapter that follows, we will cover some advanced and upcoming architecture and technology strategies for Machine learning.

14
New generation data architectures for Machine learning

This is our last chapter, and we will take a detour from our usual learning topics to cover some of the solution aspects of Machine learning. This is in an attempt to complete a practitioner's view on the implementation aspects of Machine learning solutions, covering more on the choice of platform for different business cases. Let's look beyond Hadoop, NoSQL, and other related solutions. The new paradigm is definitely a unified platform architecture that takes care of all the aspects of Machine learning, starting from data collection and preparation until the visualizations, with focus on all the key architecture drivers such as volume, sources, throughput, latency, extensibility, data quality, reliability, security, self-service, and cost.

The following flowchart depicts different data architecture paradigms that will be covered in this chapter:

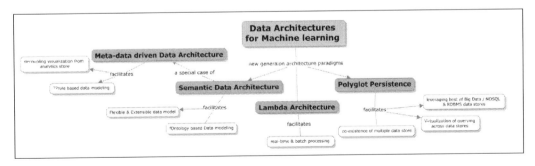

The topics listed here are covered in depth in this chapter:

- A brief history of how traditional data architectures were implemented and why they are found desirable in the current context of big data and analytics.

- An overview of the new-age data architecture requirements in the context of Machine learning that includes **Extract, Transform, and Load (ETL)**, storage, processing and reporting, distribution, and the presentation of the insights.

- An introduction to Lambda architectures that unifies strategies for batch and real-time processing with some examples.

- An introduction to Polyglot Persistence and Polymorphic databases that unify data storage strategies that include structured, unstructured, and semi-structured data stores, and centralize the querying approach across data stores. An example of how the Greenplum database supports the same and how it integrates with Hadoop seamlessly.

- Semantic Data Architectures include Ontologies Evolution, purpose, use cases, and technologies.

Evolution of data architectures

We will start with understanding how data architectures traditionally have been followed by detailing the demands of modern machine learning or analytics platforms in the context of big data.

Observation 1 — Data stores were always for a purpose

Traditionally, data architectures had a clear segregation of purpose, **OLTP (Online Transaction Processing)**, typically known to be used for transactional needs, and **OLAP (Online Analytic Processing)** data stores that typically used for reporting and analytical needs. The following table elaborates the general differences:

	OLTP databases	**OLAP databases**
Definition	This involves many small online transactions (INSERT, UPDATE, and DELETE). The fast query processing is the core requirement; maintaining data integrity, concurrency, and effectiveness is measured by the number of transactions per second. It's usually characterized by a high-level of normalization.	This involves a relatively small volume of transactions. Complex Queries involves slicing and dicing of data. The data stored is usually aggregated, historical in nature, and mostly stored in multi-dimensional schemas (usually star schema).

	OLTP databases	OLAP databases
Data type	Operational data	Integrated/consolidated/aggregated data
Source	OLTP databases usually are the actual sources of data	OLAP databases consolidate data from various OLTP databases
Primary purpose	This deals with the execution of day-to-day business processes/tasks	This serves decision-support
CUD	This is short, fast inserts and updates initiated by users	Periodic long-running jobs are refreshing the data
Queries	This usually works on smaller volumes of data and executes simpler queries	This often includes complex queries involving aggregations and slicing and dicing in the multi-dimensional structure
Throughput	This is usually very fast due to relatively smaller data volumes and quicker running queries	This usually run in batches and in higher volumes, may take several hours depending on volumes
Storage Capacity	Relatively small as historical data is archived	This requires larger storage space due to the volumes that are involved
Schema Design	Highly normalized with many tables	This is typically de-normalized with fewer tables and the use of star and/or snowflake schemas
Backup and Recovery	This requires proper backup religiously; operational data is critical to run the business. Data loss is likely to entail significant monetary loss and legal liability	Instead of regular backups, some environments may consider simply reloading the OLTP data as a recovery method

Observation 2—Data architectures were shared disk

Shared disk data architecture refers to an architecture where there is a data disk that holds all the data, and each node in the cluster has access to this data for processing. All the data operations can be performed by any node at a given point in time, and in case two nodes attempt at persisting/writing a tuple at the same time, to ensure consistency, a disk-based lock or intended lock communication is passed on, thus affecting the performance. Further with an increase in the number of nodes, contention at the database level increases. These architectures are *write* limited as there is a need to handle the locks across the nodes in the cluster.

Even in the case of the reads, partitioning should be implemented effectively to avoid complete table scans. All the traditional RDBMS databases are the shared disk data architectures.

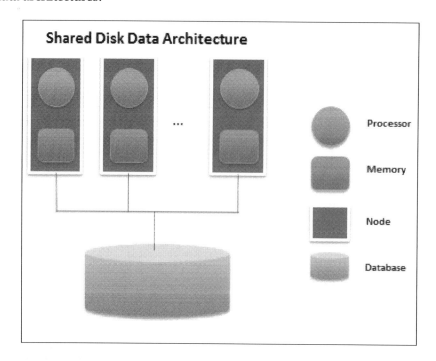

Observation 3—Traditional ETL architecture had limitations. The following list provides the details of these limitations:

- Onboarding and integrating data were slow and expensive. Most of the ETL logic that exists today is custom coded and is tightly coupled with the database. This tight coupling also resulted in a problem where the existing logic code cannot be reused. Analytics and reporting requirements needed a different set of tuning techniques to be applied. Optimization for analytics was time-consuming and costly.

- Data provenance was often poorly recorded. The data meaning was *lost in translation*. Post-onboarding, maintenance and analysis cost for the on-boarded data was usually very high. Recreating data lineage was manual, time-consuming, and error-prone. There was no strong auditing or record of the data transformations and were generally tracked in spreadsheets.

- The target data was difficult to consume. The optimization favors known analytics but was not well-suited to the new requirements. A one-size-fits-all canonical view was used rather than fit-for-purpose views, or lacks a conceptual model to consume easily the target data. It has been difficult to identify what data was available, how to get access, and how to integrate the data to answer a question.

Observation 4 — Data was usually only structured

Most of the time, the database was designed to fit the RDBMS models. If the incoming data was not actually structured, the ETLs would build a structure around for being stored in a standard OLTP or OLAP store.

Observation 5 — Performance and scalability

The optimization of a data store or a query was possible to an extent, given the infrastructure, and beyond a certain point, there was a need for a redesign.

Emerging perspectives & drivers for new age data architectures

Driver 1 — *BIG* data intervention.

We have defined big data and large dataset concepts in *Chapter 2, Machine learning and Large-scale datasets*. The data that is now being ingested and needs to be processed typically has the following characteristics:

- **Source**: Depending upon the nature of the information, the source may be a real-time stream of data (for example, trade transactions), or batches of data containing updates since the last sync

- **Content**: The data may represent different types of information. Often, this information is related to other pieces of data and is needed to be connected

The following screenshot shows the types of data and different sources that need to be supported:

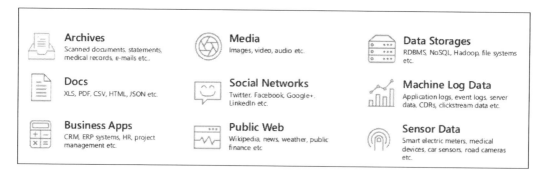

- **Volume**: Depending upon the nature of the data, the volumes that are being processed may vary. For example, master data or the securities definition data are relatively fixed, whereas the transaction data is enormous compared to the other two.

- **Lifecycle**: Master data has a fixed life and is rarely updated (such as, slowly changing dimensions). However, the transactional data has a very short life but needs to be available for analysis, audit, and so on for longer periods.

- **Structure**: While most of the data is structured, there is an advent of unstructured data in the financial industry. It is becoming increasingly critical for financial systems to incorporate unstructured data as part of their IT architectures.

The next chart depicts the complexity, velocity volume, and various aspects of each data source:

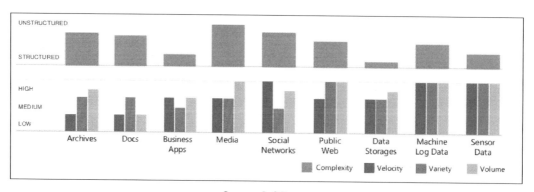

Source: SoftServe

Driver 2—Data platform requirements are advanced

The landscape of the new age-data platform requirements is drastically expanding, and the unified platforms are the happening ones. The next concept map explains it all. The core elements of data architectures include ETL (Extract, Transform, and Load), Storage, Reporting, Analytics, Visualization, and data distribution.

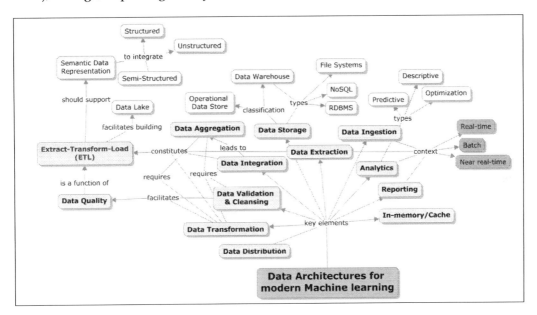

Driver 3—Machine learning and analytics platforms now have a new purpose and definition

The evolution of analytics and it repurposing itself is depicted in the following diagram:

- Historically, the focus was merely on reporting. Aggregated or preprocessed data is loaded into the warehouse to understand what has happened. This is termed as **Descriptive analytics** and was primarily a backward step.

- With the advent of ad-hoc data inclusion, the need was to understand why certain behavior happened. This is called **Diagnostic analytics** and is focused on understanding the root cause of the behavior, which is again based on the historical data.

- Now, the demand has shifted, and the need is to understand what will happen. This is called **Predictive analytics,** and the focus is to predict the events based on the historical behavior.

- With the advent of real-time data, the focus is now on do we make it happen? This goes beyond predictive analytics where remediation is a part of something. The ultimate focus is to *Make it happen!* with the advent of real-time event access. The following diagram depicts the evolution of analytics w.r.t. the value and related complexity:

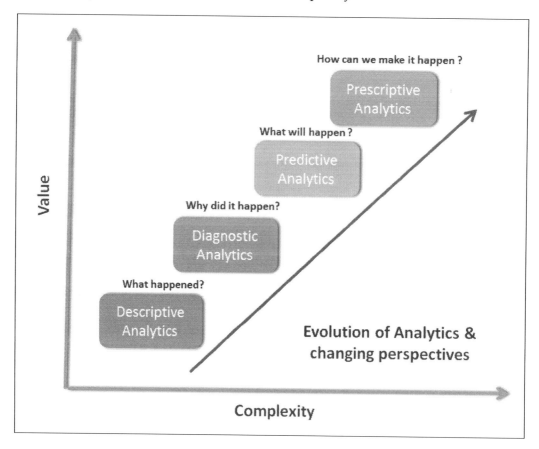

The next table differentiates the traditional analytics (BI) and the new age analytics:

Area	Traditional analytics (BI)	New age analytics
Scope	Descriptive Analytics Diagnostic Analytics	Predictive Analytics Data science
Data	Limited/Controlled volumes Preprocessed/Validated Basic models	Large volumes Diverse formats and heavy on variety Raw data that are not pre-processed The growing model complexity
Result	Here, the focus is on retrospection and the root-cause analysis	Here, the focus is on prediction/insights and the accuracy of analysis

Driver 4—It is not all about historical and batch, it is real-time and instantaneous insights

The data coming in lower volumes and higher velocity is what defines *real-time*. The new age analytics systems are expected to handle real-time, batch, and near real-time processing requests (these are scheduled and known as micro batches). The following graph depicts the properties of real-time and batch data characteristics with respect to volume, velocity, and variety being constant.

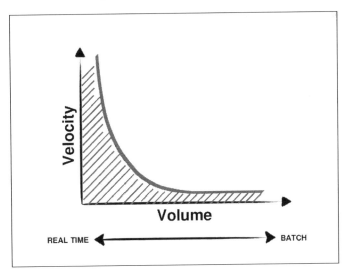

Driver 5—Traditional ETL is unable to cope with *BIG* data

The goal is to be able to lay out an ETL architecture strategy that can address the following problematic areas:

- Facilitates standardization in implementation—dealing with the need for one standard
- Supports building reusable components
- Building agnostic functions
- Improving performance and scalability using parallel processing techniques
- Reducing the total overall **cost of ownership (TCO)**
- Building a specialized skill pool

The following table provides a comparative analysis of the key data loading pattern:

	ETL **Extract, Transform, and Load**	**ELT** **Extract, Load, and Transform**	**ETLT** **Extract, Transform, Load, and Transform**
Overview	This is a traditional technique for moving and transforming data in which an ETL engine is either separated from the source or the target DBMS performs the data transformations.	This is a technique for moving and transforming data from one location and formatting it to another instance and format. In this style of integration, the target DBMS becomes the transformation engine.	In this technique, transformations are partly done by the ETL engine and partly pushed to the destination DBMS.
Highlights	A heavy work of transformation is done in the ETL engine. It uses the integrated transformation functions. Transformation logic can be configured through the GUI. This is supported by Informatica.	A heavy work of transformation is handed over to the DBMS layer. Transformation logic runs closer to the data. It is supported by Informatica.	Transformation work is split between the ETL engine and the DBMS. It is supported by Informatica.

	ETL **Extract, Transform, and Load**	ELT **Extract, Load, and Transform**	ETLT **Extract, Transform, Load, and Transform**
Benefits	This is an easy, GUI-based configuration. The transformation logic is independent, outside the database, and is reusable This works very well for granular, simple, function-oriented transformations that do not require any database calls. Can run on SMP or MPP hardware.	This leverages the RDBMS engine hardware for scalability. It always keeps all the data in RDBMS. It is parallelized according to the dataset, and the disk I/O is usually optimized at the engine level for faster throughput. It scales as long as the hardware and the RDBMS engine can continue to scale. Can achieve 3x to 4x the throughput rates on the appropriately tuned MPP RDBMS platform.	It can balance the workload or share the workload with the RDBMS.
Risks	This requires a higher processing power on the ETL side. The costs are higher. It consists of the complex transformations that would need reference data, which will slow down the process.	Transformation logic is tied to a database. The transformations that involve smaller volume and simple in nature will not gain many benefits.	This will still have a part of the transformation logic within the database.

Fact 6—No "one" data model fits advanced or complex data processing requirements; there is a need for multi-data model platforms

Different databases are designed to solve different problems. Using a single database engine for all of the requirements usually leads to non-performant solutions. RDBMSs are known to work well-transactional operations, OLAP databases for reporting, NoSQL for high-volume data processing, and storage. Some solutions unify these storages and provide an abstraction for querying across these stores.

Modern data architectures for Machine learning

From this section onwards, we will cover some of the emergent data architectures, challenges that gave rise to architectures of this implementation architecture, some relevant technology stacks, and use cases where these architectures apply (as relevant) in detail.

Semantic data architecture

Some of the facts covered in the emerging perspectives in the previous section give rise to the following core architecture drivers to build semantic data model driven data lakes that seamlessly integrate a larger data scope, which is analytics ready. The future of analytics is semantified. The goal here is to create a large-scale, flexible, standards-driven ETL architecture framework that models with the help of tools and other architecture assets to enable the following:

- Enabling a common data architecture that can be a standard architecture.
- Dovetailing into the Ontology-driven data architecture and data lakes of the future (it is important to tie this architecture strategy with the data aggregation reference architecture). This will ensure there is a single data strategy that takes care of the data quality and data integration.
- Enabling product groups to integrate rapidly into the data architecture and deliver into and draw from the common data repository.
- Enabling ad-hoc analytics on need basis.
- Reducing time needed to implement the new data aggregation, ingestion, and transformation.
- Enabling *any format to any format* model (a format-agnostic approach that involves data normalization sometimes).

- Complying with emerging semantic standards. This will bring in the flexibility.

- Enabling the common IT management and reduction of the TCO.

- Enabling a consolidated cloud (that can be a proprietary) for the Broadridge Master Business Data Repository.

- Enabling all the applications and products to "talk to a common language" and building the Broadridge data format.

- Reduce, and in some cases eliminate, the proliferation of too many licenses, databases, implementations, stacks, and more.

- Data Semantification: It is important to analyze the underlying schemas in order to unlock the meaning from them. The semantification process is always iterative and evolves over the period of time. The metadata definitions in this context will be elaborated or expanded in this process.

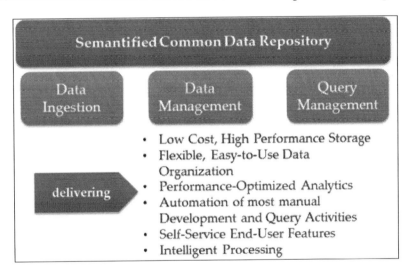

Setting up an enterprise-wide aggregate data mart is not the solution to problems outlined previously. Even if such a data mart was set up, keeping it updated and in line with the rest of the projects would be a major problem. As stated earlier, the need is to lay out the common reference architecture of a system that can accumulate data from many sources without making any assumptions on how, where, or when this data will be used.

There are two different advances in the field that we leverage to address the issues at an architecture level. These are the evolution of a data lake as an architecture pattern, and the emergence of Semantic Web and its growing relevance in e-business.

The business data lake

The enterprise data lake gives the concept of an enterprise data warehouse a whole new dimension. While the approach with a data warehouse has always been to design a single schema and aggregate the minimum information needed to fulfill the schema, data lake turns both these premises of traditional data warehouse architectures on its head. The traditional data warehouse is designed for a specific purpose in mind (for example, analytics, reporting, and operational insights). The schema is designed accordingly, and the minimum information needed for the purpose is aggregated. This means that using this warehouse for any other objective is only incidental if at all, but it is not designed for such a use.

The business data lake promotes the concept of an appropriate schema — the warehouse is not constrained by a fixed, predetermined schema. This allows the data lake to assimilate information as and when it becomes available in the organization. The important direct implication of this is that rather than assimilating the minimum information — the data lake can assimilate all the information produced in the organization. Since there are no assumptions made about what the data is, options remain open to use the information for any purpose in the future. This enables the data lake to power business agility by being able to serve newer ideas with the data that is already available in the data lake.

The business data lake addresses the following concerns:

- How to handle unstructured data?
- How to link internal and external data?
- How to adapt to the speed of business change?
- How to remove the repetitive ETL cycle?
- How to support different levels of data quality and governance based on differing business demands?
- How to let local business units take the initiative?
- How to ensure the deliverance of platform and that it will it be adopted?

Semantic Web technologies

When using external data that are most often found on the web, the most important requirement is understanding the precise semantics of the data. Without this, the results cannot be trusted. Here, Semantic Web technologies come to the rescue, as they allow semantics ranging from very simple to very complex to be specified for any available resource. Semantic Web technologies do not only support capturing the passive semantics, but also support active inference and reasoning on the data.

Semantic Web technologies allow data to be annotated with additional metadata (as RDF). One of the most fundamental capabilities that this adds is the **AAA principle** of Semantic Computing is—*Anyone can add anything about anything at any time*. As the information is made up of metadata, adding more metadata can enrich the information at any time.

Querying RDF data is done using SPARQL, which allows navigating complex relationship graphs to extract meaningful information from the data store. Reasoner (or an inference engine) works with the RDF metadata to deliver inferences at the top of the data. This allows the system to extract newer insights, which were originally not available in the incoming data.

Today, enormous amounts of information are becoming available over the web and over corporate and regulatory networks. However, access to all the available information remains limited as long as the information is stored separately without easy means to combine them from different sources.

This exacerbates the need for suitable methods to combine data from various sources. This is termed as the *cooperation of information systems*. This is defined as the ability to share, combine, and exchange information between heterogeneous sources in a transparent way to the end users. These heterogeneous sources are usually known to have always handled data in silos, and thus, they are inaccessible. To achieve data interoperability, the issues posed by data heterogeneity needs to be eliminated. Data sources can be heterogeneous in the following ways:

- **Syntax**: Syntactic heterogeneity is caused by the use of different models or languages
- **Schema**: Schematic heterogeneity results from structural differences

- **Semantics**: Semantic heterogeneity is caused by different meanings or interpretations of data in various contexts

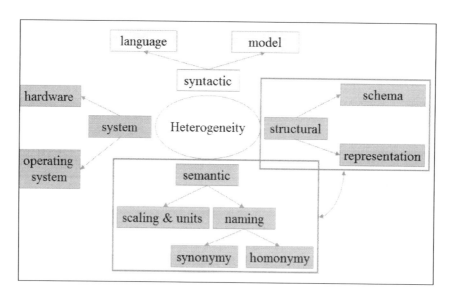

Data integration provides the ability to manipulate data transparently across multiple data sources. Based on the architecture, there are two systems:

- **Central Data Integration**: A central data integration system usually has a global schema, which provides the user with a uniform interface to access information stored in the data sources.

- **Peer-to-peer**: In contrast, in a peer-to-peer data integration system, there are no general points of control on the data sources (or peers). Instead, any peer can accept user queries for the information distributed in the entire system.

The cooperation of information systems is the ability to share, combine, and/or exchange information from multiple information sources, and the ability to access the integrated information by its final receivers transparently. The major problems that hinder the cooperation of information systems are the autonomy, the distribution, the heterogeneity, and the instability of information sources. In particular, we are interested in the heterogeneity problem that can be identified at several levels: the system, the syntactic, the structural, and the semantic heterogeneity. The cooperation of information systems has been extensively studied, and several approaches have been proposed to bridge the gap between heterogeneous information systems, such as: database translation, standardization, federation, mediation, and web services. These approaches provide appropriate solutions to the heterogeneity problem at syntactic and basic levels.

However, in order to achieve semantic interoperability between heterogeneous information systems, the meaning of the information that is interchanged has to be understood in the systems. Semantic conflicts occur whenever two contexts do not use the same interpretation of the information.

Therefore, in order to deal with semantic heterogeneity, there is a need for more semantic-specialized approaches, such as ontologies. In this chapter, our focus is to demonstrate how information systems can cooperate using semantics. In the next section, let us look at the constitution of semantic data architecture.

Ontology and data integration

The diagram here represents the reference architecture for Semantic data architecture-based analytics:

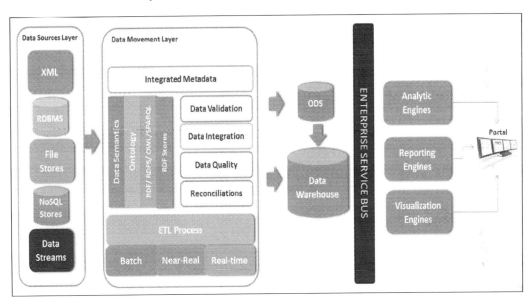

The key features of semantic data architecture are as follows:

- **Metadata representation**: Each of the sources can be represented as local ontologies supported by a meta-data dictionary to interpret the nomenclature.

- **Global conceptualization**: There will be a global ontology definition that maps the local ontologies and provides a single view or nomenclature for a common view.

- **Generic querying**: There will be a support for querying at a local of a global ontology levels depending on the need and purpose of the consumer / client.

- **Materialised view**: A high level querying strategy that masks querying between nomenclatures and peer sources.

- **Mapping**: There will be support for defining the thesaurus based mapping between ontology attributes and values.

Vendors

Type	Product/framework	Vendor
Open source and commercial versions	MarkLogic 8 is the NoSQL graph store that supports storing and processing RDF data formats and can serve as a triple store.	MarkLogic
Open source and commercial versions	Stardog is the easiest and the most powerful graph database: search, query, reasoning, and constraints in a lightweight, pure Java system.	Stardog
Open source	4Store is an efficient, scalable, and stable RDF database.	Garlik Ltd.
Open source	Jena is a free and open source Java framework for building Semantic Web and Linked Data applications.	Apache
Open source	Sesame is a powerful Java framework for processing and handling RDF data. This includes creating, parsing, storing, inferencing, and querying of such data. It offers an easy-to-use API that can be connected to all the leading RDF storage solutions.	GPL v2
Open Source	Blazegraph is SYSTAP's flagship graph database. It is specifically designed to support big graphs offering both Semantic Web (RDF/SPARQL) and graph database (TinkerPop, blueprints, and vertex-centric) APIs.	GPL v2

Multi-model database architecture / polyglot persistence

We could never have imagined, even five years ago, that relational databases would become only a single kind of a database technology and not the database technology. Internet-scale data processing changed the way we process data.

The new generation architectures such as Facebook, Wikipedia, SalesForce, and so on, are found in principles and paradigms, which are radically different from the well-established theoretical foundations on which the current data management technologies are developed.

The major architectural challenges of these architectures can be characterized next:

- Commoditizing information:

  Apple App Store, SaaS, Ubiquitous Computing, Mobility, and the Cloud-Based Multi-Tenant architectures have unleashed, in business terms, an ability to commoditize information delivery. This model changes almost all the architecture decision making, as we now need to think in terms of what the "units of information" that can be offered and billed as services are, instead of thinking in terms of the TCO of the solution.

- Theoretical limitations of RDBMS:

  What Michael Stonebraker, an influential Database theorist, has been writing in recent times at the heart of the Internet Scale Architectures is a new theoretical model of data processing and management. The theories of database management are now more than three decades old, and when they were designed, they were designed for the mainframe-type computing environments and very unreliable electronic components. Nature and the capabilities of the systems and applications have since evolved significantly. With reliability becoming a quality attribute of the underlying environment, systems are composed of parallel processing cores, and the nature of data creation and usage has undergone tremendous change. In order to conceptualize solutions for these new environments, we need to approach the designing solution architectures from a computing perspective, not only from an engineering perspective.

Six major forces are driving the data revolution today. They are as follows:

- Massive Parallel Processing
- Commoditized Information Delivery
- Ubiquitous Computing and Mobile Devices
- Non-RDBMS and Semantic Databases
- Community Computing
- Cloud Computing

Hadoop and MapReduce have unleashed massive parallel processing of data on a substantial basis and have made complex computing algorithms in a programmatic platform. This has changed analytics and BI forever. Similarly, web services and API-driven architectures have made information delivery commoditized on a substantial basis. Today, it is possible to build extremely large systems in such a way that each subsystem or component is a complete platform in itself, hosted and managed by a different entity altogether.

The previous innovations have changed the traditional Data Architecture completely. Especially, semantic computing and the ontology-driven modeling of information have turned data design on its head.

Philosophically, the data architecture is going through a factual underpinning. In traditional data models, we first design the *data model*—a fixed, design-time understanding of the world and its future. A data model fixes the meaning of data forever into a fixed structure.

A table is nothing but a category, a set of something. As a result, data has meaning only if we understand the set/category to which it belongs. For example, if we design an automobile processing system into some categories such as four-wheelers, two-wheelers, commercial vehicles, and so on, this division itself has some significant meaning embedded into it. The data that is stored in each of these categories does not reveal the *purpose of the design* that is embedded in the way the categories are designed. For example, another system might view the world of automobiles in terms of its drivetrain—electric, petroleum powered, nuclear powered, and more. This categorization itself reveals the purpose of the system in some manner, which is impossible to obtain from the attributes of any single record.

The term *polyglot* is typically used to define a person who can speak many languages. In the context of big data, this term refers to a set of applications that use many database technologies where each database technology solves a particular problem. The basic premise of this data architecture is that different database technologies solve various problems and since complex applications have many problems, picking one option to solve a particular issue is better than trying to solve all the problems using one option. When we talk about a data system, it is defined as a system that takes care of storage and querying of data, which has a runtime of several years and needs to address every possible hardware and maintenance complexities.

Polyglot persistence data architecture is used when there is a complex problem, broken down into smaller problems and solved by applying different database models. This is followed by aggregating the results into a hybrid data storage platform followed by analysis. Some factors influencing the choice of database are as follows:

Factor 1—Data Models:

- What type of data sources do we want to integrate?
- How would we want to manipulate/analyze the data?
- What is the volume, variety, and velocity of data?
- Examples—Relational, Key-Value, Column-Oriented, Document-Oriented, Graph, and so on.

Factor 2—Consistency, availability, and partitioning (CAP):

- **Consistency**: Only one value of an object to each client (Atomicity)
- **Availability**: All objects are always available (Low Latency)
- **Partition tolerance**: Data is split into multiple network partitions (Clustering)

CAP theorem requires us to choose any of the two features depicted here:

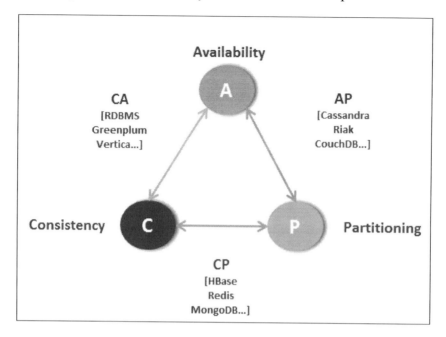

The following diagram is an example of a system that has multiple applications with a data model built for its purpose:

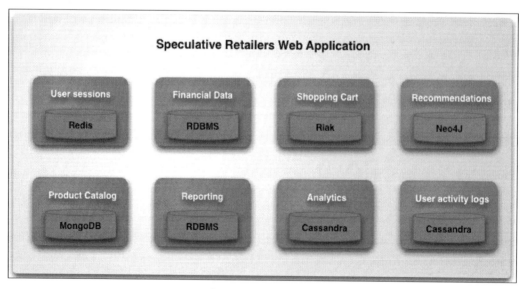

Source: ThoughtWorks

Some important aspects that affect this solution are listed next:

- It is important that the proposed hybrid environment be clearly understood to ensure that it facilitates taking the right decision about data integration, analytics, data visibility, and others, and thus, how the solution fits into the entire big data and analytics implementation umbrella.

- Since there is more than one data model, there will be a need for a unified platform that can interface with all the databases identified for solution and aggregation. This platform should address some bare minimum big data platform expectations like; fault tolerance high-availability, transactional integrity, data agility and reliability, scalability and performance are addressed.

- Depending on the specific requirements, it is important for us to know/understand what sort of a data model works both: for the particular problem and the overall solution.

- Data ingestion strategies address the real-time and batch data updates and how they can be made to work in the context of the multi-model database. Since there will be a variety of data stores, what will the **System of Record (SOR)** be? And how do we ensure that data across all the data sources is in sync or up-to-date?

So overall, this is probably a big data challenge at its best. Multiple sources of data with very different structures need to be collected, integrated, and analyzed to solve a particular business problem. Then, the key is to identify whether the data needs to be pushed to the client on-demand or in real-time. And obviously, this type of problem cannot be solved easily or cost-effectively with one type of database technology. There could be some cases where a straightforward RDBMS could work, but in cases where there is non-relational data, there is a need for different persistence engines such as NoSQL. Similarly, for an e-commerce business problem, it is important that we have a highly available and a scalable data store for shopping cart functionality. However, to find products bought by a particular group, the same store cannot help. The need here is to go for a hybrid approach and have multiple data stores used in conjunction that is known as polyglot persistence.

Vendors

Type	Product/framework	Vendor
Commercial	FoundationDB is a rock-solid database that gives NoSQL (Key-Value store) and SQL access.	FoundationDB
Open source	ArangoDB is an open source NoSQL solution with a flexible data model for documents, graphs, and key-values.	GPL v2

Lambda Architecture (LA)

Lambda Architecture addresses one important aspect of Machine learning; that is, providing a unified platform for real-time and batch analytics. Most of the frameworks that we have seen until now support batch architecture (for example, Hadoop), in order to support real-time processing integration with specific frameworks (for example, Storm).

Nathan Marz introduced the concept of Lambda Architecture for a generic, scalable, and fault-tolerant data processing architecture that addresses a real-time stream-based processing and batch processing as a unified offering.

Lambda Architecture facilitates a data architecture that is highly fault-tolerant, both: against hardware failures and human mistakes. At the same time, it serves a broad range of uses and workloads, where low-latency reads and updates are required. The resulting system should be linearly scalable, and it should scale out rather than up.

Here's how it looks from a high-level perspective:

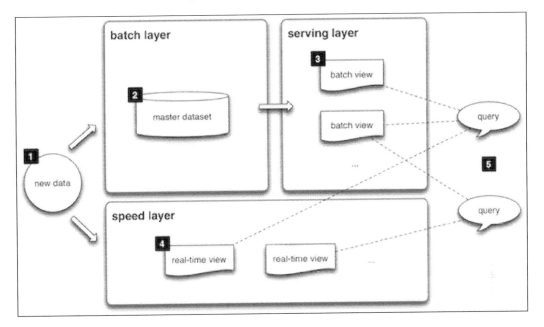

- **Data Layer**: All of the data entering the system is dispatched to both the batch layer and the speed layer for processing.

- **Batch layer**: This manages master data and is responsible for batch pre-computation. It handles heavy volumes.

- **Speed layer**: Speed layer is responsible for handling recent data and compensates for the high latency of updates to the serving layer. On an average, this layer does not deal with large volumes.

- **Serving layer**: Serving layer handles indexing the batch views and facilitates ad hoc querying demonstrating low-latency.

- **Query function**: This combines the results from batch views and real-time views.

Vendors

Type	Product/framework	Vendor
Open source and commercial	Spring XD is a unified platform for a fragmented Hadoop ecosystem. It's built at the top of the battle-tested open source projects, and dramatically simplifies the orchestration of big data workloads and data pipelines.	Pivotal (Spring Source)
Open source	Apache Spark is a fast and conventional engine for big data processing with built-in modules for streaming, SQL, Machine learning, and graph processing.	Apache
Open source	Oryx is a simple, real-time, and large-scale Machine learning infrastructure.	Apache (Cloudera)
Open source	The storm is a system used to process streaming data in the real time.	Apache (Hortonworks)

Summary

In this concluding chapter, our focus has been on the implementation aspects of Machine learning. We have understood what traditional analytics platforms have been and how they cannot fit the modern data requirements. You have also learned the architecture drivers that are promoting the new data architecture paradigms such as Lamda Architectures and polyglot persistence (multi-model database architecture), and how Semantic architectures help seamless data integration. With this chapter, you can assume that you are ready for implementing a Machine learning solution for any domain with an ability to not only identify what algorithms or models are to be applied to solve a learning problem, but also what platform solutions will address it in the best possible way.

Index

Symbol

Avro
  about 102
  URL 102

B

Backpropagation algorithm 326-330
bagging
  about 385
  example 387
  over-fitting cases 387
  testing step 386
  training step 386
  under-fitting cases 387
basic RL model 355-357
Bayesian learning 240
Bayesian method based algorithms
  about 35
  Averaged one-dependence
    estimators (AODE) 35
  Bayesian belief network (BBN) 35
  Naive Bayes 35
Bayes theorem 257-259
bell curve 256
Bellman Equation 344, 358
Bernoulli distribution 253
Bernoulli Naïve Bayes classifier 262, 263
bias 27
big data
  about 42
  characteristics 43
binary threshold neurons 314
Binomial distribution
  about 254
  exponential distribution 255
  normal distribution 256
  Poisson probability distribution 254, 255
Blazegraph 410
boosting
  about 381
  characteristics 381
Bootstrap Aggregation 385
browser
  Julia, using via 140, 141
Business Intelligence (BI) 77

C

C4.5 166, 175
CAL5 177
case-based reasoning (CBR) 186, 194, 195
CHAID 176
Checkpoint 84
Chukwa
  about 102
  URL 102
Classification and Regression Tree
    (CART) 34, 174
clustering
  examples 227
  hierarchical clustering 228, 229
  partitional clustering 230, 231
  types 228
clustering-based learning 226, 227
clustering methods
  Expectation maximization (EM) 35
  Gaussian mixture models (GMM) 35
  K-means 35
clusters 226
cluster sampling 242
command line
  Julia code, running from 141
command line version
  downloading, of Julia 139
  using, of Julia 139
complexity measure, k-means clustering
    algorithm 237
complimenting fields, Machine learning
  about 29
  Artificial intelligence (AI) 30
  data mining 30
  data science 32
  statistical learning 31
components, MapReduce 95
concurrency 54
concurrent algorithms
  developing 55, 56
conditional probability 247, 248
Configurable Logical Blocks (CLB) 61
confounder 282
confounding 281-283

Deep learning methods
  implementing 340
  implementing, Julia used 341
  implementing, Mahout used 340
  implementing, Python (scikit-learn)
    used 341
  implementing, R used 340
  implementing, Spark used 340
Deep learning taxonomy
  about 332
  autoencoders 339, 340
  convolutional neural networks
    (CNN/ConvNets) 333
  Deep Boltzmann Machines (DBMs) 338
  Recurrent Neural Networks (RNNs) 336
  Restricted Boltzmann Machines
    (RBMs) 337
Deep learning, techniques
  Convolutional Networks 23
  Deep Belief Networks (DBN) 23
  Restricted Boltzmann Machine (RBM) 23
  Stacked Autoencoders 23
default block placement policy 87
dendogram 228
denoising autoencoder (DA) 340
dense vectors 125
dependent events 246, 247
Descriptive analytics 399
Diagnostic analytics 399
dimensionality reduction methods
  about 36
  Multidimensional scaling (MDS) 36
  Partial least squares (PLS) regression 36
  Principal component analysis (PCA) 36
  Projection pursuit (PP) 36
  Sammon mapping 36
discrete quantity 253
disjoint events 246
distance measures, in KNN
  about 192
  Euclidean distance 193
  Hamming distance 193
  Minkowski distance 193
distance measures methods, k-means
    clustering algorithm
  average link 236

  centroids 236
  complete link 236
  single link 236
distributed processing 47
distribution
  about 250-253
  Bernoulli distribution 253
  Binomial distribution 254
  relationship between 257
Divisive clustering algorithm 229
Dynamic Learning Vector Quantization
    (DLVQ) networks 325
Dynamic Programming (DP) 359, 360

E

Eclipse
  URL 119
Eclipse IDE
  used, for setting up Mahout 119, 120
ecosystem components, Hadoop 100-103
effect modification 281, 283
Elman networks 323
ensemble learning methods
  about 369
  key use cases 374
  Wisdom of Crowds 369-374
Ensemble method algorithms
  about 36
  AdaBoost 36
  Bagging 36
  Bootstrapped Aggregation (Boosting) 36
  Gradient boosting machines (GBM) 37
  Random forest 36
  Stacked generalization (blending) 37
ensemble methods
  about 377, 378
  implementing 392
  implementing, Julia used 392
  implementing, Mahout used 392
  implementing, Python (scikit-learn)
    used 392
  implementing, R used 392
  implementing, Spark used 392
  supervised ensemble methods 379, 380
Enterprise Service Bus (ESB) 49

singularity 286
skewed data 269
smart data 70
Softmax regression technique 331
solution architecture, Machine
        learning 32, 33
solution methods, Reinforcement
        Learning (RL)
  about 359
  actor-critic methods (on-policy) 364
  Dynamic Programming (DP) 359, 360
  Monte Carlo methods 361
  Q-Learning technique 363
  R Learning (Off-policy) 365
  temporal difference (TD) learning 362
Spark
  used, for implementing ANNs 340
  used, for implementing Apriori and
        FP-growth 223
  used, for implementing decision trees 184
  used, for implementing Deep learning
        methods 340
  used, for implementing ensemble
        methods 392
  used, for implementing k-means
        clustering 237
  used, for implementing KNN 196
  used, for implementing linear
        regression 302
  used, for implementing logistic
        regression 302
  used, for implementing Naïve Bayes
        algorithm 264
  used, for implementing Support Vector
        Machines (SVM) 204
Spark SQL 151
Spark Streaming 151
sparse vectors
  about 125
  random access sparse vectors 125
  sequential access sparse vectors 125
specialized trees
  about 178
  evolutionary trees 182
  Hellinger trees 183

oblique trees 178, 179
random forests 180-182
Spring XD
  about 114, 155, 418
  features 155
Spring XD architecture, layers
  about 156
  Batch Layer 156
  Serving Layer 156
  Speed Layer 156
Sqoop
  about 103
  URL 103
SSE (Sum Squared Error) 290
SSL (Secure Socket Layer) 81
standard deviation 243
Stardog 410
state 348
statistical learning
  versus Machine learning 31
statisticians
  objective 241
stochastic binary neurons 316-318
stratified sampling 242
stream mining 377
String manipulations, Julia
  working with 143
sum of squared error of prediction
        (SSE) 232
supervised ensemble methods
  about 368, 379
  bagging 385-387
  boosting 381, 382
  wagging 388
supervised learning 345
Support Vector Machines (SVM)
  about 185, 198-202
  implementing 204
  implementing, Julia used 204
  implementing, Mahout used 204
  implementing, Python (scikit-learn)
        used 204
  implementing, R used 204
  implementing, Spark used 204
  Inseparable Data 202, 203
symmetric distribution 269
synapses 311, 312

T

Tableau 151
Tajo
  about 103
  URL 103
task dependency graph 55
task parallelization 49
TaskTracker 92
Temporal Credit Assignment 357
temporal difference (TD) 344
temporal difference (TD) learning
  about 362
  Sarsa 362
terms, Reinforcement Learning (RL)
  action 348
  agent 348
  environment 348
  policy 348
  reward 348
  state 348
  value 348
top-K recommendation 187
Total Cost of Ownership (TCO) 43
Total Lifetime Value (TLV) 16
traditional ETL architecture
  limitations 396, 397
transfer learning 376
tree Induction method
  CAL5 177
  CHAID 176
  FACT 177
  ID3 176
  LMDT 177
  MARS 177
  QUEST 177

U

Ubuntu-based Hadoop Installation
  IPv6, disabling 106
  Jdk 1.7, installing 104
  prerequisites 104
  system user, creating for Hadoop 106
uncertainty
  sources 243

Unique Transaction Identifier (UTI) 208
unlabelled data set 346
unsupervised ensemble methods 390, 391

V

value 348
variables, Julia 141
variance
  about 268
  properties 274, 275
vectors
  implementing, in Mahout 124
Visualizations
  about 78
  data, exploring with 79, 80
Voronoi cell 189

W

wagging 388
WebHDFS REST API
  URL 91
Wisdom of Crowds
  about 369, 370
  aggregation 370
  cross inducers 371
  decentralization 370
  dependency between classifiers 371
  diversity, generating 371
  diversity of opinion 370
  independence 370
  size of ensemble 371
  usage of combiner 371

Y

YARN (Yet Another Resource
  Negotiator) 65

Z

ZooKeeper
  about 103
  URL 103

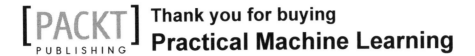

Thank you for buying
Practical Machine Learning

About Packt Publishing

Packt, pronounced 'packed', published its first book, *Mastering phpMyAdmin for Effective MySQL Management*, in April 2004, and subsequently continued to specialize in publishing highly focused books on specific technologies and solutions.

Our books and publications share the experiences of your fellow IT professionals in adapting and customizing today's systems, applications, and frameworks. Our solution-based books give you the knowledge and power to customize the software and technologies you're using to get the job done. Packt books are more specific and less general than the IT books you have seen in the past. Our unique business model allows us to bring you more focused information, giving you more of what you need to know, and less of what you don't.

Packt is a modern yet unique publishing company that focuses on producing quality, cutting-edge books for communities of developers, administrators, and newbies alike. For more information, please visit our website at www.packtpub.com.

Writing for Packt

We welcome all inquiries from people who are interested in authoring. Book proposals should be sent to author@packtpub.com. If your book idea is still at an early stage and you would like to discuss it first before writing a formal book proposal, then please contact us; one of our commissioning editors will get in touch with you.

We're not just looking for published authors; if you have strong technical skills but no writing experience, our experienced editors can help you develop a writing career, or simply get some additional reward for your expertise.

Building Machine Learning Systems with Python

ISBN: 978-1-78216-140-0   Paperback: 290 pages

Master the art of machine learning with Python and build effective machine learning systems with this intensive hands-on guide

1. Master Machine Learning using a broad set of Python libraries and start building your own Python-based ML systems.

2. Covers classification, regression, feature engineering, and much more guided by practical examples.

3. A scenario-based tutorial to get into the right mind-set of a machine learner (data exploration) and successfully implement this in your new or existing projects.

Machine Learning with Spark

ISBN: 978-1-78328-851-9   Paperback: 338 pages

Create scalable machine learning applications to power a modern data-driven business using Spark

1. A practical tutorial with real-world use cases allowing you to develop your own machine learning systems with Spark.

2. Combine various techniques and models into an intelligent machine learning system.

3. Use Spark's powerful tools to load, analyze, clean, and transform your data.

Please check **www.PacktPub.com** for information on our titles

Mastering Machine Learning with scikit-learn

ISBN: 978-1-78398-836-5   Paperback: 238 pages

Apply effective learning algorithms to real-world problems using scikit-learn

1. Design and troubleshoot machine learning systems for common tasks including regression, classification, and clustering.

2. Acquaint yourself with popular machine learning algorithms, including decision trees, logistic regression, and support vector machines.

3. A practical example-based guide to help you gain expertise in implementing and evaluating machine learning systems using scikit-learn.

Machine Learning with R
Second Edition

ISBN: 978-1-78439-390-8   Paperback: 452 pages

Discover how to build machine learning algorithms, prepare data, and dig deep into data prediction techniques with R

1. Harness the power of R for statistical computing and data science.

2. Explore, forecast, and classify data with R.

3. Use R to apply common machine learning algorithms to real-world scenarios.

Please check **www.PacktPub.com** for information on our titles